FLAGS OF THE CONFEDERACY
AN ILLUSTRATED HISTORY

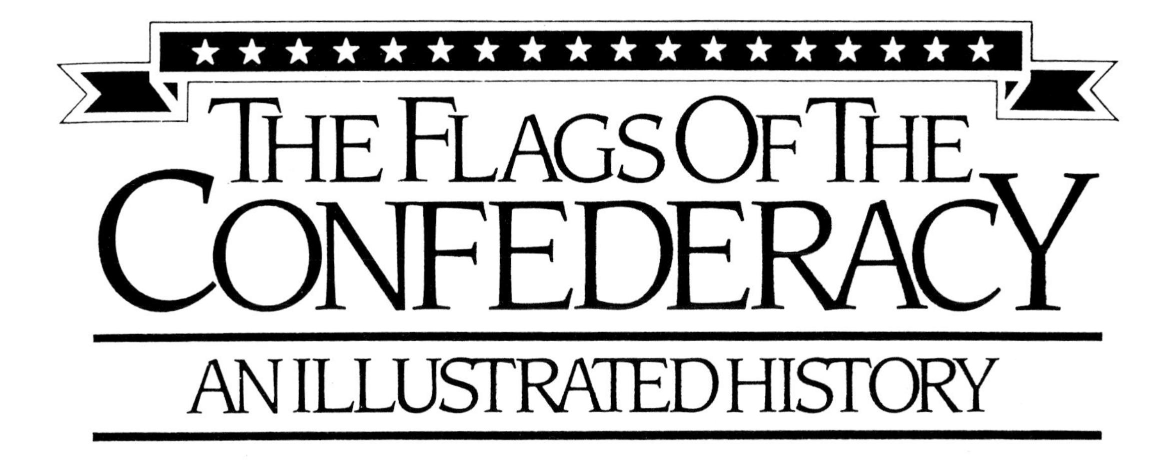

BY

Devereaux D. Cannon, Jr.

PELICAN PUBLISHING COMPANY
GRETNA 2005

Published by St. Lukes Press, 1988
Published by arrangement with the author by
Pelican Publishing Company, Inc., 1994

First Pelican printing, 1994
Second Pelican printing, 1997
Third Pelican printing, 2005

Library of Congress Cataloging-in-Publication Data

Cannon, Devereaux D., 1954-
The flags of the Confederacy : an illustrated history / by
Devereaux D. Cannon, Jr.
p. cm.
Originally published: Memphis, TN : St. Lukes Press, 1988.
Includes index.
ISBN 9781565541092
1. Flags—Confederate States of America. 2. United States—
History—Civil War, 1861-1865—Flags. I. Title.
[CR113.5.C58 1994]
929.9'2'0975—dc20
94-28637
CIP

Cover design by Larry Pardue

Printed in China
Published by Pelican Publishing Company, Inc.
1000 Burmaster Street, Gretna, Louisiana 70053

This book is dedicated to
DEVEREAUX D. CANNON, III
whose enthusiasm is unbounded,
and to his mother,
who has the patience to put up with
two unreconstructed rebels.

ACKNOWLEDGEMENTS

Special thanks are due to the following individuals and institutions who rendered invaluable assistance in the preparation of this book:

Nora T. Cannon, Esquire, Nashville, Tennessee;

Mark Lea "Beau" Cantrell, Esquire, El Reno, Oklahoma for assistance on flags in the Trans-Mississippi Department;

Confederate Research Center, Hill College History Complex, Hillsboro, Texas

John Hudson, Tennessee State Museum, Nashville, Tennessee;

Timothy Kelly, Nashville, Tennessee;

Howard Michael Madaus, Milwaukee Public Museum, Milwaukee, Wisconsin for general assistance on a variety of details;

Dr. John McGlone, Tennessee State Library and Archives, Nashville, Tennessee;

Bill Pitts, Confederate Memorial Hall, Oklahoma Historical Society, Oklahoma City, Oklahoma;

Col. Frank R. Rankin, Louisville, Kentucky for information on the Kentucky seal; and

Rebecca R. Tickle, Lucy, Tennessee.

Table of Contents

List of Illustrations

FLAGS OF THE CONFEDERACY
AN ILLUSTRATED HISTORY

CHAPTER 1
IN THE BEGINNING . . . FLAGS

Flags are fond symbols, popular with people of all ages. They can be just pretty pieces of colored bunting snapping in the breeze to give an event a festive air, or they can be the charismatic expression of a cause.

National flags are the history and glory of a people expressed in the art of the seamstress. The flags of States which are members of a federation are more difficult to deal with on so general a basis. As an expression of the sovereignty of each member State, they tend, in happy times, to be lost in the patriotism felt for the federation and symbolized in its flag. Regardless of politics, battle flags, while they existed for the ordinary and necessary purposes of recognition and the direction of armies, came to be totems. For the soldiers who followed them, they acquired a personality of their own and often became the object of battle, rather than its markers. In the Confederate States of America, which had an independent political existence of only four years before they were conquered and reincorporated into the United States, all these variations found full play.

All revolutionary movements breed a wide variety of flags. This was certainly true in the early days of the Southern independence movement, and it would continue to be true for the military forces of the Confederacy in the Western and Trans-Mississippi theatres. Yet the Confederate revolution was a conservative revolution in that the forms of government remained intact in the States, and the new federal government established by them was almost a carbon copy of that from which they had separated. In part as a result of the conservative and legalistic manner in which the Confederacy was established, the first national flag of the Confederate States was adopted sooner and promulgated in a more uniform and regular manner than is usual with flags associated with other revolutions.

In order to have a good understanding of the Confederate flags in this book, it is helpful to have an understanding of the civil and political structure of the Confederate States government. When the Southern States seceded from the United States of America in 1860 and 1861, they believed that they were acting in a perfectly legal and acceptable manner. The Constitution of 1787 had been drafted by delegates from the States and had been voluntarily ratified by the people of the several States. No State had been forced into the union, and any State whose people did not wish to join the union could go its own way. Logically, it followed therefore that any State could also voluntarily leave the union when its people believed that the union was no longer serving its purpose of establishing justice and/or insuring domestic tranquility.

Secession did not change the State governments in their internal operations, and they continued to function in their daily activities. It was recognized, however, that the purposes for which the old union had been formed in 1788 were good, and that the failure of the system in 1860 could be remedied by the formation of a new and southern confederacy. Accordingly, the newly independent States called a convention to form a new federal government.

The Convention met in Montgomery, Alabama on February 4, 1861 where the Confederate founding fathers proceeded to form a provisional or temporary government to preside over the new country until a permanent government could be established. The Convention also drafted a new Constitution very similar to the United States Constitution and created the machinery for the establishment of a permanent government a year later. After toying with the names "Republic of Washington" and "Federal Republic of America," the Convention named the new country the Confederate States of America.

Over the years, considerable confusion in the historical record has been created by the existence of both a provisional and a permanent government. For example, Jefferson Davis was inaugurated President twice: first as the President of the provisional government that existed from February 8, 1861 to February 18, 1862; and a second time as President of the government established by the Constitution of the Confederate States of America as the permanent government which began to function on February 18, 1862.

The Provisional Congress was the legislature of the provisional government and was unicameral. Under the permanent government, the Congress was bicameral, as in the United States, with a Senate and a House of Representatives. The Congresses of the permanent government were numbered, the number changing every two years with the election of a new House of Representatives, just as is done in the United States. For this reason, we say that the United States Congress which was elected in 1986 was the One Hundredth Congress, and the First Congress of the United States was elected in 1788.

In the Confederate States there were two numbered Congresses. The First Congress was elected in 1861 and served from February 1862 until February 1864. The Second Congress was elected in 1863 and served from February 1864 until the destruction of the government in 1865. If, therefore, in our discussion of Confederate flag laws, we mention the "Provisional Congress," the reference is to the Congress of the temporary government in

1861; if to the "First" or "Second Congress," the reference is to one of the Congresses of the permanent government from 1862 to 1865.

The Confederate Flag is properly the official flag of the Confederate States; i.e., the national flag. Often people will use the term "Confederate Flag" to describe one of the flags used by the army as a battle flag. In the course of this book the term "Confederate Flag" will only be used in reference to the national flags of the Confederate States of America.

The discussion of flags will of necessity use some vexillological terms which may not be familiar to you. "Vexillology" is a rather difficult word to pronounce, and sounds like some great technical field of science. As it is derived from the Latin word "vexillum," meaning flag, the suffix "ology" meaning "The study of," the word "vexillology" means quite simply the study of flags. In order to help the reader understand these terms, a glossary is provided here.

GLOSSARY OF VEXILLOLOGICAL TERMS

BORDER: An edging to a flag which is of a different color than the field of the flag and is used for either decorative purposes or to prevent fraying.

CANTON: This is also known as the union of the flag. It refers to the upper left-hand corner of the flag.

ENSIGN: The national flag as used on a ship.

FIMBRATION: A narrow edging, often white, used to separate different colored features on a flag. The rules of heraldry prohibit the placing of color upon color.

FLY: The length of the flag.

FLY END or FLY EDGE: The width of the flag at the point farthest from the staff.

HOIST: The width of the flag at the point nearest the staff.

JACK: A small flag designating nationality and flown at the bow of a naval vessel while in port.

FLAGS OF THE CONFEDERACY

MULLETT: An heraldic device said to have originally represented the rowel of a spur, more often referred to now as a star. It is most often shown with five points, although more are used at times.

SAINT GEORGE'S CROSS: An upright cross in "+" form, this feature was derived from the flag of England.

SALTIER or SALTIRE: A cross traversing a flag from corner to corner in "x" form. Also referred to as a Saint Andrew's cross, this feature was derived from the flag of Scotland.

PART I—THE NATION

CHAPTER 2
"STARS AND BARS"

Adoption

For the first twenty-four days of the existence of their government, the Confederate States of America had no officially approved flag. When Jefferson Davis was inaugurated President of the provisional government on February 18, 1861 the capitol building in Montgomery flew the flag of the State of Alabama, and the inaugural parade was lead by a company of infantry carrying the flag of Georgia.

The Provisional Congress had established a Committee on Flag and Seal, the chairman of which was William Porcher Miles of South Carolina. The Committee received hundreds of designs for flags which were submitted to it by citizens from all parts of the country. Even citizens of States still among the United States sent in proposals. An unwritten deadline for the adoption of a flag was March 4, 1861 because on that date Abraham Lincoln was to be inaugurated president of the now foreign United States; and on that date the Southern States were determined to fly a flag which expressed their own sovereignty.

As the deadline neared, the Committee continued to examine and debate designs without being able to reach a consensus. The patterns submitted could be divided generally into two categories: those which bore some resemblance to the flag of the United States and flags of intricate and complex design. The Committee, and especially Chairman Miles, discredited all those imitating the United States' flag as being too easily confused with the flag of the old union. A sentimental attachment to "the old flag" felt by the public at large, however, made it impossible to ignore the elements of its design. The category of intricate designs was ruled out as being too difficult and expensive to render into bunting flags. The Committee finally had to admit its inability to agree on a flag and chose four patterns to present to the full Congress for a final decision.

On the morning of March 4, large cambric models of the proposed flags were hung up on the walls of the Congressional chamber. The models of the three rejected patterns did not survive the War, but we are able to reconstruct them from a description given by Chairman Miles in an 1872 letter to General P.G.T. Beauregard.

The first of these three is now a familiar design: a blue saltier fimbrated in white on a red field, with white stars upon the saltier. This flag was designed by Chairman Miles, whose inspiration may have been the banner

Figure 1: Proposed Flag of the Confederate States,
Submitted to Congress March 4, 1861 by William Porcher Miles.

of the South Carolina Secession Convention. The Convention flag had been red with a blue Saint George's cross which bore fifteen stars representing the slaveholding States. Its canton featured the crescent and palmetto of the State. The Congress rejected Miles' flag: one member even ridiculed it as resembling "a pair of suspenders." The difficulty of achieving a symmetrical arrangement of the seven stars (one for each of the seven Confederate States in March 1861) on the arms of the cross may have prejudiced Congress' consideration of this proposal.

Miles' flag would not die, however, and in various alterations went on to become the battle flag of the Confederate armies. Before the end of the War, Miles' "pair of suspenders" would be incorporated into the flag of the Confederate States and, as the canton of the ensign of the CSS *Shenandoah*, would circumnavigate the globe.

The other proposals rejected by the Confederate Congress were never to be seen again. One of these was closely patterned on the flag of the United States. Its blue union displayed a star for each of the Confederate States, but the stripes were changed from red and white to red and blue. Mr. Miles could not remember, in 1872, how many stripes were on the model. Probably there were seven to represent the original Confederate States in keeping with the precedent of thirteen stripes to represent the thirteen original United States.

The third flag rejected by Congress bore no resemblance to the flag of the United States. It was described by Chairman Miles as "a red field with a blue ring or circle in the center." Presumably the ring is representative of the solidarity of the Southern States, but there is no statement of its symbolism in Miles' 1872 letter to Beauregard.

STARS AND BARS

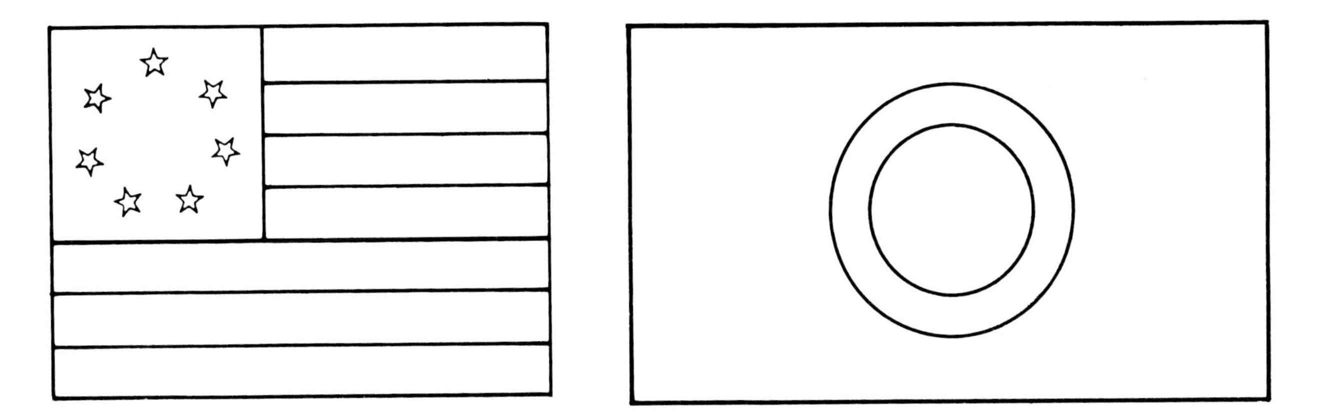

Figures 2-3: Two of the Flags Submitted to the Provisional Congress on March 4, 1861.

The flag which received the blessing of Congress was described in the following language:

> The flag of the Confederate States of America shall consist of a red field with a white space extending horizontally through the center, and equal in width to one-third the width of the flag. The red space above and below to be the same width as the white. The union blue extending down through the white space and stopping at the lower red space. In the center of the union a circle of white stars corresponding in number with the States in the Confederacy.

The text of this description was inserted into a report of the Committee on Flag and Seal which may have already been prepared save for the description of the flag. The report was then written into the journal of the Congress.

Arrangements had already been made for a flag-raising ceremony to be held on the afternoon of March 4; but a flag had just that day been decided upon. "Thanks to fair and nimble fingers," however, to quote Chairman Miles from his 1872 letter again, a flag made of merino was completed within two hours of its adoption. This very first flag of the Confederate States of America was hoisted over the capitol building in Montgomery by Miss Letitia Christian Tyler, the granddaughter of President John Tyler.

In their hurry to adopt the flag and have it prepared for the ceremony to be held that afternoon, Congress neglected to formally enact a flag law. The journal of the Congress reflects the report of the Committee on Flag and Seal, but indicates nothing with regard to a vote. Nor do the statute books of the Confederate States contain a Flag Act of 1861. Despite official use for over two years, the "Stars and Bars" was never established as the Confederate Flag by the laws of the land.

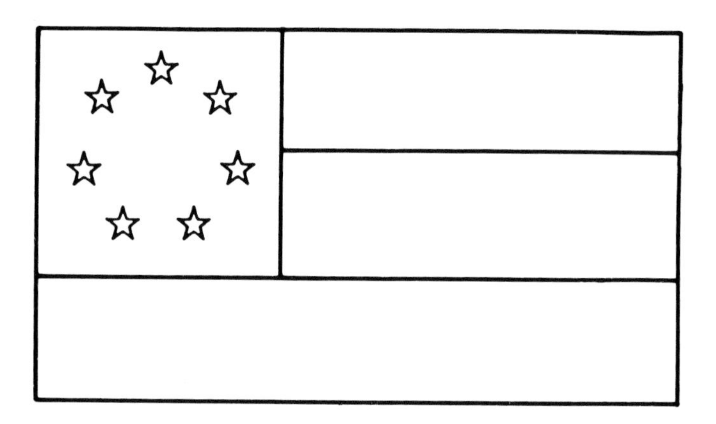

Figure 4: Flag of the Confederate States of America,
Adopted by the Provisional Congress, March 4, 1861.

The use of this new flag not only spread rapidly across the Confederate States but also among Confederate sympathizers in States still in the old Union. Six weeks later, it was flying over Fort Sumter in Charleston harbor as a flag of a nation at war. With war came alterations in the flag because, by the third week in May, Virginia and Arkansas had been admitted to the Confederacy adding two more stars to the flag. The circle grew to eleven with the addition of North Carolina and Tennessee in July. Missouri in November and Kentucky in December brought to the flag a new constellation of thirteen stars. In this final form, the "Stars and Bars" would see official use until its replacement in 1863.

Designer

In the first half of the Twentieth Century, a great controversy erupted over the origin of the design of the first flag of the Confederate States. The claimants to the honor were Nicola Marschall, a Prussian artist who lived in Montgomery, Alabama and Orren Randolph Smith of North Carolina. Both men claimed to have submitted to the Provisional Congress the design destined to later become famous as the "Stars and Bars." Mr. Marschall also claimed to have submitted two other unsuccessful patterns.

The controversy between Marschall and Smith seems to have arisen about 1911, but it was not until 1915 that it was officially investigated. At

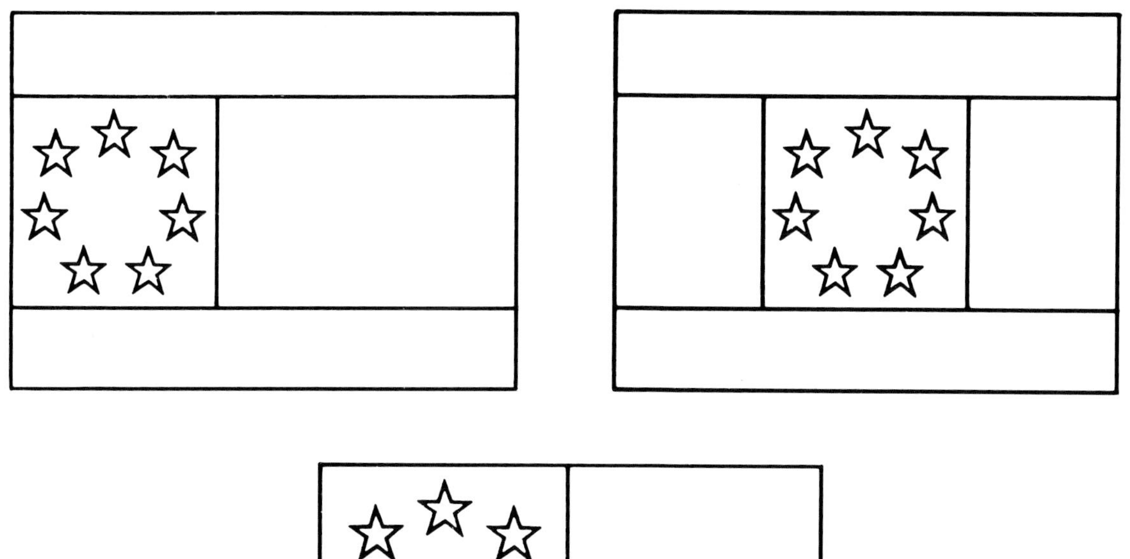

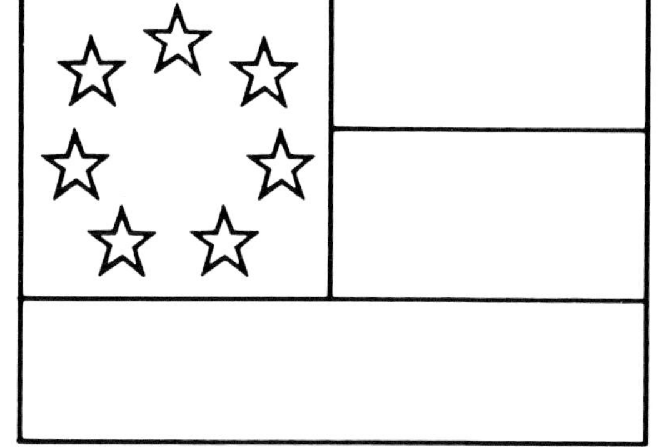

Figures 5-7: Three Flag Designs Submitted to the Provisional Congress by Nicola Marschall.

that time the Stars and Bars Committee of the United Confederate Veterans at their Richmond reunion held during June 1-3 of 1915 found in favor of Mr. Smith's claim, as evidenced by the published report of the committee. The debate continued, however, and in 1931 the Alabama Department of Archives and History published the results of an investigation by the Alabama legislature which determined that Mr. Marschall had in fact designed the flag.

Both sides produced convincing evidence as well as contradictions during these investigations. Contradictions should always be expected when attempting to reconstruct from memory events which have transpired more than fifty years earlier. However a recently discovered letter dated March 2, 1861 seems definitely to establish Marschall's claim. Given simplicity of the design and the early enthusiasm for the flag bearing some resemblance to that of the United States, it is possible that Mr. Smith also submitted a very similar proposal. The evidence presented to the United Confederate Veterans and the Alabama legislature may well entitle both men to claim the honor of being "Father of the Stars and Bars."

Specifications

The report of the Committee on Flag and Seal established some, but not a complete set of, specifications for the relative proportions of the elements of the "Stars and Bars." The canton or union was to be equal in width to two-thirds the width of the flag. Each bar was to be equal to one-third the width of the flag. No direction was given as to the length of the canton or the overall length of the flag.

An exhaustive survey of surviving Confederate Flags done by Howard Michael Madaus of the Milwaukee Public Museum and reported in the monograph *"Rebel Flags Afloat" (Flag Bulletin,* No. 115, Vol. XXV, Nos. 1-2, January-April 1986) found that by far the largest number of first national pattern flags had cantons which were square, or nearly so.

Only about a quarter of the flags studied had cantons which were definitely rectangular; on some the width exceeded the length, and on others the length exceeded the width.

There was no definite pattern with regard to length. Over 70 percent of the "Stars and Bars" flags in the Madaus survey fell into the rather broad category of having lengths between one and one-half and two times their widths.

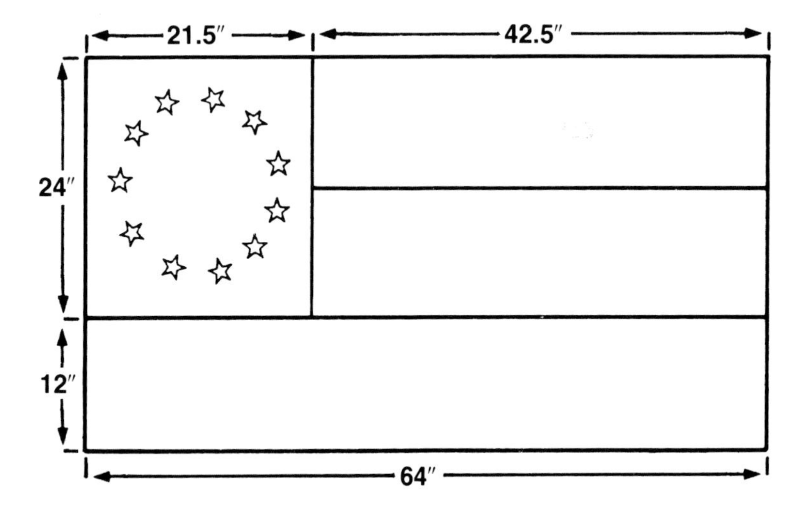

Figure 8: Specifications of a Representative Example of the "Stars and Bars."

STARS AND BARS

The flag shown in the illustration is a representative example but should by no means be taken as definitive of proportions. The Committee report left a lot of room for interpretation.

The illustrated flag has eleven stars in the canton and would have been official from the time Tennessee was admitted to the Confederacy on July 2, 1861 until the admission of Missouri on November 28 of that year. Kentucky was admitted as one of the Confederate States on the following December 10, and the thirteen-star flag was official from that date until the "Stars and Bars" was replaced as the Confederate Flag on May 1, 1863.

CHAPTER 3
"STAINLESS BANNER"

Towards A More Confederate Flag

William Porcher Miles was not satisfied with the "Stars and Bars." He did not share in the sentimental attachment to the old flag and wished the adoption of a new symbol which could not in any way be thought similar to that of the United States. To his chagrin, his desires were not reflected in the mood of the people or of their representatives in Congress in 1861.

As the War extended from weeks into months, the sentimental feelings felt for the "Stars and Stripes" began to wane. More and more Confederate citizens came to see what one member of Congress referred to as "the old gridiron" as the symbol of oppression and imperialistic aggression. In February, 1862 the First Congress of the Confederate States assembled in Richmond. Its recently elected membership reflected the changing attitudes of the people towards the flag.

Among the first actions of the new Senate and House of Representatives was the appointment of a Joint Committee on Flag and Seal with instructions to consider and propose a new Confederate Flag. On April 19, 1862 the Joint Committee submitted its report to both Houses of Congress. The report, introduced in the form of a joint resolution, read as follows:

> A JOINT RESOLUTION adopting the flag of the Confederate States of America
>
> *Resolved by the Congress of the Confederate States of America,* That the flag of the Confederate States shall be as follows: A red field, charged with a white saltier, having in the centre the device of a sun, in its glory, on an azure ground, the rays of the sun corresponding with the number of the States composing the Confederacy.

In its report on the flag, the Committee stated that the azure (blue) ground on which the sun was charged would be in the form of a shield. The symbolism of the flag was described in these words:

> The red field denotes nautical powers, boldness, courage, valour.
>
> The saltier, an "honourable ordinary" in heraldry, is the emblem of progress and strength; its white indicating purity, innocence, and gentleness.
>
> The blue of the shield represents justice and faith, perseverance

and vigilance.

The sun manifests the dominion, generosity and stability of the Confederacy.

Nearly all the designs submitted to the committee contained a combination of stars. This heraldic emblem, however, has been descended as a manifestation of our entire and absolute severance from the United States at the complete annihilation of every sentiment indicating the fainted hopes of reconstruction.

Figure 9: Flag Proposal of the Joint Committee on Flag and Seal—April 19, 1862.

The Senate designated the resolution Senate Resolution No. 11, but took no vote while the House of Representatives began immediate debate on the resolution. Congressman Miles expressed his approval of the design, saying that he was "glad that a flag had been adopted [by the committee] so dissimilar to the old."

Some members of the House of Representatives received the Committee's flag proposal favorably and urged immediate adoption. Others resisted the proposal. Representative Charles M. Conrad of Louisiana's second congressional district did not consider the flag attractive and expressed concern that, since it had no canton, the Committee's design could not be inverted as a signal of distress at sea. The observation by Mr. Miles that the flags of most maritime nations had no cantons did not impress the Louisianian.

A number of members of the House of Representatives wanted to put off consideration of the flag. Some were more inclined to adopt a Confederate flag that more nearly resembled the battle flag used by the army in Virginia. Others were concerned about the lack of a consensus in favor of the

Committee's flag. April 19, 1862 would not see the birth of a new Confederate flag. The House of Representatives voted 39 to 21 to postpone consideration of the resolution. It was never again brought up for discussion in the halls of Congress.

The change would be made in 1863. On April 22 of that year, the Committee on Flag and Seal of the Confederate States Senate reported a bill which was designated Senate Bill No. 132. It read as follows:

> AN ACT to establish the flag of the Confederate States.
>
> *The Congress of the Confederate States of America do enact,* That the flag of the Confederate States shall be as follows: a white field with the battle flag for a union, which shall be square and occupy two thirds of the width of the flag, and a blue bar, one third of the flag in its width, dividing the field lengthwise.

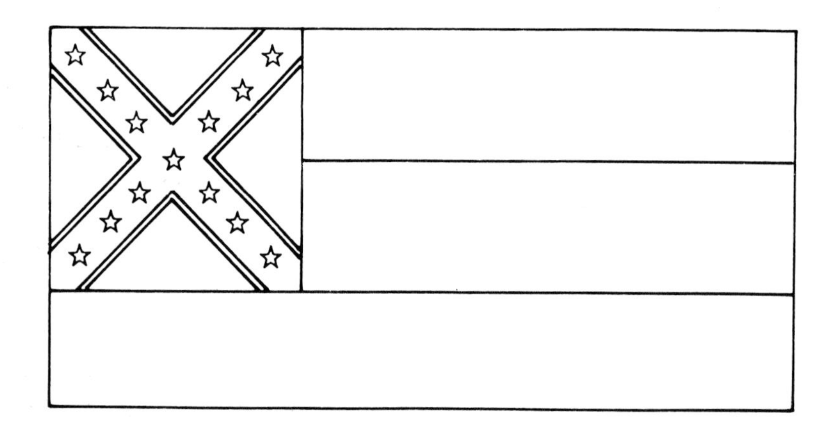

Figure 10: Original Version of the Flag in Senate Bill No. 132, 1863.

The bill was passed by the Senate on the same day and sent to the House of Representatives.

The flag which this bill proposed sought to cure the similarity between the "Stars and Bars" and the "Stars and Stripes" by reversing the colors of the former. Rather than a blue union and bars of red, white and red, the new Confederate flag proposed by the Senate would have a red union with bars of white, blue and white. The red battle flag of the Army of Northern Virginia would provide the canton of this new flag.

Although Senate Bill No. 132 passed the Senate with little debate and on a voice vote on the day that it was reported out of committee, it would not receive such easy approval in the House of Representatives. The House was much more radical on the flag issue than the Senate. The Representatives demanded even less resemblance to the Northern flag than that which had been approved in Senate Bill No. 132.

Figure 11: A Proposed Amendment of Senate Bill No. 132, 1863.

The House of Representatives took up the debate on May 1, 1863. Motions were immediately made to effect various amendments to the bill. The first successful motion removed the bars altogether and replaced them with a white field bordered in red, with the battle flag still in canton. The canton itself was reduced in size by another motion from two-thirds to three-fifths the width of the flag. Congressman Ethelbert Barksdale of Mississippi made a motion to remove the stars from the cross. He believed that "the flags of the two countries [should be] as distinct as the character of the two people." The majority of the House did not wish to go as far as the Mississippian, and the stars stayed.

Figure 12: Congressman Swan's Proposed Amendment to Senate Bill No. 132.

FLAGS OF THE CONFEDERACY

William G. Swan of Tennessee's second congressional district wished to substitute the following language:

> That the flag of the Confederate States shall be as follows: A red field with a Saint Andrew's cross of blue edged with white and emblazoned with stars.

Swan, who before secession had been mayor of Knoxville and attorney general of Tennessee, had adapted his proposal from the battle flag of the Army of Northern Virginia, but it was in fact identical to the flag proposed by William Porcher Miles in March 1861. But in the intervening years, the battle flag had been sanctified by the blood of Southern soldiers in the struggle for independence. Swan wished to adopt it for use by the nation now as a tribute to the valor of the Confederate fighting man.

William Porcher Miles rose to speak on the subject. He was quite proud that the flag which he had designed and urged upon Congress in 1861 had been adopted by the military with such success. In recording Representative Miles' address, the Minutes of the Third Session of the First Congress (*Southern Historical Society Papers,* Volume 49, p. 272) outlined his argument:

> The country was aware how it had been received by the army—it had been consecrated. The battle flag should be used then with simplicity, but to the demand that it should be taken alone, he would reply that it was necessary to emblazon it. The battle flag, on a pure white field, he thought was the best they could find. The white flag could be easily distinguished, and would not be taken as a flag of truce—it was the old French Bourbon flag. They should abandon the border—it was unusual. It was not intended to follow strictly the requirements of heraldic art, but some attention should be paid to good taste. He trusted that the battle flag on a pure white field, discarding the blue bar and border (a monstrosity), would be adopted.

Robert P. Trippe of Georgia's seventh congressional district urged postponing consideration of a new flag. This was the last day of the session and he believed that it was precipitous to be "deciding on the flag of a great nation in fifty-five minutes, what remains of the actual session." Congress would not be put off, though time would give the appearance of prophesy to Congressman Trippe's words.

"STAINLESS BANNER"

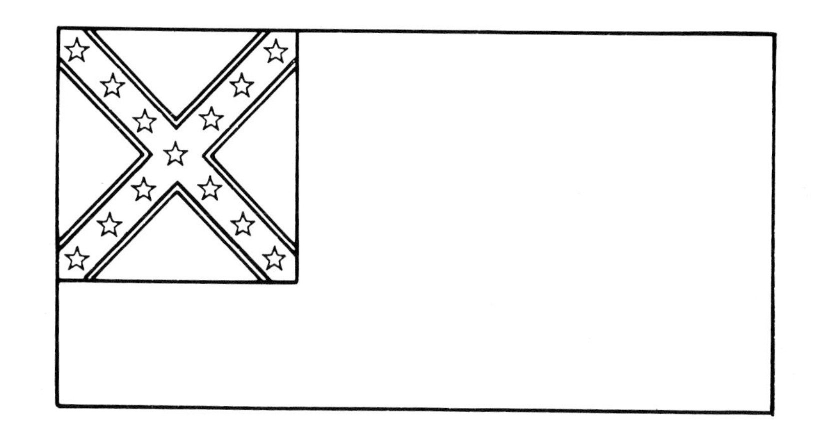

Figure 13: Flag of the Confederate States of America, May 1, 1863 to March 4, 1865.

Finally, Representative Peter W. Gray of Houston, Texas put into formal language an amendment to Senate Bill No. 132 which read as follows:

> AN ACT to establish the flag of the Confederate States.
>
> *The Congress of the Confederate States of America do enact,* That the flag of the Confederate States shall be as follows: The field to be white, the length double the width of the flag, with the union (now used as the battle flag) to be a square of two-thirds the width of the flag, having the ground red; thereon a broad saltier of blue, bordered with white, and emblazoned with white mullets or five-pointed stars, corresponding in number to that of the Confederate States.

In this form Senate Bill No. 132 passed the House of Representatives and was returned to the Senate for concurrence in the amendment. The Senate approved the amendment with little or no debate. Later that afternoon President Davis' signature gave a new national flag to the Confederate States of America.

This second Confederate Flag was referred to as the "Stainless Banner" because of its pure white field, and was proclaimed emblematic of the purity of the Cause which it represented. Regrettably, one of its first uses was to drape the coffin of General Thomas J. "Stonewall" Jackson. On the evening of May 2, 1863 General Jackson was fired upon by one of his own regiments at the Battle of Chancellorsville. His left arm was amputated, and his health seemed to improve until May 7, by which time he had developed pneumonia. On May 10, the hero of the Southern nation was dead and on May 12, his body lay in state in the Confederate House of Representatives chamber. His coffin, by order of the President, was draped with the first of the new national flag to be manufactured. This very first "Stainless Banner" is now on display in the Museum of the Confederacy in Richmond.

Figure 14: Confederate States Treasury Note Decorated with the Confederate Flag and a Portrait of Stonewall Jackson.

Because the first use of the new Confederate flag was connected with Jackson's funeral, it is at times referred to as the "Jackson flag." This identification of the flag with Jackson would be strengthened by the use of the Stainless Banner and Jackson's portrait together on Confederate bonds and currency issued in 1864 and 1865.

Specifications

The Flag Act of 1863 gives a bit more detail on relative proportions than did the report adopting the "Stars and Bars." When combined with further details set out in regulations issued by the Secretary of the Navy on May 26, 1863 for the construction of the naval ensign, full and complete specifications are available for almost every detail of the flag.

The Flag Act of 1863 specified that the length of the flag was to be twice its width. For example, a 54 inch wide flag would have a length of 108 inches. The canton of this 108 inch long flag would be a 36 inch square. The proportions of the cross and stars are not provided in the act, but they are set out in some detail in the naval regulations. The arms of the cross were to be proportioned in width as 1/4.8 the width of the canton; i.e., seven and one-half inches in our example. The white border of the cross of our flag will be one and three-fifths inches wide at a specified size of 1/22 the width of the canton. Finally, the stars are to have a diameter of 1/6.4 the width of the canton, or about five and one-half inches on our example. Using the Flag Act of 1863 in combination with the naval regulations, it is quite possible to construct in accurate detail the official dimensions of the "Stainless Banner."

During the War these detailed specifications were not very strictly followed. A large number of the surviving flags have lengths much less than twice their widths. In a number of cases, the canton is rectangular rather than square. Very little effort seems to have been made to measure the stars to their regulation sizes.

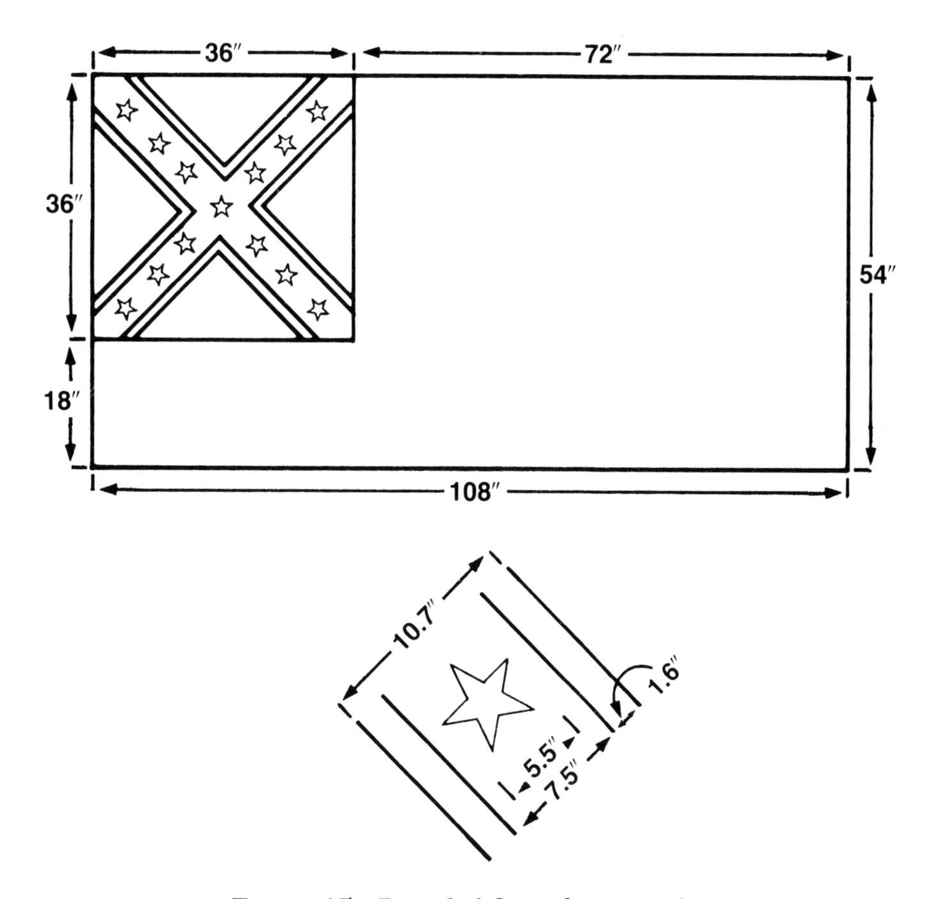

Figure 15: Detailed Specifications for the Construction of the Stainless Banner.

CHAPTER 4
THE CONFEDERATE FLAG — FINAL EDITION

Revision Of The "Stainless Banner"

The Flag Act of 1863 solved the problem of clear national identity and a complete vexillological separation from the United States, but the new flag would present new problems. Congressman Miles had argued in the 1863 flag debate that "the white flag . . . would not be taken for a flag of truce—it was the old French Bourbon flag"; but the flag had been considered by many as looking too much like a flag of truce. As a result, the flag was often manufactured with a shorter fly length in order to minimize the white field.

To address this problem, a new flag bill was introduced in the Confederate States Senate on December 13, 1864. Senator Thomas J. Semmes of Louisiana introduced Senate Bill No. 137 with the statement that "naval officers objected to the present flag—that in a calm it looked like a flag of truce." The text of the bill was as follows:

> AN ACT to establish the flag of the Confederate States.
>
> *The Congress of the Confederate States of America do enact,* That the flag of the Confederate States of America shall be as follows: The width two-thirds of its length, with the union (now used as the battle flag) to be in width three-fifths of the width of the flag, and so proportioned as to leave the length of the field on the side of the union twice the width of the field below it; to have the ground red and a broad blue saltier thereon, bordered with white and emblazoned with mullets or five-pointed stars, corresponding in number to that of the Confederate States; the field to be white, except the outer half from the union to be a red bar extending the width of the flag.

Senate Bill No. 137 was referred to the Naval Committee on December 13. Senator Albert G. Brown of Mississippi read the Committee's report, which included a recommendation for passage, to the Senate on December 16. This time, however, the Congress would not pass a flag law without a great deal of consideration. Senator Edward Sparrow of Louisiana recommended that opinion of officers of the army should be obtained on the matter. Senator Semmes replied that he had received a letter from "the most distinguished officer" of the army (General Lee?) expressing the opinion that the officers of the navy were the proper parties to resolve the flag question. Nevertheless, in an abundance of caution, the Senate referred the bill to the Military Committee.

The Military Committee considered the bill for seven weeks and made its report recommending passage without amendment on February 5, 1865. The Senate passed Senate Bill No. 137 on February 6 and sent it on to the House of Representatives.

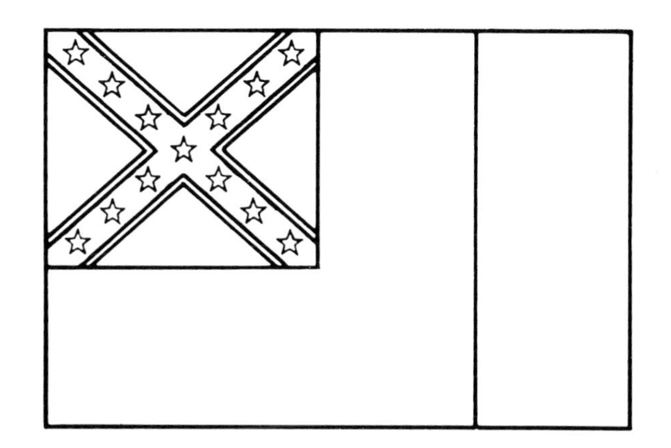

Figure 16: Flag of the Confederate States of America Since March 4, 1865.

On February 7 the new flag bill was referred to the House Committee on Flag and Seal. That committee kept the bill for twenty days and also reported favorably on it. The House passed Senate Bill No. 137 on February 27. On March 4, 1865, President Jefferson Davis signed the bill into law, and the Confederate States of America acquired their third and last national flag. The Flag Act of 1865 became law exactly four years after the Provisional Congress had adopted the "Stars and Bars" as the first Confederate Flag.

Specifications

The Flag Act of 1865 made fairly detailed changes in the proportions of the flag, as well as in its general appearance. In addition to adding the broad red bar to the fly end, it shortened the fly length of the flag and changed the canton from a square to a rectangular shape.

The 1865 law specifies that the width of the flag shall be two-thirds its length. In the case of a flag 60 inches wide, the proper length would be 90 inches. The canton of a 60 inch wide flag at a specified width of three-fifths that of the flag will be 36 inches wide. The law specifies that the canton will be so proportioned as to leave the length of the field beyond it "twice the width of the field below it." On a 60 inch wide flag, this will leave a canton length of 42 inches, thus creating a width to length ratio for the canton of 6/7.

The red bar on our illustrated flag would be 24 inches wide at a specified width of one-half the area of the fly beyond the canton.

It seems proper to apply the navy regulations of 1863 to this new flag for a determination of the cross and star proportions. Since our 60 inch flag under the 1865 law has the same canton width as the 54 inch wide flag under the 1863 law, the cross and star proportions on the two flags would be the same: a seven and one-half inch wide cross with a one and three-fifths inch wide border and stars with a five and one-half inch diameter.

Unlike the existing War period flags of the earlier patterns, there are very few survivors of the 1865 version. Of the ones which do exist, most are the 1863 flag with the fly shortened and a red bar added.

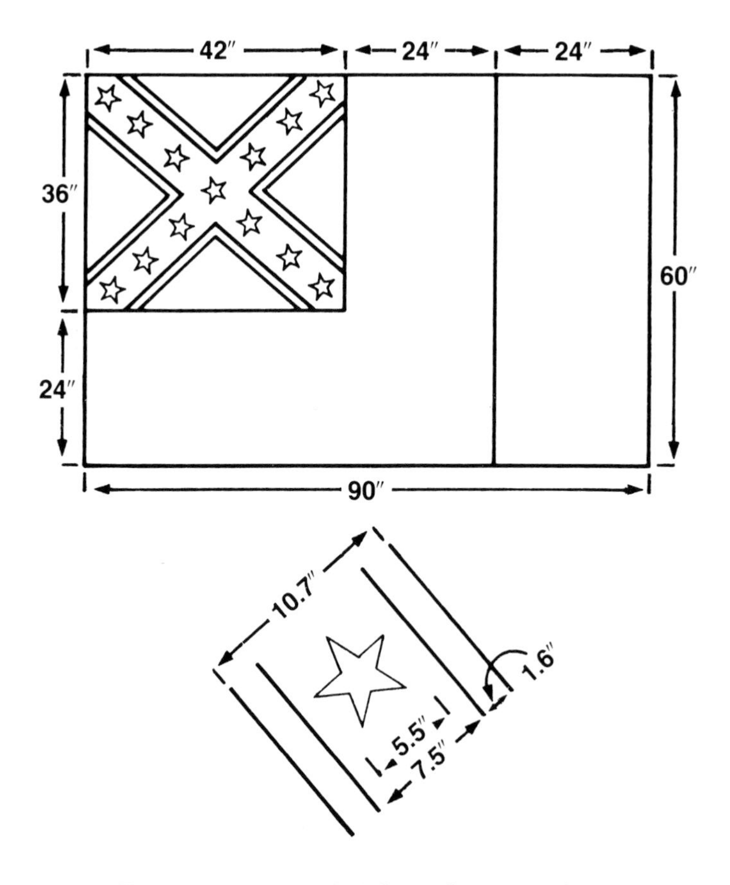

Figure 17: Detailed Specifications for the Construction of the Last Confederate Flag.

CHAPTER 5
EVOLUTION OF THE FLAG

While it may not be immediately apparent, the national flag of the Confederate States of America has evolved by a direct and traceable lineage from the flag of the United Kingdom of Great Britain.

In 1606, King James VI of Scotland, also known as King James I of England, established a new flag for the United Kingdoms of England and Scotland. The king combined the Saint George's flag of England with the Saint Andrew's flag of Scotland to form the Union flag of Great Britain. At sea, this Union flag was placed as a canton hence also called a union, on a red flag to become known as the "British red ensign." Because of the maritime nature of American colonization, it was this red ensign which became best known in British America.

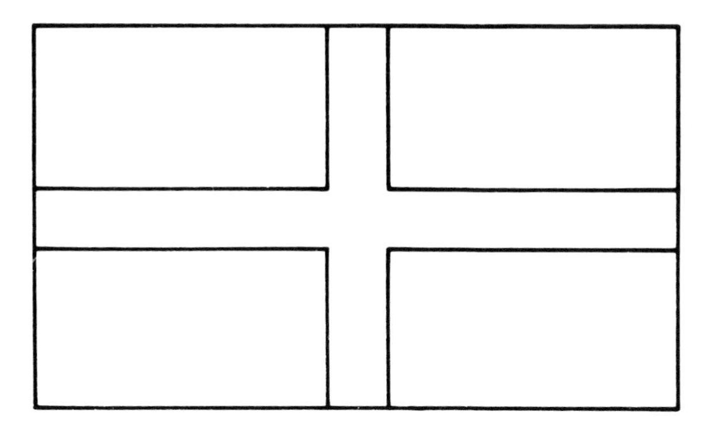

Figure 18: St. George's Cross of England

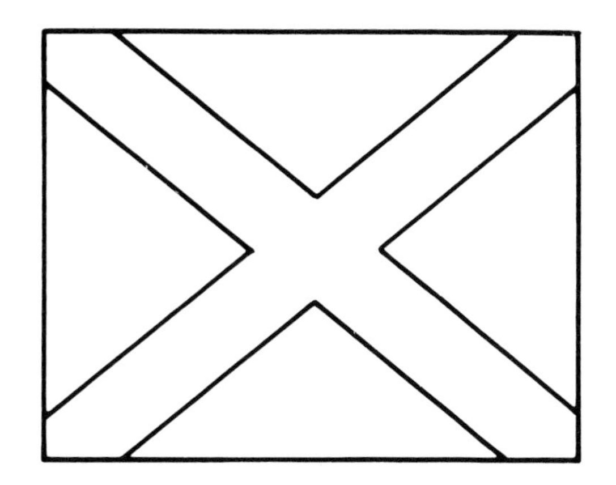

Figure 19: St. Andrew's Cross of Scotland

FLAGS OF THE CONFEDERACY

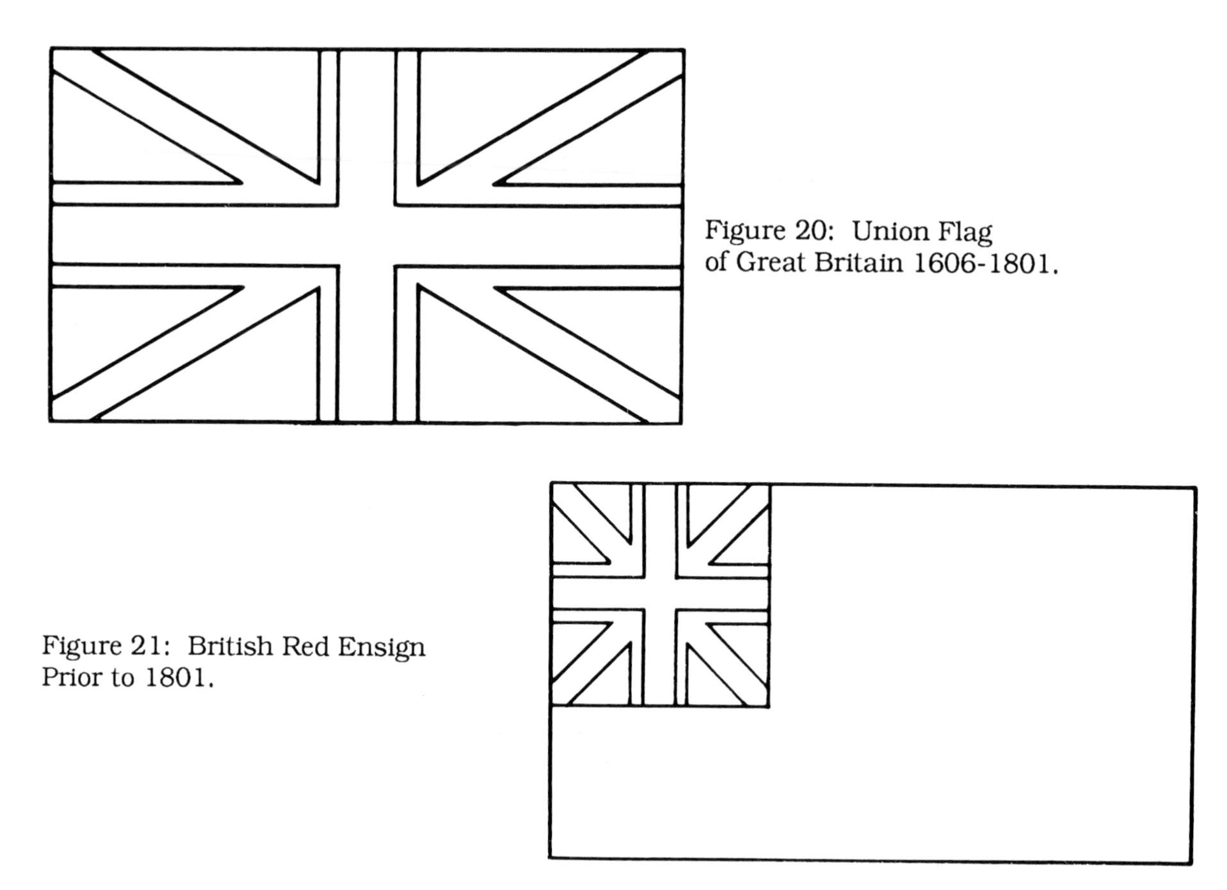

Figure 20: Union Flag of Great Britain 1606-1801.

Figure 21: British Red Ensign Prior to 1801.

When the Revolution broke out in 1775, the Americans adopted various banners to display their political sentiments. Among those often appeared the British red ensign charged with some motto such as "LIBERTY." In December 1775, John Paul Jones hoisted upon an American ship a red ensign which had been altered by the addition of white stripes, creating thirteen red and white stripes to represent the rebel colonies. A similar flag was raised in the American lines outside of Boston by General George Washington just after the turn of the new year in 1776. This striped ensign, which was called the Grand Union Flag, came to be accepted as the common flag of the united colonies. With the Declaration of Independence on July 4, 1776 it became the first national flag of the United States of America and served that role until June 14, 1777.

In June, 1777, the Continental Congress decided that the flag should be altered by removing from the blue union the crosses of England and Scotland. In their stead were placed the stars of the American States, and thus was born the "Stars and Stripes." Over time new States were admitted to the American union, which in turn were represented by new stars in the union of the flag. Custom came to prefer five-pointed stars, though stars with more points would be used until the middle of the nineteenth century.

In 1861, when the Southern States left the American union and formed the new Confederacy, they chose for the new nation a flag with the same elements as the old, but reduced the thirteen stripes to three bars. As in the case of the Continental Congress in 1777, by 1863 the Confederate Congress was ready to remove from their flag reminders of the old government. An initial proposal to reverse the colors of the "Stars and Bars" was amended by removing the bars altogether, leaving the red battle flag of the army as a canton on a "stainless" white field.

Figure 22: Flag of the United States—1776 to 1777

In 1865, with concern expressed by naval officers that the flag of 1863 could be mistaken for a flag of truce, the dimensions were altered and a red bar was added to the fly creating the last flag of the Confederate States of America.

Figure 23: Flag of the United States—1777 to 1795

FLAGS OF THE CONFEDERACY

Thus was established the long and proud heritage of the Confederate Flag. One could say that the British Union flag, in the form of the red ensign, was the great-great-great grandfather of the Confederate Flag of 1865. In the tradition of biblical genealogy, we could fashion a geneaology of the Confederate Flag as follows:

The Union flag of 1606 and its red ensign begat the Grand Union flag of 1775, the symbol of American liberty;

the Grand Union flag begat the "Stars and Stripes" of 1777, the symbol of American independence;

the "Stars and Stripes" begat the "Stars and Bars" of 1861, the symbol of Southern liberty;

the "Stars and Bars" begat the "Stainless Banner" of 1863, the symbol of Southern independence; and

the "Stainless Banner" begat the Confederate Flag of 1865, the final expression in bunting of the sovereignty of the Confederate States of America.

PART II—THE STATES

CHAPTER 6
THE BONNIE BLUE FLAG

On January 9, 1861, the Convention of the People of Mississippi adopted an Ordinance of Secession. With the announcement of the Ordinance, a large blue flag bearing a single white star was raised over the capitol building in Jackson. One of the witnesses to this event, an Irish-born actor named Harry Macarthy, was so inspired by the spectacle that he wrote a song entitled "The Bonnie Blue Flag" which was destined to be the second most popular patriotic song in the Confederacy. (See Appendix D)

The first recorded use of a lone star flag dates to 1810. At that time the portion of Louisiana east of the Mississippi River, along with the southern portions of Mississippi and Alabama, made up the Spanish province of West Florida. This area had once been part of the French province of Louisiana. In 1763, after the French and Indian War, France ceded New Orleans and all of Louisiana west of the Mississippi to Spain. That portion of Louisiana east of the river was ceded to the English, who established therein the British province named West Florida. West Florida was conquered by Spain during her campaigns as an American ally in the Revolutionary War. When France later re-acquired Louisiana from Spain, there was a dispute about whether or not the transaction included West Florida. Spain refused to relinquish control of the province, and the United States inherited the dispute when they purchased Louisiana from France in 1803.

The inhabitants of West Florida were in large part English-speaking people on whom the authoritarian rule of Spain did not wear well. They were disappointed in the failure of the United States to annex the territory, and in 1804 an unsuccessful revolt was lead by the brothers Reuben, Nathan, and Sam Kemper. In the years following the Kemper Rebellion, the English-speaking people of West Florida attempted to secure some degree of traditional English liberties within the framework of their Spanish government. This culminated in a convention of the people meeting in 1810 to press for some form of constitutional guarantees. Governor de Lassus pretended to cooperate with the convention while sending to the Governor of East Florida for troops to put down this perceived threat to his authority.

Upon learning of the Governor's duplicity, the supporters of the convention turned to open rebellion. On Saturday, September 11, 1810, a troop of dragoons under the command of Major Isaac Johnson set out for the provincial capitol at Baton Rouge. At the head of the column rode a color sergeant carrying a blue flag with a single, white five-pointed star. This flag had been made a few days before by Mrs. Melissa Johnson. Together with other republican forces under the command of Colonel Philemon Thomas, these men captured Baton Rouge without loss to themselves, imprisoned the Governor, and on September 23, 1810 raised their Bonnie Blue flag over the Fort of Baton Rouge. Three days later, John Rhea, president of the West Florida Convention, signed a Declaration of Independence, and the lone star flag became the emblem of a new republic.

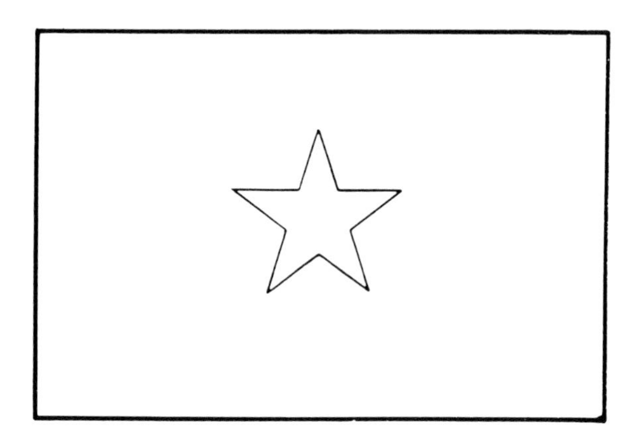

Figure 24: The Bonnie Blue Flag.
- Flag of the Republic of West Florida September 16 to December 10, 1810.
- Flag of the Republic of Texas, December 10, 1836 to January 25, 1839.
- Flag of the Republic of Mississippi January 6 to January 26, 1861.

The Republic of West Florida was short-lived. When Spanish rule was removed from the country with neither the use of American troops nor risk to itself, the government of the United States was interested in asserting its claim to the little republic. On October 27, 1810, President Madison issued a proclamation declaring West Florida under the jurisdiction of the Governor of the Louisiana Territory. On December 10, the flag of the United States replaced the Bonnie Blue flag over Baton Rouge, and The Republic of West Florida passed into history.

The memory of the West Florida movement lived on in Southern tradition, and the flag of the little nation became the flag of the Republic of Texas from 1836 to 1839. It would rise again as the unofficial flag of the Republic of Mississippi for a few weeks in 1861; and Harry Macarthy's song would spur it on into the romantic lore of the South. When the song was first played in New Orleans before a mixed audience of Texans and Louisianians, it was received with an outburst of approval that was nearly riotous. Thereafter, the Bonnie Blue flag spread across the nation and into the hearts of the people. Although the Confederate government did not adopt it, the Confederate people did, and lone star flags were adopted in one form or another in five of the southern States which adopted new flags in 1861.

CHAPTER 7
STATE FLAGS

The secession movement saw the first large-scale use of flags by the American States. After the Revolution, most of the States retired their revolutionary colors and displayed only the flag of the Union. With the resumption of their independence, the Southern States adopted new banners to reflect their new status among the States of the earth. Of the Confederate States which had adopted official State flags by the end of 1861, only one had a flag in use before she seceded from the Union. Three of those States—Virginia, South Carolina, and, of course, Texas—still fly the flags which were flown in 1861.

South Carolina

South Carolina was the first State to leave the United States and was among the first to adopt a new national flag. The design chosen was drawn from South Carolina's revolutionary heritage.

The crescent had been the symbol of South Carolina in the days of the colonial government. During the Revolution, South Carolina troops wore silver crescents as hat badges and fought under blue flags with a white crescent in the upper corner. The other emblem of South Carolina is the palmetto tree. Its use also dates from the Revolution and is said to have been inspired by the palmetto logs used in the construction of Fort Moultrie

Figure 25: Flag of South Carolina,
January 26, 1861 to January 28, 1861.

on Charleston harbor. Because palmetto is resilient, the logs absorbed the shock from British cannon balls instead of shattering under them; they are credited with contributing to the successful defense of Charleston on June 28, 1776. Shortly after this battle, the palmetto was adopted as the central device of the Great Seal of South Carolina.

Figure 26: Flag of South Carolina,
January 28, 1861 to Present.

Prior to secession, South Carolina patriots had often displayed palmetto flags. Secession saw these multiply, with each flag-maker designing the flag according to her own fancy. On January 26, 1861 the legislature adopted an official flag which embraced both of the State's historic devices. The new emblem was the old revolutionary flag with the white crescent. Added to the center of the field was a large white oval on which appeared a palmetto tree in natural colors. Two days later the legislature altered the flag by removing the oval and placing a white palmetto tree on the blue field. In this final form, the palmetto flag has served South Carolina to the present.

Mississippi

On January 9, 1861, Mississippi became the second State to secede from the United States. To celebrate her new role as an independent republic, the Bonnie Blue flag was freed to the wind from the flagpole of the State capitol in Jackson.

Mississippi adopted an official State flag on January 26, 1861. Her new flag incorporated the Bonnie Blue flag as a canton on a white field. In the center of the field was a representation of a magnolia tree in natural colors,

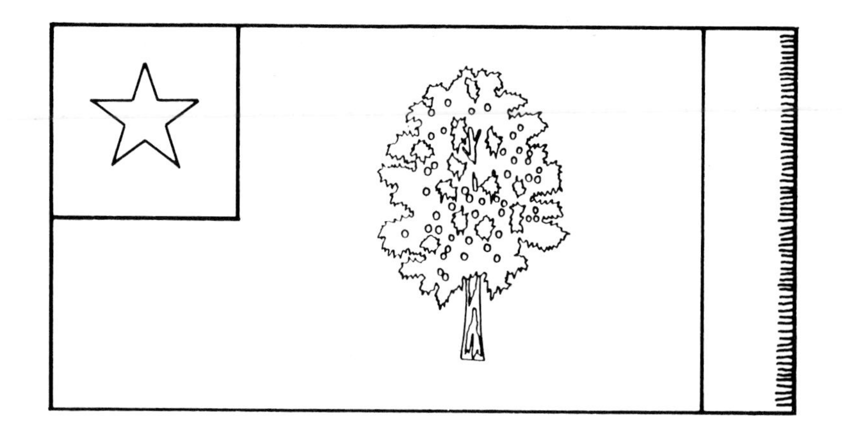

Figure 27: Flag of Mississippi Adopted January 26, 1861.

an association so permanent that the State is still known as the Magnolia State. The fly end of the magnolia flag was decorated with a red fringe.

Florida

Florida withdrew "from the confederacy of States existing under the name of the United States of America" by the adoption of her Ordinance of Secession on January 10, 1861. Some time passed before she acquired an official State flag, in part because the legislature was unable to agree on a design. On February 8, 1861 a law was enacted delegating to the governor the power to designate a flag.

Figure 28: Provisional Flag of Florida, January 13, 1861 to September 13, 1861.

In the meantime, the Military Department of the State adopted a provisional flag to be used until the governor provided a State flag. This provisional flag was promulgated by an order dated January 13, 1861 and was simply the flag of the United States with a single star in the union.

Figure 29: Flag of Florida Adopted September 13, 1861.

The Governor finally issued an executive order establishing the State flag on September 13, 1861. The flag adopted by the Confederate Congress on March 4, 1861 was altered to serve Florida's needs by extending the canton to form a vertical bar the entire width of the flag. Centered on the blue bar was a new seal for the State, displaying in natural colors a stand of arms and flags beneath an oak tree, with ships at sea in the background.

Alabama

In anticipation of the secession of Alabama, some ladies of Montgomery painted a beautiful flag for presentation to the State. The Alabama Convention approved the flag and, upon the adoption of the Ordinance of Secession, the new Alabama flag was raised over the capitol of the independent republic.

Alabama's banner was unique among Southern State flags in being two-sided; that is, the front and back had different designs. The central device on the front of the blue flag was the goddess Liberty dressed in red with a sword in her right hand and a Bonnie Blue flag in her left. This Bonnie Blue flag was edged in yellow and had a yellow star. Above the star in yellow letters was the name "ALABAMA." Also in yellow letters and arched over the goddess was the legend "INDEPENDENT NOW AND FOREVER."

Figure 30: Flag of Alabama.

The reverse of the flag was also a field of blue. Featured on the reverse was a cotton plant guarded by a rattlesnake, below which appeared the Latin motto "NOLI ME TANGERE." The motto translates "Don't Touch Me" and together with the snake was reminiscent of the "Don't Tread On Me" flags of the Revolution.

Figure 31: Reverse of the Alabama State Flag.

Attractive as this flag was, it was not easy to make, and Alabamians apparently borrowed one of its details to serve as a simpler flag. This was the Bonnie Blue flag with the yellow star held by the Liberty on the official standard. It may have appeared at times with the word "ALABAMA" over the star, but the most common form seems to have been with the yellow star alone on the blue field.

STATE FLAGS

Georgia

On the day that Georgia's Convention adopted "An Ordinance to dissolve the union between the State of Georgia and other States united with her under the compact of government entitled 'The Constitution of the United States of America,' " a new flag was raised over the capitol in Milledgeville. This flag has been described as the arms of Georgia on a white field. The arms feature the arch of the Constitution being supported by the pillars of Justice, Wisdom, and Moderation.

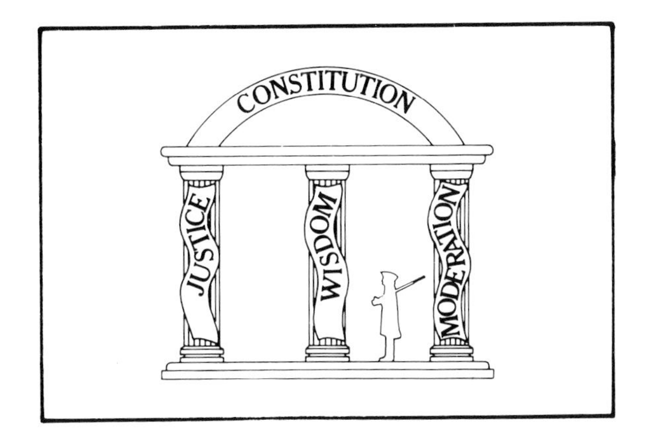

Figure 32: The Flag of Georgia.

Over the years, tradition has placed this device more often on a blue field, and it may have been used on a blue field as a military color. Georgia's State flags in this century have continued the tradition of displaying the State seal on blue. A surviving Georgia flag in the collection of the Museum of the Confederacy in Richmond, however, places the arms on a red field.

Georgia's flag had a position of honor on the occasion of Jefferson Davis' inauguration as President of the provisional government. On February 18, 1861 the Confederate States did not yet have a flag, and the President-elect's inaugural parade was led by a company of re-coated Georgia militia marching under the flag of the State of Georgia.

FLAGS OF THE CONFEDERACY

Louisiana

The pelican has been the symbol of Louisiana for almost as long as there has been such a place. The bird which now graces the flag of the State has been the device of the Seal of Louisiana since its territorial status under the United States. While the current flag has only been official since 1912,

Figure 33: Pelican Flag.

pelican flags are known to have existed before the War Between the States. One such flag was used at the Louisiana Secession Convention on the occasion of the adoption of the Ordinance of Secession on January 26, 1861.

When she adopted an official flag to proclaim her independence after secession, Louisiana turned away from the pelican. Instead, she chose a flag

Figure 34: Flag of Louisiana, Adopted February 11, 1861.

which combined the sentimental attachment she felt for the United States flag with the lone star symbol of sovereignty and colors from her heraldic past.

Like the flag of the old Union, the new flag adopted by Louisiana on February 11, 1861 had thirteen stripes. These were altered from the red and white of the United States to the blue, white and red of France, Louisiana's mother country. The canton of the flag placed a single yellow star on a field of red, the colors of the flag of Spain which had also once held dominion over Louisiana.

Texas

Texas had the richest vexillological heritage of any American State. The flags of six independent powers have flown over her territory. During the period which Texans consider to have been their glory—the era of the Republic--six flags flew to represent Texan nationalism.

Figure 35: Flag of the Texas Revolution, 1835.

When the Texas Revolution began in 1835, the predominant sentiment was not for independence, but for liberty under the law, as established by the Mexican Constitution of 1824. The flag of the Revolution proclaimed this, and Texas was represented by the flag of Mexico, the green-white-red tri-color, with the national arms replaced by the date "1824."

The response of Santa Anna to the demands of the Texans left little room for reconciliation, and by 1836 the revolution had become a secession movement. On March 2, 1836 the independence of Texas was proclaimed, and

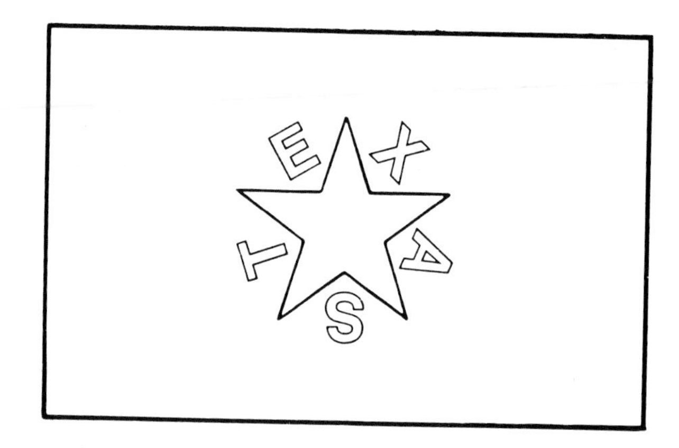

Figure 36: Texas Flag, March 11, 1836
to December 10, 1836.

on March 11 the Republic adopted a new flag devoid of Mexican symbolism. This standard was the Bonnie Blue flag with letters spelling out the name "TEXAS" arrayed around and between the points of the star. On December 10, 1836, the flag was modified by removing the letters, and the unadorned Bonnie Blue flag of the late Republic of West Florida with a yellow star served as the national flag of Texas for the next two years.

Figure: 37: Texas Flag, December 10, 1836 to January 25, 1839; and unofficial variant of the Alabama State Flag, 1861.

On January 25, 1839 the Republic of Texas made a final modification of its flag. The blue field was reduced to a vertical bar, its width approximately one half the width of the flag, but still carrying the lone star of the Republic. The remainder of the flag became two broad bars of white over red. This flag has served Texas ever since: first as the flag of the Republic until 1845; then as the flag of the State under the United States; and finally as the flag of the State under the Confederate States of America.

During the era of the Republic, Texas also had distinctive flags for use at sea. During the pre-independence period of the revolution, Texas privateers

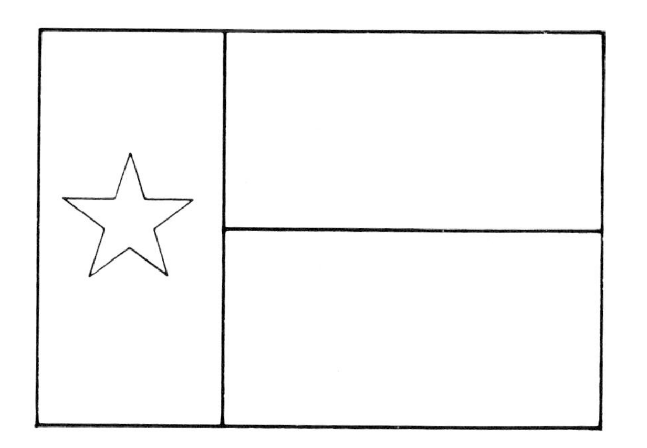

Figure 38: Texas Flag, January 25, 1839 to Present.

flew the "1824" flag. In 1836, this was replaced by the ensign of the Texas Navy. The Texas naval ensign proclaimed the attachment of Texas to the United States, both symbolically and diplomatically, and was in fact the flag of the United States with a lone star in the union. This ensign graced the naval vessels of the Republic until Texas became one of the United States in 1845.

During the time the Bonnie Blue flag served as the national flag of Texas,

Figure 39: Texas Naval Ensign.

it probably also served as the national ensign for private and merchant ships belonging to Texans. With the adoption of the new national flag in 1839, a new and distinctive civil ensign was also adopted by the Congress of Texas. The civil ensign rearranged the features of the national flag to form a horizontal tri-color with bars of white, blue and red. The lone star was displayed in the center of the blue bar, which was twice as wide as the white

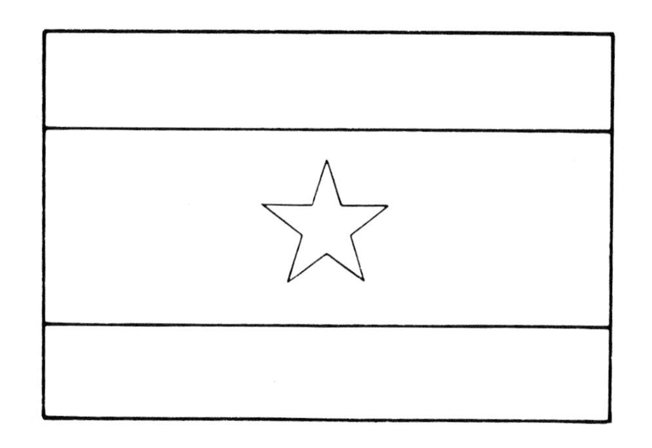

Figure 40: Texas Civil Ensign.

or red bars. Although the civil ensign ceased to be used after Texas joined the American union in 1845, the Flag Law of 1839 does not appear to have been amended. It would still be appropriate for Texans who wished to fly a Texas flag from their boats or ships to display the civil ensign of 1839. Texas is therefore one of the few American States to have a distinctive civil ensign.

Virginia

On April 15, 1861 Lincoln's Secretary of War called upon Virginia to supply regiments for the invasion and conquest of the Confederate States. The Old Dominion responded by withdrawing from the United States on the 17th of April; and on the 30th of that month, a flag was adopted for the independent Commonwealth of Virginia.

Virginia's banner is the Bonnie Blue flag with the star replaced by the seal of the Commonwealth. The seal, which had been adopted during the Revolution, represents the goddess Liberty striking down an allegorical tyrant, his crown dashed to the earth. Both the seal and flag display the Latin

Figure 41: Virginia State Flag.

motto "SIC SEMPER TYRANNIS": which translates as "Ever Thus to Tyrants." The symbol which had been adopted as Virginia's response to monarchial and parliamentary tyranny in the 1770s would serve as her reply to aggression in the 1860s. In slightly modified form, the flag of 1861 still serves the Commonwealth of Virginia.

North Carolina

On May 20, 1861 exactly eighty-six years after North Carolina is said to have expressed her determination for independence from Great Britain in the Mecklenburg Resolves, the people of North Carolina assembled in convention once again declared their independent spirit and removed themselves from the jurisdiction of the United States government. On June 22, 1861 North Carolina adopted a flag which commemorated both of these events.

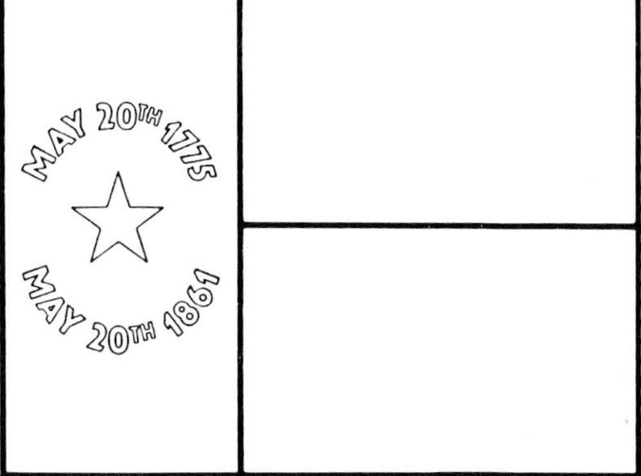

Figure 42: North Carolina State Flag.

The North Carolina State flag followed the lone star theme which had been adopted in Alabama, Florida, Louisiana, Mississippi and Texas. The Old North State was inspired by the flag of Texas in choosing a pattern, but the Carolinians reversed the colors. Carolina's star was placed on a broad red vertical bar from which flowed horizontal bars of blue over white. Around the star were placed the dates on which North Carolina celebrates her independence: May 20, 1775 for independence from Great Britain and May 20, 1861 for independence from the United States.

Tennessee

On April 25, 1861 the Tennessee General Assembly convened in Nashville in the second extraordinary session of the legislature to be called since the turn of the year. The first extra session had put to a vote of the people the question of joining the deep South in seceding from the Union. Taking a wait-and-see attitude towards the Lincoln government, the people rejected secession in the February election; but in April, war had become a reality, and the questions was again to be placed before the voters.

On the first day of the session, the speaker of the Senate, Tazewell B. Newman, offered Senate Resolution No. 2 to establish a flag for the State of Tennessee. The resolution called for the Secretary of State to have a flag of the Confederate States made which would be modified by replacing the stars with the Great Seal of Tennessee. Senate Resolution No. 2 was referred to the Committee on Federal Relations, but was never acted upon further and never became a law. The committee thought it impolitic to fly an obviously Confederate flag while Tennessee was still one of the United States.

Figure 43: Proposed Tennessee State Flag, 1861.

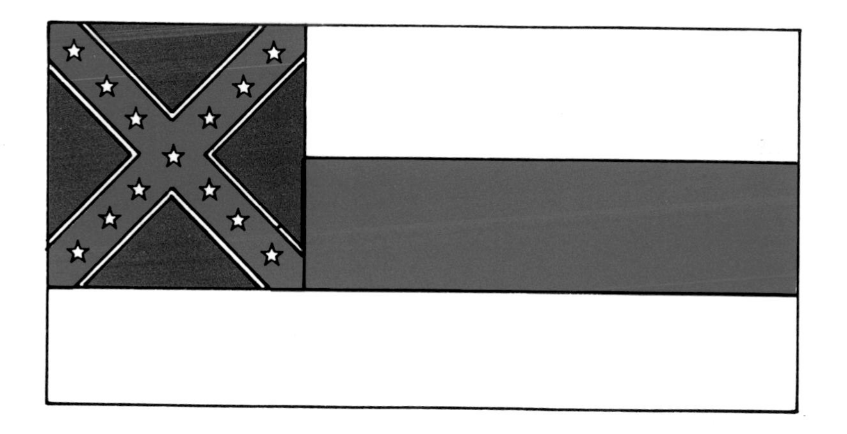

Figure 10: Original Version of the Flag in Senate Bill No. 132, 1863.

Figure 11: A Proposed Amendment of Senate Bill No. 132, 1863.

Figure 12: Congressman Swan's Amendment to Senate Bill No. 132.

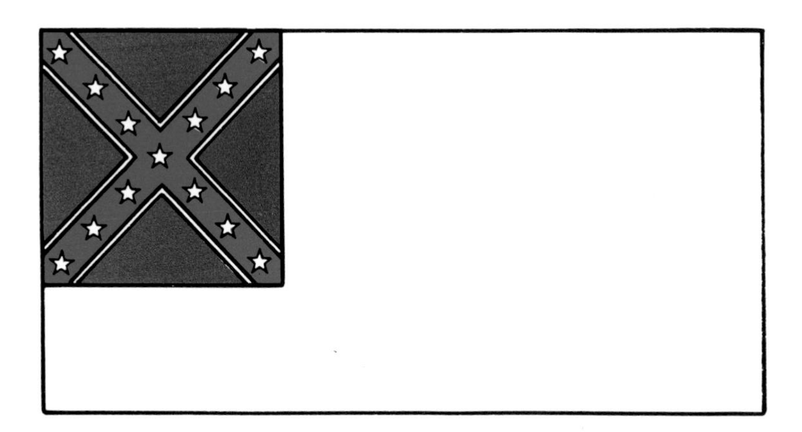

Figure 13: Flag of the Confederate States of America, May 1, 1863 to March 4, 1865.

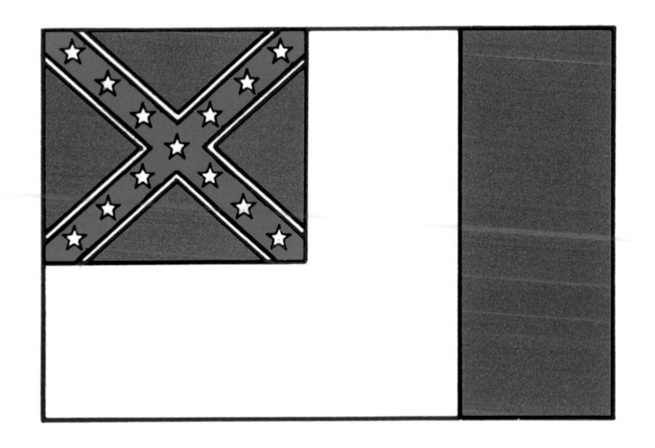

Figure 16: Flag of the Confederate States of America Since March 4, 1865.

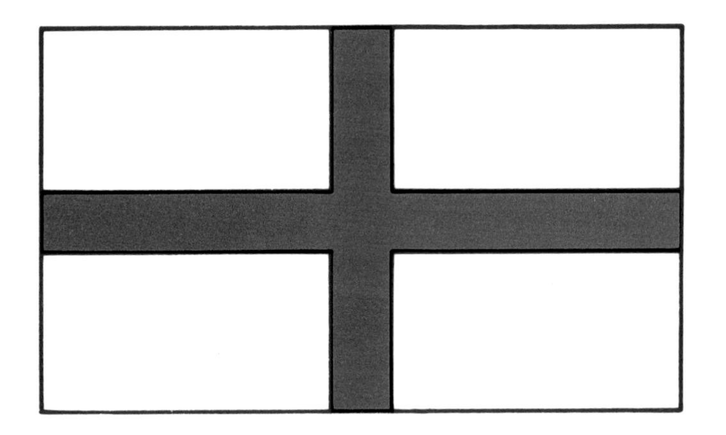

Figure 18: St George's Cross of England.

Figure 19: St. Andrew's Cross of Scotland.

Figure 20: Union Flag of Great Britain 1606-1801.

Figure 21: British Red Ensign Prior to 1801.

Figure 22: Flag of the United States—1776 to 1777.

Figure 23: Flag of the United States—1777 to 1779.

Figure 24: The Bonnie Blue Flag.

Figure 25: Flag of South Carolina, January 26, 1861 to January 28, 1861.

Figure 26: Flag of South Carolina, January 28, 1861 to Present.

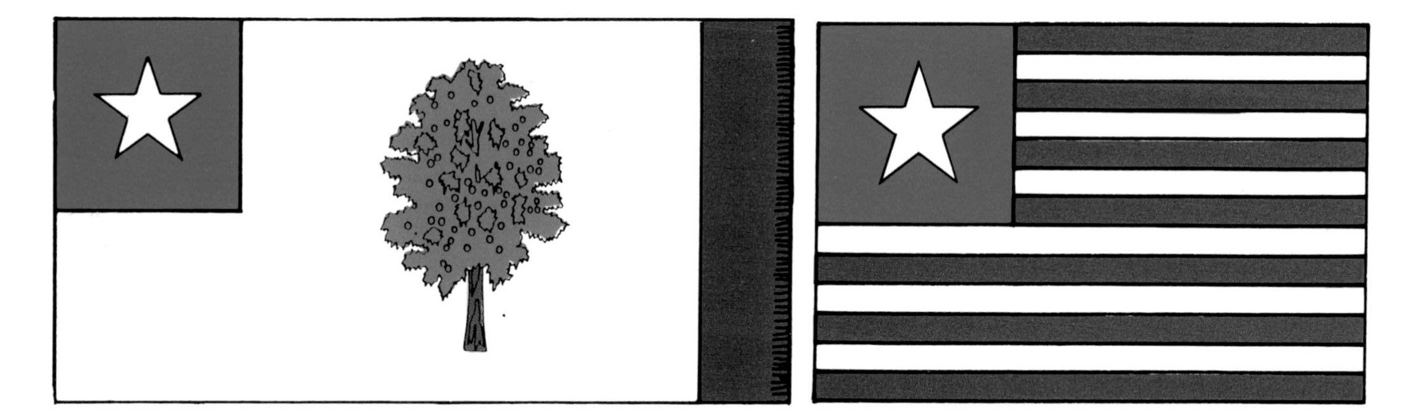

Figure 27: Flag of Mississippi, Adopted January 26, 1861.

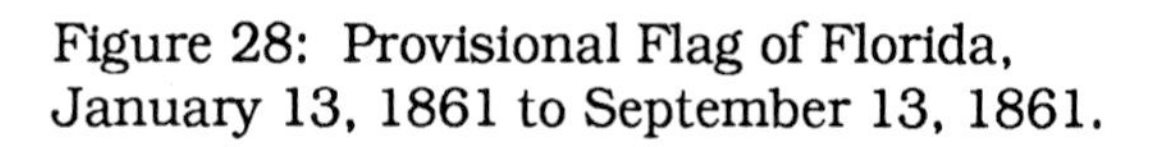

Figure 28: Provisional Flag of Florida, January 13, 1861 to September 13, 1861.

Figure 29: Flag of Florida, Adopted September 13, 1861.

Figure 30: Flag of Alabama.

Figure 31: Reverse of the Alabama State Flag.

Figure 32: The Flag of Georgia.

Figure 33: Pelican Flag.

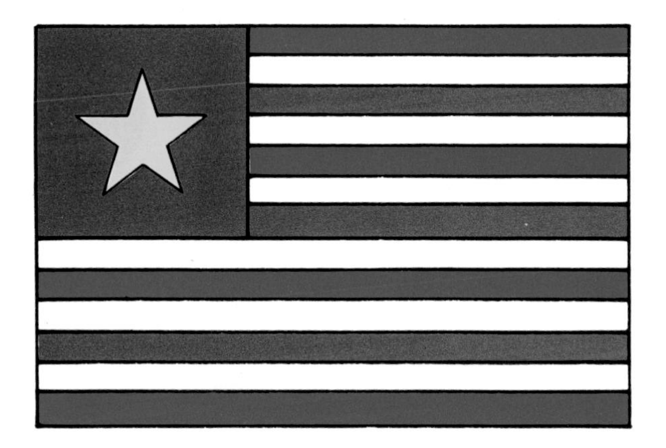

Figure 34: Flag of Louisiana, Adopted February 11, 1861.

Figure 44: The Seal of the State of Kentucky.

Figure 45: Flag of Missouri.

Figure 46: General Beauregard's Prototype of the Battle Flag.

Figure 47: Silk Battle Flag, Issued November 1861.

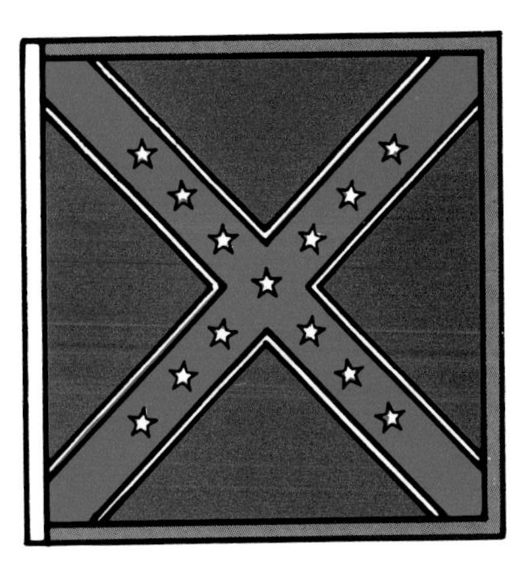

Figure 48: First Bunting Issue, 1862.

Figure 49: Third Bunting Issue, 1863, Army of Northern Virginia.

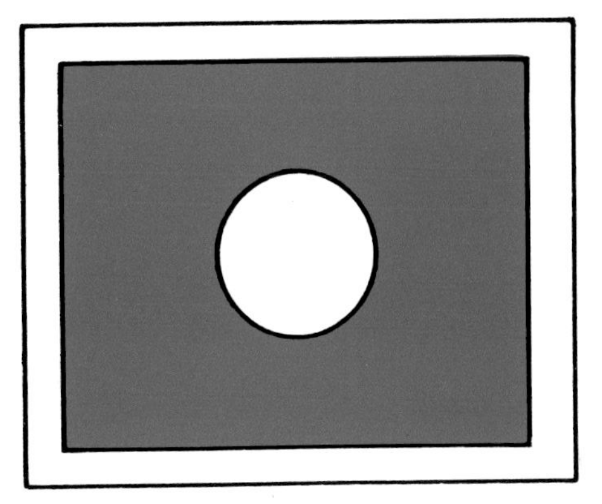

Figure 50: Hardee's Corps, Army of Tennessee.

Figure 51: Polk's Corps Battle Flag, Army of Tennessee.

Figure 60: Battle Flag of General Richard Taylor's Army.

Figure 61: Trans-Mississippi Department, Van Dorn's Corps.

Figure 62: Trans-Mississippi Department, The "Missouri Battle Flag."

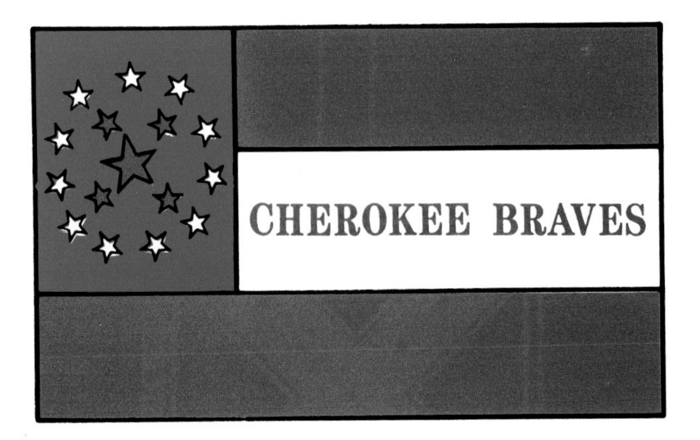

Figure 63: Trans-Mississippi Department, Cherokee Nation.

Figure 64: Flag of the Choctaw Brigade.

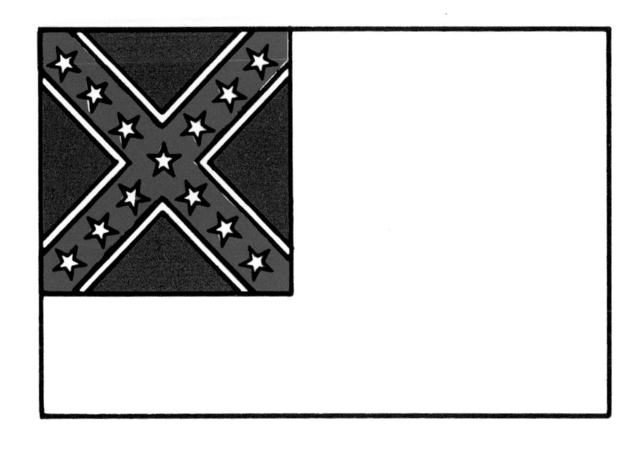

Figure 66: Confederate States Naval Ensign After May 26, 1863.

Figure 67: Confederate Navy Jack March 4, 1861 to May 26, 1863.

Figure 68: Confederate Navy Jack After May 26, 1863.

Figure 69: Confederate Commission Pennant, March 4, 1861 to May 26, 1863.

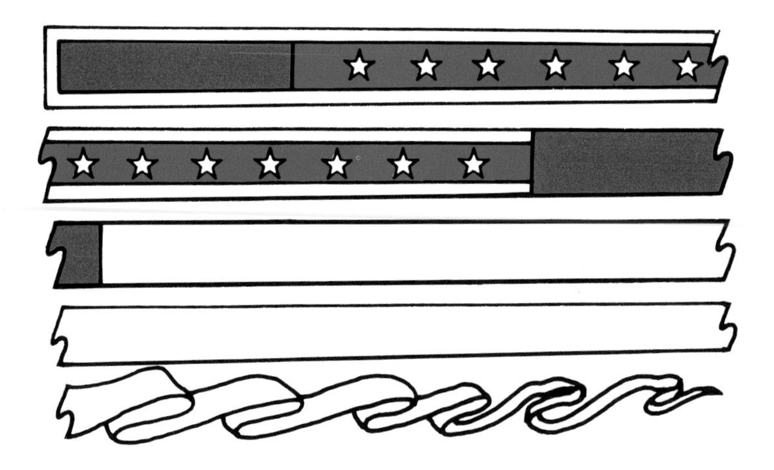

Figure 70: Confederate Commission Pennant, After May 26, 1863.

Figure 71: Variant Confederate Commission Pennant, Used After May 1, 1863.

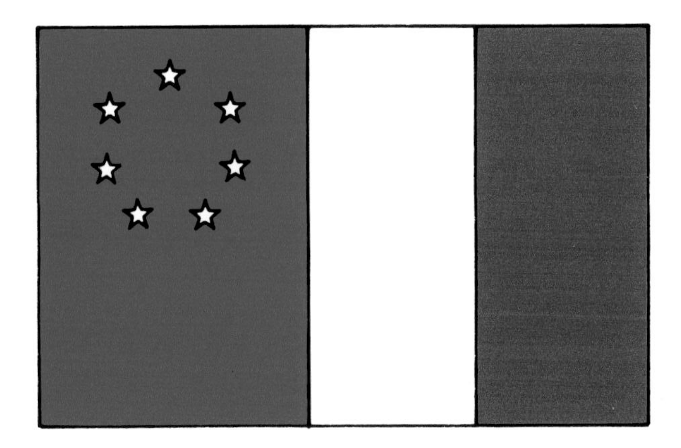

Figure 72: Confederate States Revenue Service Ensign.

CHAPTER 8
BATTLE FLAGS

The use of distinctive battle flags by units of the army is not unique to the Confederacy. For centuries British regiments have carried, in addition to the King's Colors, a distinctive regimental flag. From the War of 1812 through the War Between the States, infantry regiments of the United States carried a blue battle flag emblazoned with the eagle and shield of the Union.

In the Confederate States, there were a number of battle flags used by the army. Those used in the Eastern theatre, where the army tended to get more support from the government, were fairly uniform. The armies in the Western theatre and Trans-Mississippi, more remote from the government in distance and attention, had greater diversity in the styles and patterns of battle flags. Uniformity of flags among the Western troops was never truly achieved and only approached realization in the last year of the War.

The Army of Northern Virginia

The Confederate Army in Virginia was always considered the grand army of the South. Called the Army of the Potomac while under the leadership of General Joseph E. Johnston in 1861 and early 1862, it gained immortality under the command of General Robert E. Lee as the Army of Northern Virginia. Its legendary position in history was guaranteed by the greatness of its commander and by the pre-eminence placed upon it by the government in Richmond.

The first great battle of the army was the Battle of Manassas fought on July 21, 1861. Nominally commanded by General Johnston, the greatest part of the planning and actual field operations were handled by General P.G.T. Beauregard, the "hero of Fort Sumter." On numerous occasions during the course of the battle, confusion was caused by the inability of commanders to distinguish their troops from those of the enemy. There was no distinct uniform for either army at this time, both sides having units clothed in grey and blue along with other more exotic and spectacular colors. The heat and dust of battle combined to obscure visibility. Added to these difficulties was the fact that the "Stars and Bars" were so similar to the "Stars and Stripes" that many men in both armies believed the other side had used the flag of his opponent as a *ruse de guerre.* Time would remedy the uniform confusion; the obscurity caused by battle smoke and dust could never be eliminated; but Beauregard was determined to remedy the flag problem at once.

General Johnston sought initially to solve the problem by having the troops use their State flags, but only the Virginia regiments were sufficiently supplied to accomplish this. General Beauregard contacted Congressman William Porcher Miles to attempt to have the Confederate flag changed. Miles was sympathetic, but informed the General that Congress would not agree to a change. Miles suggested that the army address the issue by adopting for its own use a distinctive battle flag and recommended the design which he had urged upon the Congress as the Confederate Flag on March 4, 1861.

Figure 46: General Beauregard's Prototype of the Battle Flag.

Beauregard liked the red flag with its blue cross and stars. Johnston liked it too, but recommended that it would be more convenient for military use if made square. Three prototypes were made by Hettie, Jennie, and Constance Cary and presented to Generals Johnston, Beauregard and Earl Van Dorn. Johnston approved the issuance of these battle flags in September 1861 and ordered the quartermaster of the army to have flags made up in silk and distributed to the regiments. By tradition, the silk for these flags was dress material donated by the ladies of Virginia. November 1861 would see the first issue to the army of the flag to become known as the "Southern Cross." On the crosses were twelve stars for the eleven States then in the Confederate States, and Missouri, which had seceded but was not yet admitted as a member of the Confederacy. The outer edges were bordered in yellow, and the flag was attached to its staff by a dark blue sleeve.

Figure 47: Silk Battle Flag, Issued November 1861.

The heavy campaigning of the army was hard on these silk flags, requiring a new issue to be made in 1862. The replacement battle flags were made of a high quality English wool bunting, designed to last and wear well. All subsequent issues of battle flags to the Army of Northern Virginia would be made of wool bunting.

Figure 48: First Bunting Issue, 1862.

The first two issues of bunting flags differed from their silk predecessors in several design details. The number of Confederate States had increased to thirteen, and all subsequent battle flags issued in Virginia would have a thirteenth star at the junction of the cross. The yellow border on the outer edges was replaced by an orange border, and the sleeve was replaced by a white canvas heading with eyelets through which cord could pass to attach

FLAGS OF THE CONFEDERACY

Another corps which had adopted its own battle flag was that of Major General Leonidas Polk. His standard, like Beauregard's, had as its major feature a cross adorned with stars. Polk, however, appears to have been influenced by his non-military vocation in the design of his flag. In addition to his role as a Confederate general, Polk was the Episcopal Bishop of Louisiana. The emblem of the Episcopal Church is the red cross of Saint George, the national emblem of England, and this cross became the central device of Polk's battle flag. The red cross was separated from the blue field of the flag by a white fimbration and carried white stars on its arms to represent the States in the Confederacy.

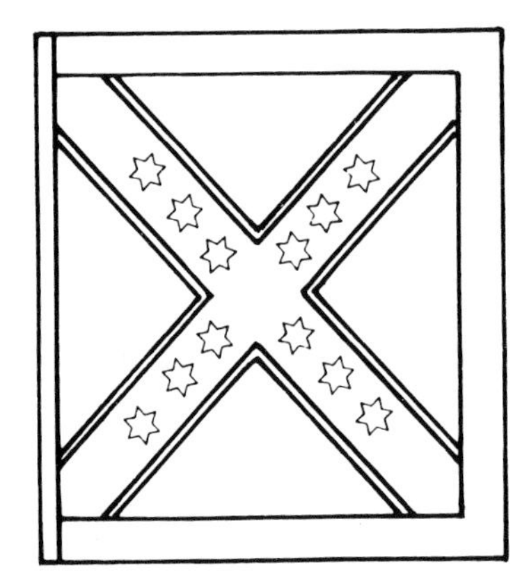

Figure 52: Bragg's Corps Battle Flag,
Army of the Mississippi, First Pattern.

When General Braxton Bragg's corps was added to the army in February 1862 its regiments had no distinctive battle flag. Beauregard took advantage of this lack by having flags of the "Southern Cross" pattern made for these troops. Bragg's new battle flags corresponded closely to those issued in Virginia in November 1861. They were made of wool bunting instead of silk, and the twelve stars had six points. This first Western version of the "Southern Cross" was bound on its outer edges by a broad pink border.

After the first shipment of these flags was received, Beauregard apparently ordered another set to be issued as needed in the future. This second set was of the same material and construction as the first, but the pink border was on all four sides of the flags, which were made oblong instead of square.

The remaining corps of the Confederate Army of the Mississippi was the reserve corps commanded by General John C. Breckinridge of Kentucky, the former Vice President of the United States. Breckinridge's regiments continued to use the "Stars and Bars" national flag of the Confederate States.

Thus were set the basic patterns used by the Army of the Mississippi when it gathered to meet the enemy near Shiloh Church; a distinctive battle flag for each of the main army corps and the national flag for the reserve corps. The multiplicity of flags continued through 1862, in November of which the army was re-named the Army of Tennessee, and only increased after Congress adopted a new Confederate national flag in 1863. [Note: The main Confederate army in the Western theatre was called the "Army of the Mississippi" from March 5, 1862 to November 20, 1862. See, *Official Records of the Union and Confederate Armies in the War of the Rebellion*, Series I, Volume 10, Part I, pp. 596-7, and Volume 16, pp. 886.]

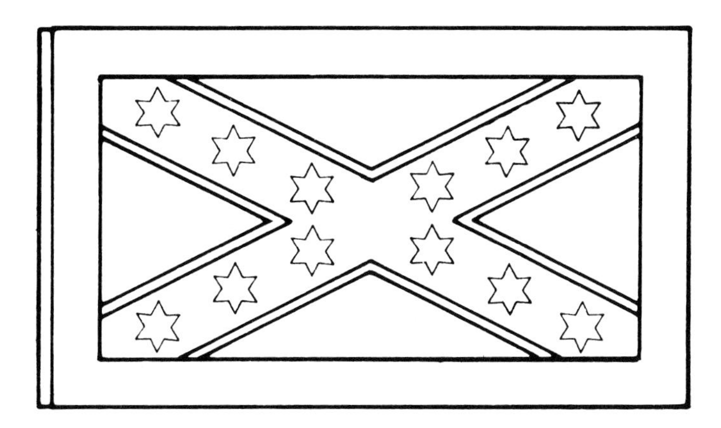

Figure 53: Bragg's Corps Battle flag, Army of the Mississippi, Second Pattern.

On December 18, 1864, following Braxton Bragg's disastrous defeat at Chattanooga, command of the Army of Tennessee was transferred to General Joseph E. Johnston. Johnston's first goal was to restore the morale and *esprit d'corps* of the army. One of the ways by which he effected this revitalization was by the issuance of new and uniform battle flags to his regiments during the months of March and April 1864.

The Army of Tennessee battle flag was of the "Southern Cross" pattern and differed from its Virginia parent mainly in being rectangular instead of square. The Army of Tennessee flag had average dimensions of 36 inches in width by 52 inches in length. Those issued to artillery batteries were about 30 inches wide and 42 inches long. They had thirteen stars and no border.

General Johnston's flag did not achieve uniformity for the Army of Tennessee. The regiments of General Patrick Cleburne's division reacted so strongly to the ordered change of flags that they were allowed to keep their old Hardee pattern banners, though new flags of this pattern were issued to them. The flag of the Army of Tennessee is now the most commonly encountered form of the "Southern Cross," and the flag sold at souvenir stands throughout the South.

Figure 54: Army of Tennessee Battle Flag, 1864.

The Department Of South Carolina, Georgia And Florida

In addition to their field armies, the Confederate States were divided into a number of geographical military departments. Troops within those departments were based at permanent forts, camps and stations and used for the defense of their departments.

The Department of South Carolina, Georgia, and Florida was one of the

Figure 55: Battle Flag of the Department of South Carolina, Georgia and Florida

first military departments created during the war effort. While its boundaries changed at times, for the most part it encompassed all of South Carolina along with tidewater Georgia and eastern Florida. In the first year of the war, the regiments in that department primarily used their State flags. In September, 1862, General Beauregard assumed command of the department and replaced the State flags with the "Southern Cross."

The battle flag of this department was very similar to that used in Virginia after the middle of 1863. It was a square bunting flag with a white border and thirteen five-pointed stars. The main difference between the flags was that the stars of the battle flag of the Army of Northern Virginia were grouped towards the junction of the cross, leaving the outer reaches of the arms unoccupied, while the stars of the department's flags were evenly spaced on the arms of the cross. Also, unlike the Virginia battle flags, which were tied to their staffs through several eyelets, the battle flags of the Department of South Carolina, Georgia, and Florida were attached by means of a sleeve sewn to the heading of the flag.

The flags of this department were issued in different sizes for the different branches of the service, as were those in Virginia. Service branch was also indicated by the color of the pole sleeve with blue for infantry and red for artillery.

Department of East Tennessee

The Department of East Tennessee was under the command of General Edmund Kirby Smith in 1862. During Bragg's Kentucky campaign, Kirby Smith's troops left their department and were called the Army of Kentucky. There is evidence that during this time the regiments of the Department of East Tennessee carried a distinctive battle flag.

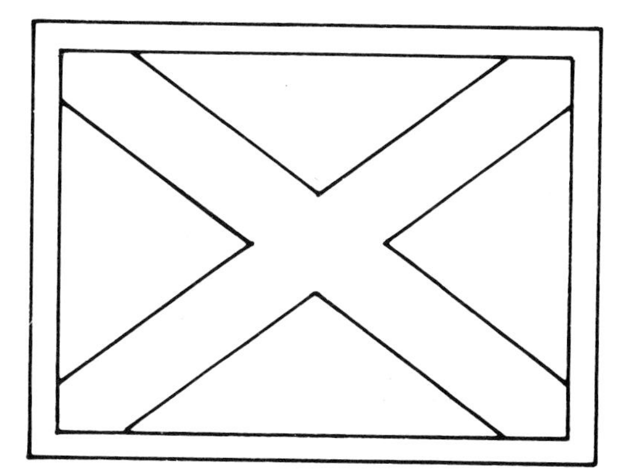

Figure 56: Battle Flag of the Department of East Tennessee.

The East Tennessee battle flags were apparently the traditional Saint Andrew's Cross of Scotland: an unadorned white saltier on a blue field. Borders and edgings on these flags seem to have varied, and there is no uniformity of size or construction among those which survive.

Department Of Alabama, Mississippi, and East Louisiana

The Department of Alabama, Mississippi, and East Louisiana existed in 1864 and 1865. It covered all of Alabama, Mississippi, and that portion of Louisiana which lies to the east of the Mississippi River.

Figure 57: Battle Flag of the Department of Alabama, Mississippi, and East Louisiana.

Battle flags used by the regiments of this department were regularly issued and were manufactured in Mobile, Alabama, from a standard pattern. Generally following the "Southern Cross" flag of the Army of Tennessee, this battle flag was unbordered, made of wool bunting, and made with the leading edge folded over to form a pole sleeve. The white stars were equally spaced on the arms of the fimbrated blue cross. Instead of the thirteen stars found on the flags of the Army of Tennessee, however, the battle flags of this department omitted the star at the junction of the cross. This seems to be characteristic of flags made in Mobile. Even second national pattern Confederate Flags manufactured in this area omitted the thirteenth star.

The department's battle flag was generally 45 inches wide and about 52 inches long. A smaller version, measuring 37 inches in width by 46 inches in length, was issued to the regiments of Lieutenant General Nathan Bedford Forrest's cavalry corps.

The Trans-Mississippi Department

The Trans-Mississippi Department was geographically the largest military department in the Confederate States. It was composed of all of Louisiana west of the Mississippi River, the entire States of Arkansas, Missouri and Texas, the Indian nations in what is now Oklahoma, and the Confederate Territory of Arizona which included the southern portions of modern Arizona and New Mexico. After the fall of Vicksburg in July, 1863, the Department was isolated from the rest of the Confederate States and in large measure operated independently of the authorities in Richmond in military matters. It was also the last part of the Confederate States to fall to the Yankee invasion. At the beginning of 1865, Texas was almost entirely free of Northern soldiers.

Figure 58: Battle Flag of Shelby's Brigade.

The Trans-Mississippi was unique among Confederate military departments in that its military forces were significantly bi-racial. In 1861 the Confederate States entered into nine treaties with the Indian nations and tribes in the area now known as the State of Oklahoma. The treaties with those Indians known as the "civilized nations" — the Cherokee, Chickasaw, Choctaw, Creek, and Seminole — included mutual defense provisions under which an estimated three thousand Indian soldiers served in the Confederate army. These soldiers fought valiantly and provided valuable service in the Trans-Mississippi Department. The last Confederate general to surrender his command was Stand Watie of the Cherokee Nation, and the last Confederate civil authorities to submit to the invaders were Governor Winchester Colbert and the Council of the Chickasaw Nation.

Several incarnations of the "Southern Cross" battle flag were used in the Trans-Mississippi Department. One very close to that used by the Army of Northern Virginia was a surviving flag from General Jo Shelby's Missouri Brigade. The silk flag was bordered in white, as were the later issue battle flags in Virginia, and added to the white border on three sides is a red silk fringe. It is fortunate that this flag survives. General Shelby did not surrender his division at the end of the War. With two hundred volunteers who did not wish to be reconstructed, he rode across Texas for Mexico. On July 4, 1865 Shelby had his survivors weight their battle flags with stones and sink them in the Rio Grande before they crossed into Coahuila. One of Shelby's men rescued this flag from its watery grave before crossing over.

Figure 59: Battle Flag of Parson's Texas Cavalry.

Other far western troops used flags of the "Southern Cross" pattern more nearly resembling those of the Army of Tennessee. Flags such as the one used by Parson's Texas Cavalry Brigade were borderless and oblong. They also tended to violate the rules of heraldry by omitting the white edging of the cross. Another feature often found on flags from the Trans-Mississippi, especially those associated with Texas, was that the central star was larger than the other stars of the cross.

In March 1864 the forces of General Richard Taylor defeated their Northern opponents and re-established Confederate control over western Louisiana. The battle flags under which these men fought were also patterned on the "Southern Cross," but these had the colors reversed, with red crosses on

Figure 60: Battle Flag of General Richard Taylor's Army.

blue grounds. Like other flags in this Department, the cross was not separated from the field by a white edging. At least one of Taylor's regiments, the First Arkansas Cavalry, used a variant with a Saint George's Cross similar to those used by the regiments of General Leonidas Polk in Tennessee in 1862.

Figure 61: Trans-Mississippi Department,
Van Dorn's Corps.

A number of Trans-Mississippi commands used more singular standards. One such was the flag of Earl Van Dorn's Army of the West. The Van Dorn battle flag had a red field adorned with thirteen white stars arranged in five rows, with a white crescent in the upper corner. The flags were bordered in yellow or white. When General Van Dorn brought his regiments to the east side of the river in 1862 to join Beauregard's army at Corinth, Mississippi, they brought these flags with them and fought under them at the Battle of Corinth in October of that year.

Figure 62: Trans-Mississippi Department,
The "Missouri Battle Flag".

Another distinctively Trans-Mississippi flag was associated almost exclusively with Missouri regiments in that Department, resulting in its identification as the Missouri battle flag. The blue flag was bordered in red on its outer edges. A white Roman cross adorned the field near the hoist of the flag.

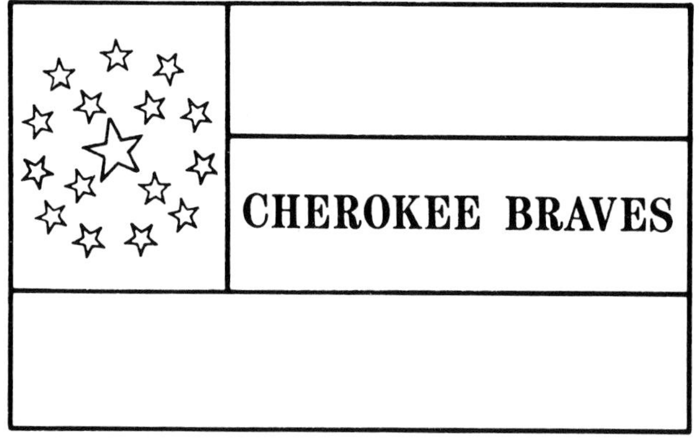

Figure 63: Trans-Mississippi Department,
Cherokee Nation.

When Confederate Indian Commissioner Albert Pike signed the treaty with the Cherokee Nation on October 7, 1861, he presented to Principal Chief John Ross a special flag. This "Stars and Bars" Confederate flag had added within its circle of white stars a cluster of five red stars to represent the five "civilized nations" of Indians with whom the Confederate States had a special relationship. A similar flag survives which was credited to the First Cherokee Mounted Rifles and suggests that this design may have had unofficial use as a national flag by Confederate Cherokees.

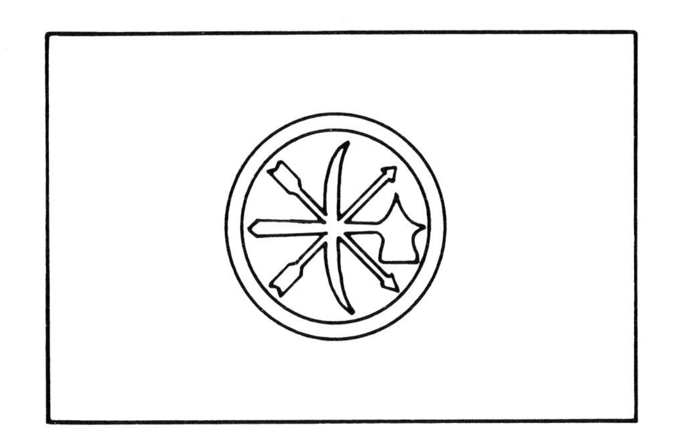

Figure 64: Flag of the Choctaw Brigade.

Another Confederate Indian flag was that of the Choctaw Brigade. Centered on the blue field of the flag was a red disk edged in white. In white silhouette on the red disk were represented traditional weapons of the Choctaw Nation—a bow, arrows, and a tomahawk.

CHAPTER 9
THE FLAG AT SEA

Navies have their own specific flags and flag terminology, and it will be helpful in understanding this chapter to be familiar with that terminology.

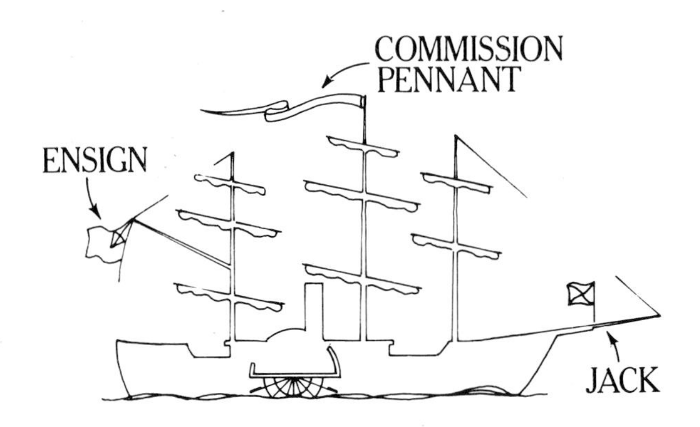

Figure 65: Illustration of a Three Masted Ship Demonstrating Placement of the Ensign, Jack and Commission Pennant.

An ensign is the national flag as flown on a sea-going vessel. It is normally found at the stern of a ship as shown in the accompanying illustration. On special occasions a ship will be "dressed," meaning that it will be decorated with a number of national and signal flags; at such times the ensign may also be displayed at other masts. It is the custom of some nations that the ensign be of a pattern different from the national flag. A case in point is the Royal Navy of Great Britain, the ensign of which is a white flag with a red Saint George's cross and the Union flag of Britain as the canton. In America the "Stars and Stripes" evolved from the red British merchant ensign. As a result the national flag was also used as the ensign, and this practice was carried over by the Confederate States.

The other distinctively naval flags are the jack and the commission pennant. The jack is a flag, designating the nationality, which is flown from the jack staff at the bow of the ship. It is flown only on a ship of war and then only when the vessel is in port. The Royal Navy flies the canton of its white ensign as a jack, which tradition was carried over into the navies of both the United States and the Confederate States.

THE FLAG AT SEA

The commission pennant is flown from the main mast of a ship and designates its status as a commissioned vessel of its country's navy. This pennant may only be displayed by a ship in the national service.

The National Ensign

The ensign of the Confederate States conforms to the design of the Confederate Flag for the appropriate time period: the "Stars and Bars" from March 4, 1861 to May 1, 1863; the "Stainless Banner" from May 1, 1863 to March 4, 1865; and the last Confederate Flag after March 4, 1865.

There are no regulations extant for the ensign of 1861, and the evidence is that it conformed exactly to the national flag. Some sources have indicated that a naval ensign was used which arranged the stars in rows rather than a circle. Although a few ensigns do exist with such a star pattern, the vast majority of surviving flags have their stars in a circular arrangement.

On May 26, 1863, Secretary of the Navy Stephen R. Mallory promulgated regulations adopting a new set of naval flags to conform with the Flag Act adopted by Congress on May 1 of that year. In these regulations, Mallory modified the "Stainless Banner" for its role as a national ensign by reducing its proportional length. While the Flag Act of 1863 called for the flag's width to be half its length, the naval regulations specified a width for the ensign of two-thirds its length. A 72 inch wide ensign would have a length of 108 inches as compared to a 144 inch length for national flag of the same width.

Figure 66: Confederate States Naval Ensign
After May 26, 1863.

FLAGS OF THE CONFEDERACY

When Congress adopted the final Confederate Flag in 1865, the naval regulations should have changed to adapt to the new law, especially since the call for the change seems to have come from the navy. The new flag's overall proportions corresponded to the regulation's specifications for the ensign, and the likelihood is that the new ensign would not have varied its details from those of the national flag. No new flag regulations are know to have been adopted by the navy after the passage of the Flag Act of 1865 and, with one exception, the Confederate States Navy ceased to exist a little over two months later.

The one exception was the CSS *Shenandoah*. While Lee and Johnston were surrendering their armies, she was sinking United States ships in the North Pacific. When General Stand Watie was surrendering his Indian division on June 23, 1865, the *Shenandoah* was in the process of capturing twenty-five ships of the New Bedford whaling fleet near the Bering Strait. Only on August 2 did Captain Waddell of the *Shenandoah* receive positive information from a British ship that his government no longer existed. Determined not to surrender to the United States authorities, Waddell set course for Britain. On November 5, 1865 the *Shenandoah* arrived at the British coast where she had begun her voyage over a year before. On November 6 she sailed into Liverpool harbor, and the white ensign of the Confederate States of America was lowered for the last time.

The Confederate Jack

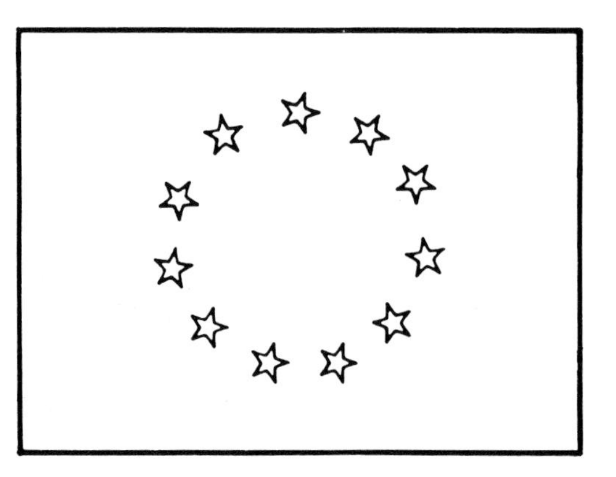

Figure 67: Confederate Navy Jack
March 4, 1861 to May 26, 1863.

THE FLAG AT SEA

As we have seen, the Confederate States followed the precedent established by Great Britain, and adopted by the United States, of using the canton of the ensign as the jack of the navy. The first Confederate jack, like the jack of the Union navy, was a blue flag on which were placed the stars corresponding with the number of States in the Confederacy.

Figure 68: Confederate Navy Jack
after May 26, 1863.

The naval flag regulations of 1863, which adopted the new national ensign, also adopted a new jack. The jack was now to be "the same as the union for the Ensign, excepting that its length shall be one and a half times its width." In design and proportions it is very similar to the battle flag issued to the Army of Tennessee in 1864. Since the Flag Act of 1865 did not change the basic design of the Confederate Flag's canton, the jack of 1863 would have remained the Confederate jack after 1865.

Commission Pennants

Naval commission pennants are designed to indicate the nationality of a ship and to indicate its commissioned status in the national service. The commission pennant of the United States Navy is blue at its head with seven white stars and has two stripes of white over red trailing out from the blue.

No published regulations exisit for the Confederate States Navy's commission pennant prior to 1863. Evidence from a surviving pennant, and from engraved plates in Admiral Raphael Semmes' book *Memoirs of Service Afloat,* however, indicates that the Confederate pennant was derived from

Figure 69: Confederate Commission Pennant,
March 4, 1861 to May 26, 1863.

that of the United States. It also had a blue head, on which was placed a star for each of the Confederate States. The stripes on this pennant were three in number and were colored red, white, and red, corresponding to the bars of the Confederate Flag.

Figure 70: Confederate Commission Pennant,
After May 26, 1863.

The naval regulations of May 26, 1863 gave the Confederate States Navy a new commission pennant in keeping with the new Confederate Flag and ensign. The proportions of the pennant are dramatic with the length to be seventy-two times the width at the head and tapering to a point. The first portion of the pennant is red, edged in white on the outer edges, with a length three times the width at the head. It is followed by a white edged, blue section twelve times longer than the width of the pennant, and decorated with stars equal in number to the States in the Confederacy. This is followed by an unbordered red section, the same length as the first red section, and the remaining three-fourths of the pennant is white.

Figure 71: Variant Confederate Commission Pennant Used After May 1, 1863.

Other commission pennants of a non-regulation character were used from time to time during the course of the War. One such example is also influenced by the Confederate Flag of 1863, but is not much influenced by the official navy regulations. Rather than having the red-blue-red sections of the official pennant, the head of this variant is in the form of the "Southern Cross" union of the ensign with the stars omitted.

The Revenue Service

The United States Revenue Service was created in the early years of the Union to collect import duties and to protect the coasts against smugglers trying to evade duties and taxes. The United States Navy was unable to

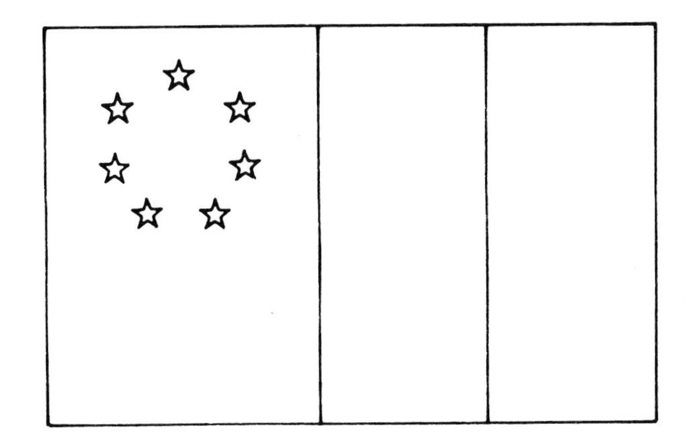

Figure 72: Confederate States Revenue Service Ensign.

provide this service while off fighting quasi-wars in European waters or pirates on the Barbary Coast. Congress, therefore, created the Revenue Service as a branch of the Treasury Department and authorized its use of ships to serve as revenue cutters.

When the Confederate States government was established, all laws of the United States which were not inconsistent with the Confederate Constitution were made laws of the Confederacy. These included the law establishing the Revenue Service, and the Confederate States Treasury Department's Revenue Service functioned in much the same way as did that of the United States. Among the privileges of the Revenue Service was that of lying its own distinctive ensign from its vessels. The ensign of the U.S. Revenue Service altered the U.S. ensign by displaying vertical stripes. Its canton was white with blue stars and the arms of the United States.

The Confederate States Revenue Service did not copy the white canton of its predecessor's ensign, but it did follow the scheme of vertical stripes and applied it to the "Stars and Bars" flag of the Confederacy. The canton was extended the entire width of the ensign, and one of its red bars was pivoted to a vertical position; the other red bar was eliminated. The resulting ensign looked very much like a French flag with a circle of stars in the upper part of the blue bar. As a rule, the blue bar was wider than the white or red bars by about one and a half times.

EPILOGUE

THE CONFEDERATE STATES OF AMERICA died a violent death at the hands of invading armies in 1865, and thus it was "proven" that secession was wrong . . . that no portion of the American people could elect a path of political self-determination so long as a more powerful section opposed them. The flags which represented the national aspirations of the Southern people were buried in the archives of the conquerors, until President Theodore Roosevelt had them returned to the people whose hopes had once been swaddled in their folds. During the time of obscurity the memory of them dimmed, and many errors have persisted about their design and usage. Over one hundred twenty-five years later, revisionists attempt to distort their meaning and place in history.

The flags of the Confederacy represented the aspirations of a brave and resourceful people who determined to strike out on their own and carve their place among the nations of the earth. Their desire to live under a government based upon "the consent of the governed" should be respected; and their tenacity in attempting to preserve their chosen government, though in vain, must be admired. The people of the Confederate States of America earned for their flags an honored place among the sacred relics of human endeavor.

FURTHER READING

Other books are available for further study of Confederate flags and of flags in general. A very detailed study of a large number of individual Confederate flags has been carried out by Howard Michael Madaus of the Milwaukee Public Museum. The results of his research has been published in the following works:

Madaus, Howard Michael. *The Battle Flags of the Confederate Army of Tennessee.* Milwaukee Wisc.: Milwaukee Public Museum, 1976.

_________. "Rebel Flags Afloat." *The Flag Bulletin,* Vol. XXV, No. 1. Winchester, Mass.: The Flag Research Center, 1986.

_________. *The Southern Cross.* [an unpublished manuscript scheduled for publication in late 1988].

For general works on flags the reader may refer to any number of references. Two of these have been written by the director of the Flag Research Center

Smith, Whitney. *The Flag Book of the United States.* New York: William Morrow & Company, Inc., 1970.

_________. *Flags Through the Ages and Across the World.* New York: McGraw-Hill, 1975.

The Flag Research Center publishes a bi-monthly journal called *The Flag Bulletin,* which is available from the Flag Research Center, 3 Edgehill Road, Winchester, Mass. 01890.

Further reading and research into the actions of the Confederate States Congress on flag and other matters may be had in a number of works. Those which would qualify as primary source materials are:

Matthews, James A., ed. *Statutes at Large of the Provisional Government of the Confederate States of America.* Richmond, Va.: R.M. Smith, 1864.

_________. *Statutes at Large of the Confederate States of America Passed at the First Session of the First Congress.* Richmond, Va.: R.M. Smith, 1862.

_________. *Statutes at Large of the Confederate States of America Passed at the Second Session of the First Congress.* Richmond, Va.: R.M. Smith, 1862.

_________. *Statutes at Large of the Confederate States of America Passed at the Third Session of the First Congress.* Richmond, Va.: R.M. Smith, 1863.

_________. *Statutes at Large of the Confederate States of America Passed at the Fourth Session of the First Congress.* Richmond Va.: R.M. Smith, 1864.

_________. *Statutes at Large of the Confederate States of America Passed at the First Session of the Second Congress.* Richmond Va.: R.M. Smith, 1864.

Journal of the Congress of the Confederate States of America, 1861-1865, Washington, D.C.: Government Printing Office, 1904.

Freeman, Douglas Southall, ed. "Proceeding of the Confederate Congress." *The Southern Historical Society Papers.* Vols. 44-52. Richmond, Va.: Southern Historical Society, 1923-1959.

APPENDIX A - CHRONOLOGY

1860

November 6: Presidential election results in Republican electors gaining a majority in the Electoral College.

November 13: South Carolina legislature passes an act calling for the assembly of a convention to consider secession.

December 6: The Electoral College elects Abraham Lincoln President of the United States of America.

December 17: South Carolina Convention assembles in Columbia.

December 18: Outbreak of smallpox causes the Convention to adjourn to Charleston.

December 20: South Carolina Convention adopts the Ordinance of Secession.

1861

January 9: Mississippi Secession Convention adopts an Ordinance of Secession.

January 10: Florida Secession Convention adopts an Ordinance of Secession.

January 11: Alabama Secession Convention adopts an Ordinance of Secession; Alabama State flag is raised at capitol in Montgomery.

January 13: Commanding general of the Florida military adopts a provisional flag for Florida.

January 19: Georgia Secession Convention adopts an Ordinance of Secession; Georgia flag is raised over capitol at Milledgeville.

APPENDIX A - CHRONOLOGY

January 26: Louisiana Secession Convention adopts an Ordinance of Secession; Pelican flag is raised at the Louisiana Secession Hall; Mississippi adopts an official State flag.

February 4: Texas Secession Convention adopts an Ordinance of Secession and submits it to a vote of the people.

February 4: Delegates of six seceded States assemble in Convention in Montgomery, Alabama.

February 8: The Montgomery Convention adopts a Constitution forming the Provisional Government of the Confederate States of America.

February 11: Louisiana adopts an official State flag.

February 18: Jefferson Davis is inaugurated President of the Provisional Government of the Confederate States.

February 23: The people of Texas ratify the Ordinance of Secession.

March 2: Texas secession becomes official. The Confederate Congress passes "An Act to admit Texas as a Member of the Confederate States of America."

March 4: The first Confederate Flag adopted and raised over the Alabama capitol.

March 11: The Confederate Convention adopts the Constitution of the Confederate States of America.

March 12: Alabama ratifies the C.S. Constitution.

March 16: Georgia ratifies the C.S. Constitution. March 21: Louisiana ratifies the C.S. Constitution.

March 23: Texas ratifies the C.S. Constitution.

March 26: Mississippi ratifies the C.S. Constitution

April 3: South Carolina ratifies the C.S. Constitution.

APPENDIX A - CHRONOLOGY

April 12: The bombardment of Fort Sumter.

April 15: Lincoln issues call for 75,000 troops to serve three months.

April 17: Virginia Secession Convention adopts an Ordinance of Secession.

April 19: Lincoln announces the blockade of Southern ports.

April 22: Florida ratifies the C.S. Constitution.

April 25: A resolution introduced in Tennessee Senate proposing a State flag.

April 30: Virginia adopts an official State flag.

May 6: Arkansas Secession Convention adopts an Ordinance of Secession; Confederate Congress passes "An act recognizing the existence of war between the United States and the Confederate States;" Tennessee legislature adopts a Declaration of Independence to be submitted to a popular vote.

May 7: Tennessee legislature ratifies a military league with the Confederate States; Virginia admitted to the Confederacy.

May 20: North Carolina Convention adopts an Ordinance of Secession.

May 21: Arkansas admitted to the Confederacy.

May 24: Resolution of neutrality adopted by Kentucky; United States troops invade Virginia.

June 1: Arkansas ratifies the C.S. Constitution.

June 6: North Carolina ratifies the C.S. Constitution.

June 8: Tennessee voters ratify the Declaration of Independence.

June 19: Virginia ratifies the C.S. Constitution.

June 22: North Carolina adopts official State flag.

APPENDIX A - CHRONOLOGY

June 24: Governor Isham G. Harris proclaims Tennessee officially out of the Union.

July 2: North Carolina and Tennessee admitted to the Confederacy.

July 10: Confederate States sign treaty with the Creek Nation.

July 12: Confederate States sign treaty with the Choctaw and Chickasaw Nations.

July 21: Battle of Manassas in Virginia.

August 1: Tennessee voters ratify the C.S. Constitution; Confederate States sign a treaty with the Seminole Nation.

August 5: Governor Claiborne F. Jackson declares the independence of Missouri.

August 12: Confederate States sign a treaty with the Pen-e-tegh-ca Band of the Commanches, and the tribes and bands of the Wichitas, A-na-dagh-cos, Ton-ca-wes, Ai-o-nais, Ki-Chais, Shawnees and Delawares; Confederate States sign a treaty with the Commanches of the Prairies and Staked Plains.

September: The "Southern Cross" battle flag is adopted for use by the Confederate Army of the Potomac in Virginia.

September 13: Florida adopts an official State flag.

October 2: Confederate States sign a treaty with the Great Osage Tribe.

October 4: Confederate States sign a treaty with the Seneca and Shawnee Tribes; Confederate States sign a treaty with the Quapaw Tribe.

October 7: Confederate States sign a treaty with the Cherokee Nation.

October 31: Missouri legislature adopts an Act of Secession.

November: First "Southern Cross" battle flags issued to the Confederate army in Virginia.

APPENDIX A - CHRONOLOGY

November 6: First general elections for members of the Confederate Presidential Electoral College and C.S. House of Representatives.

November 20: Kentucky Secession Convention adopts an Ordinance of Secession.

November 28: Missouri admitted to the Confederacy.

December 6: Confederate Electoral College elects Jefferson Davis President of the Confederate States of America.

December 10: Kentucky admitted to the Confederacy.

1862

January 19-20: Battle of Mill Springs, Kentucky.

February 6: Fort Henry in Tennessee falls to Union forces.

February 16: Fort Donelson in Tennessee is surrendered.

February 18: First Congress of the Confederate States convenes.

February 22: Jefferson Davis inaugurated President of the Confederate States.

February 23: Nashville, Tennessee is evacuated.

March 6-8: Battle of Pea Ridge, Arkansas.

March 9: Battle of Hampton Roads, Virginia between CSS *Virginia* (formerly *Merrimac)* and USS *Monitor.*

April 6-7: Battle of Shiloh, Tennessee.

April 19: Joint Committee on Flag and Seal proposes a new Confederate flag.

APPENDIX A - CHRONOLOGY

April 24: New Orleans is captured.

May 31: Battle of Seven Pines in Virginia.

June 6: Memphis, Tennessee is captured.

June 26: The Seven Days Battle begins in Virginia.

July 1: Battle of Malvern Hill in Virginia.

July 13: Forrest captures Union garrison at Murfreesboro, Tennessee.

August 9: Battle of Cedar Mountain, Virginia.

August 30: Second Battle of Manassas in Virginia.

September 16-17: Battle of Sharpsburg, Maryland.

October 3-4: Battle of Corinth, Mississippi.

October 8: Battle of Perryville, Kentucky.

November: 20 The Army of the Mississippi is re-named The Army of Tennessee.

December 31: The Battle of Murfreesboro (Stones River) in Tennessee begins.

1863

January 1: Union forces driven from Galveston, Texas.

April 22: C.S. Senate passes Senate Bill No. 132 to propose a new Confederate Flag.

May 1: The Flag Act of 1863 establishes the "Stainless Banner" as the Confederate Flag.

APPENDIX A - CHRONOLOGY

May 1-4: Battle of Chancellorsville, Virginia.

May 10: Stonewall Jackson dies.

May 14: Union forces capture Jackson, Mississippi.

May 26: Secretary of Navy Mallory issues regulations adopting a new ensign, jack and commission pennant for the Confederate States Navy.

July 1-3: Battle of Gettysburg, Pennsylvania.

July 4: Fall of Vicksburg, Mississippi.

September 19-20: Battle of Chickamauga, Georgia.

October 25: Battle of Pine Bluff, Arkansas.

November 23-25: Battles of Chattanooga, Lookout Mountain and Missionary Ridge, Tennessee.

December 18: General Joseph E. Johnston takes command of the Army of Tennessee.

1864

February 20: Battle of Olustee, Florida.

March & April: New "Southern Cross" battle flags issued to the Army of Tennessee.

March 8-9: Union Red River expedition in Louisiana defeated.

March 12: Battle of Fort Pillow, Tennessee.

May 5-7: Battle of the Wilderness in Virginia.

May 13-16: Battle of Resaca, Georgia.

May 15: Battle of New Market, Virginia.

APPENDIX A - CHRONOLOGY

June 1-3: Battle of Cold Harbor, Virginia.

June 10: Battle of Brice's Crossroads, Mississippi.

June 27: Battle of Kennesaw Mountain, Georgia.

July 22: Battle of Atlanta, Georgia.

August 5: Battle of Jonesboro, Georgia.

September 2: Sherman takes Atlanta.

October 8: CSS *Shenandoah* commissioned.

November 30: Battle of Franklin, Tennessee.

December 15-16: Battle of Nashville, Tennessee.

December 22: Savannah, Georgia evacuated.

1865

January 15: Fort Fisher, North Carolina falls.

February 17: Sherman captures and burns Columbia, South Carolina.

March 4: Flag Act of 1865 establishes the last Confederate Flag.

March 19-20: Battle of Bentonville, North Carolina.

April 1: Battle of Five Forks in Virginia.

April 2: Richmond and Petersburg evacuated.

April 9: Lee surrenders the Army of Northern Virginia.

April 12: Mobile, Alabama is captured.

APPENDIX A - CHRONOLOGY

April 13: Montgomery, Alabama is captured.

April 26: Johnston surrenders the Army of Tennessee.

May 4: The Department of Alabama Mississippi and East Louisiana is surrendered.

May 13: The last battle is fought at Palmetto Ranch near Brownsville, Texas.

May 23: The Army of the Trans-Mississippi Department is surrendered.

June 2: Galveston, Texas surrenders.

June 23: General Stand Watie surrenders his Indian Division.

June 28: CSS *Shenandoah* fires the last shots of the War.

July 4: General Jo Shelby crosses into Mexico.

July 14: Governor of the Chickasaw Nation ends resistance to the United States.

November 6: CSS *Shenandoah* lowers the last Confederate Flag at Liverpool, England.

APPENDIX B
CONFEDERATE FLAG LAWS

1861

STARS AND BARS

Mr. Miles, from the Committee on the Flag and Seal of the Confederacy, made the following report:

The committee appointed to select a proper flag for the Confederate States of America, beg leave to report:

That they have given this subject due consideration, and carefully inspected all the designs and models submitted to them. The number of these has been immense, but they all may be divided into two great classes.

First. Those which copy and preserve the principal features of the United States flag, with slight and unimportant modifications.

Secondly. Those which are very elaborate, complicated, or fantastical. The objection to the first class is, that none of them at any considerable distance could readily be distinguished from the one which they imitate. Whatever attachment may be felt, from association, for the "Stars and Stripes" (an attachment which your committee may be permitted to say they do not all share), it is manifest that in inaugurating a new government we can not with any propriety, or without encountering very obvious practical difficulties, retain the flag of the Government from which we have withdrawn. There is no propriety in retaining the ensign of a government which, in the opinion of the States composing this Confederacy, had become so oppressive and injurious to their interests as to require their separation from it. It is idle to talk of "keeping" the flag of the United States when we have voluntarily seceded from them. It is superfluous to dwell upon the practical difficulties which would flow from the fact of two distinct and probably hostile governments, both employing the same or very similar flags. It would be a political and military solecism. It would lead to perpetual disputes. As to "the glories of the old flag," we must bear in mind that the battles of the Revolution, about which our fondest and proudest memories cluster, were not fought beneath its folds. And although in more recent times — in the war of 1812 and in the war with Mexico — the South did win her fair share of glory, and shed her full measure of blood under its guidance and in its defense, we think the impartial page of history will preserve and commemorate the fact more imperishably than a mere piece of striped bunting. When the colonies achieved their independence of the "mother country" (which up to the last they fondly called her) they did not desire to retain the British flag or anything at all similar to it. Yet, under that flag they had been planted, and nurtured, and fostered. Under that flag they had fought in their infancy for their very existence against more than one determined foe; under it they had repelled and driven back the relentless savage, and carried it farther and farther into the decreasing wilderness as the standard of civilization and religion; under it the youthful Washington won his spurs in the memorable and unfortunate expedition of Braddock, and Americans helped to plant it on the heights of Abraham, where the immortal Wolfe fell, covered with glory, in the arms of victory. But our forefathers, when they separated themselves from Great Britain — a separation not on account of their hatred of the English constitution or of English institutions, but in consequence of the tyrannical and unconstitutional rule of Lord North's administration, and because their destiny beckoned them on to independent expansion and achievement — cast no lingering, regretful looks behind. They were proud of their race and lineage, proud of their heritage in the glories and genius and language of old England, but they were influenced by the spirit and the motto of the great Hampden, *"vestigia nulla retrorsum,"* They were determined to build up a new power among the nations of the world. They therefore did not attempt "to keep the old flag." We think it is good to imitate them in this comparatively lively little matter as well as to emulate them in greater and more important ones.

The committee, in examining the representations of the flags of all countries, found that Liberia and the Sandwich Islands had flags so similar to that of the United States that it seemed to them an additional, if not itself a conclusive, reason why we should not "keep," copy, or imitate it. They felt no inclination to borrow, at second hand, what had been pilfered and appropriated by a free negro community and a race of savages. It must be admitted, however, that something was conceded by the committee to what seemed so strong and earnest a desire to retain at least a suggestion of the old "Stars and Stripes." So much for the mass of models and designs more or less copied from, or assimilated to, the United States flag.

With reference to the second class of designs - those of an elaborate and complicated character (but many of them showing considerable artistic skill and taste) — the committee will merely remark, that however pretty they may be, when made up by the cunning skill of a fair lady's fingers in silk, satin, and embroidery, they are not appropriate as flags. A flag should be simple, readily made, and, above all, capable of being made up in bunting. It should be different from the flag of any other country, place, or people. It should be readily distinguishable at a distance. The colors should be well contrasted and durable, and, lastly, and not the least important point, it should be effective and handsome.

The committee humbly think that the flag which they submit combines these requisites It is very easy to make. It is entirely different from any national flag. The three colors of which it is composed — red, white, and blue — are the true republican colors. In heraldry they are emblematic of the three great virtues — of valor, purity, and truth. Naval men assure us that it can be recognized and distinguished at a great distance. The colors contrast admirably and are lasting. In effect and appearance it must speak for itself.

Your committee, therefore, recommend that the flag of the Confederate States of America shall consist of a red field with a white space extending horizontally through the center, and equal in width to one-third the width of the flag. The red spaces above and below to be the same width as the white. The union blue extending down through the white space and stopping at the lower red space. In the center of the union a circle of white stars corresponding in number with the States of the Confederacy. If adopted, long may it wave over a brave, a free, and a virtuous people. May the career of the Confederacy, whose duty it will then be to support and defend it, be such as to endear it to our children's children, as the flag of a loved, because just and benign, government, and the cherished symbol of its valor, purity, and truth.

Respectfully submitted.
Wm. Porcher Miles,
Chairman

1863
FLAG ACT OF 1863

ACT to establish the flag of the
Confederate States

The Congress of the Confederate States of America do enact, That the flag of the Confederate States shall be as follows: The field to be white, the length double the width of the flag, with the union (now used as the battle flag) to be a square of two-thirds the width of the flag, having the ground red, thereupon a broad saltier of blue, bordered with white and emblazoned with mullets or five-pointed stars, corresponding in number to that of the Confederate States.

Approved May 1, 1863

NAVY REGULATIONS OF 1863

The new Ensign, Pennant, and Jack, by order of the Secretary of the Navy, May 26, 1863, as follows:

THE NEW ENSIGN.

The new Ensign will be made according to the following directions,

The field to be white, the length one and a half times the width of the flag, with the union (now used as the Battle Flag) to be square, of two-thirds of the width of the flag, having the ground red, thereon a broad saltier of blue, to the union as 1 : 4 4/5, bordered with white, to the union as 1 : 22, and emblazoned with white mullets, or five-pointed stars, diameter of stars to the union as 1 : 6 2/5 corresponding in number to that of the Confederate States.

THE PENNANT.

A white ground, its size to be as 1 : 72, or its length seventy-two times its width at the head, and tapering to a point.

The union of the Pennant to be as follows: All red from the head for three times its width, with a white border equal to half its width, then all blue in length equal to twelve times its width, to be emblazoned with stars, in number equal to those in the Ensign, with a white border equal to half the width, and then red three times the width, with the fly all white.

THE JACK.

To be the same as the union for the Ensign, except that its length shall be one and a half times its width.

1865
FLAG ACT OF 1865

AN ACT to establish the flag of the
Confederate States.

The Congress of the Confederate States of America do enact, That the flag of the Confederate States of America shall be as follows: The width two-thirds of its length, with the union (now used as the battle flag) to be in width three-fifths of the width of the flag, and so proportioned as to leave the length of the field on the side of the union twice the width of the field below it; to have the ground red and a broad saltier thereon, bordered with white and emblazoned with mullets or five-pointed stars, corresponding in number to that of the Confederate States; the field to be white, except the outer half from the union to be a red bar extending the width of the flag.

Approved March 4, 1865

APPENDIX C

CONFEDERATE FLAG DAY
AND
THE SALUTE TO THE CONFEDERATE FLAG.

CONFEDERATE FLAG DAY

In recent years efforts have been undertaken by various Confederate hereditary and patriotic organizations to promote a greater knowledge of and respect for the flags of the Confederate States. This activity has increased since the 125th anniversary of the adoption of the first Confederate Flag occurred on March 4, 1986. One form which this effort has taken is the recognition of Confederate Flag Day.

The first formal acknowledgment of Confederate Flag Day was a resolution adopted by the Tennessee Division of the Sons of Confederate Veterans. At their 1987 State Convention a motion was passed to declare the fourth day of March in each year as Confederate Flag Day in the State of Tennessee. March 4 was chosen because it marked the common date of the adoption of the first Confederate Flag in 1861 and of the last Confederate Flag in 1865.

SALUTE TO THE CONFEDERATE FLAG.

In the early days of the Confederate veterans' and descendants' organizations, a salute to the flag of the Confederate States was adopted. This is not a pledge of allegiance, but rather, an affectionate greeting to the emblem of a Cause fondly remembered.

> I salute the Confederate Flag
> with affection, reverence, and
> undying devotion to the Cause
> for which it stands.

To
Albert G. Pike, Esq.,
The Poet Lawyer of Arkansas

THE

BONNIE BLUE FLAG
COMPOSED, ARRANGED,
And Sung
AT HIS
PERSONATION CONCERTS
BY
HARRY MACARTHY.
THE ARKANSAS COMEDIAN.
NEW ORLEANS
Published by A.E. BLACKMAR & BRO. 74. Camp St

THE BONNIE BLUE FLAG.

trea - sure, blood and toil; And when our rights were threaten'd, The cry rose near and
far,......... Hur-rah for the Bonnie Blue Flag, that bears a Sin - gle Star!
CHORUS.
Hur - rah!........ Hur - rah!........ for South- ern Rights hur - rah!........ Hur-rah! for the
Bonnie Blue Flag that bears a Sin-gle Star..........

THE BONNIE BLUE FLAG.

3 First, gallant South Carolina nobly made the stand;
Then came Alabama, who took her by the hand;
Next, quickly Mississippi, Georgia and Florida,
All rais'd on high the Bonnie Blue Flag that bears a Single Star.

4 Ye men of valor, gather round the Banner of the Right,
Texas and fair Louisiana, join us in the fight;
Davis, our loved President, and Stephens, Stateman rare,
Now rally round the Bonnie Blue Flag that bears a Single Star.

5 And here's to brave Virginia! the Old Dominion State
With the young Confederacy at length has linked her fate;
Impell'd by her example, now other State prepare
To hoist on high the Bonnie Blue Flag that bears a Single Star.

6 Then cheer, boys, raise the joyous shout,
For Arkansas and North Carolina now have both gone out;
And let another rousing cheer for Tennessee be given,
The Single Star of the Bonnie Blue Flag has grown to be Eleven.

7 Then here's to our Confederacy, strong we are and brave,
Like patriots of old, we'll fight our heritage to save;
And rather than submit to shame, to die we would prefer,
So cheer for the Bonnie Blue Flag that bears a Single Star.

CHORUS.—Hurrah! Hurrah! for Southern Rights, hurrah!
Hurrah! for the Bonnie Blue Flag has gain'd th' Eleventh Star!

INDEX

"As it is my design to make those that can scarcely read understand, I shall therefore avoid every literary ornament and put it in language as plain as the alphabet."

THOMAS PAINE

"There are only two mistakes one can make along the road to truth; not going all the way, and not starting."

BUDDHA

"Ye shall know the truth, and the truth shall make you free."

JOHN 8:32

How Millennial Youth Are Taking Over America
And Changing Our World Forever

GENERATION WE

By ERIC H. GREENBERG
with KARL WEBER

Published by Pachatusan™

Pachatusan™
1285 66th St.
Suite 100
Emeryville, CA 94608

Printed in the United States of America
at Quebecor World

First Printing: October 2008

ISBN-13: 978-0-9820931-0-8

Book Design: Designpool, www.designpoolstudio.com

AT LEAST 40 PERCENT OF THE FIBER USED IN THIS PRODUCT LINE COMES FROM INDEPENDENTLY CERTIFIED FORESTS
WWW.SFIPROGRAM.ORG
PWC-SFICOC-260

Note: *This label only applies to the text stock.*

To my children, Jackson and Charlie, the two souls whose lives mean more to me than my own and are the reason I am compelled to work toward making our world a better place;

To the love of my life, my wife Carmel, who has blessed me with unconditional love and has given me the support and understanding that allows me to evolve into a better human being and pursue my life's work;

To Mother Earth, our sustainer, to whom we must return the favor;

And to our Creator who, through love, has bestowed the miracle of life upon us and with whom we are all One.

"Behold, O Monks,
this is my last advice to you.
All conditioned things
in the world are changeable.
They are not lasting.
Try to accomplish your own
salvation with diligence."

(BUDDHA'S LAST WORDS)

CONTENTS

introduction:

A GIFT FOR A BETTER WORLD

Who Am I to Write This Book?

A Message from Eric Greenberg

I have been blessed to live the American Dream. I have been fortunate enough to be endowed with some personal gifts—a degree of intelligence, a strong work ethic, and, most important, an ability to make things happen. I have been able to parlay these gifts into an incredible life journey, where I have gained financial success, the chance to help others, and some wonderful opportunities to experience the world. My life almost seems too good to be true—but it is true.

I did not have much when I was young. I remember going without haircuts, taping together my broken glasses, and having only one pair of sneakers that would be replaced once my socks were starting to show through the holes.

The home in which I was raised was unhappy and emotionally chaotic. We lived in a succession of lower middle-class neighborhoods, rife with prejudice, violence, and crime. Racial and class tension were everyday facts of life. The schools I attended were mediocre and infused with a dog-eat-dog spirit.

I began working at 14 and spent seven years selling shoes to support myself. I left home at 16 years of age, and was for all practical purposes, on my own.

Through hard work and a little luck, I was able to go to fine universities and gain an incredible education. At the time tuition at the University of Texas at Austin was only 800 dollars per semester for a nonresident. I could not afford a graduate degree, so I went to work and was able to get a great job in information technology, despite having no education or training in the subject. Back in 1985, one did not have to have an advanced degree and technical training just to find an

> In central Australia with Aboriginal elder

entry-level job, and opportunities for good jobs, especially in growth sectors such as technology, were not exported overseas. People got hired based on talent, intelligence, and desire to succeed.

Back in 1985, banks were not pushing debt onto students like drug dealers, so I left college owing less than 10,000 dollars. Unlike many middle-class students today, I was not enslaved to financial institutions and was able to start my life with a more or less clean slate. I had only the future to worry about.

As a Reagan Republican, I did not believe I should have anything provided to me. Rather, I knew I had to earn everything through my individual effort. But I did not understand the American social contract that had been built over 200 years by many brave souls. I attended a land grant school whose low tuition was made possible by public support. Business was not focused solely on quarterly earnings. Companies still believed they had obligations to their employees; decent healthcare and a reliable pension were considered rights, not privileges. It was a time of greater human decency.

Through hard work, applied intelligence, and good timing, I was able to prosper. By the turn of the century, I was a paper billionaire at 35 years of age. I flew around the world in private jets. Sir Elton John played at my wedding. I had every material good one could ever dream for—but it came with a price. Overindulgence created chaos at every turn in my life. Although I was lucky enough to have a stable relationship with my wife, everything else around me devolved into a pit of misfortune, conflict, and poor health.

I was miserable. By 2004, I weighed 275 pounds, was dependent on prescription medication, depressed, and sometimes selfish and thoughtless. I was imploding from my ambition-driven ego. The world was giving me a valuable lesson: Life is not about things and what you do for yourself.

My life was unsustainable. Eventually, one of my friends saw me and told me I looked horrible and would be dead in six months if I did not get my act together. He took me to his hotel suite in New York and lectured me for two hours. The message sank in. The next day, I closed my business and stopped working.

I immediately started the long road back to redemption. I was so unfit, I couldn't walk uphill facing forward because of the back pain from gravity pulling my stomach. I spent a full year building my fitness to the point where I could trail-run 20 miles. I went on to lose more than 60 pounds, get off prescription drugs, and completely change my diet and lifestyle, becoming an outdoor enthusiast and a lover of the environment.

I also began spiritual study, endeavoring to understand the meaning of life and what my life should mean. I became a nicer person and a better husband and father, changing from being spiritless to spiritual and switching political affiliations.

By 2006, I was ready to re-emerge from my two-year-long makeover. Retirement was not for me, so I had to find out what the meaning of my life should be, and I had to learn how to live again. I traveled to remote places, challenging my mental, physical, and spiritual strengths to their capacities. I visited many ancient and sacred places and spent a lot of time with indigenous people, learning their customs and receiving their wisdom. I rediscovered the joy of living and became truly happy for the first time.

MY EPIPHANY: *A LIFE OF SERVICE*

On September 29, 2006, I was in the belly of Earth, the Amazon jungle. Then and there my life was changed forever. I had my epiphany.

I was pondering my future in a hut in the middle of the rainforest, several hours by motorized boat from the nearest jungle port. A dear friend of mine, who was instrumental in leading me into my spiritual path, had once shared with me his reason for existence: unconditional service to mankind. I never quite understood what that meant until that night.

I came to understand that we are all connected, as a species and as a planet. We are all related, genetically proven to be descendants of a single ancestral woman who lived in Africa some 140,000 years ago. Thus, there is no separateness of people from our Creator or each other. We are here to learn and evolve as souls, and this journey we call life is about having a higher purpose and meaning beyond satisfaction of our senses and accumulating possessions. Life is about working on behalf of others, taming our egos, and sharing our talents to make the planet a better place. This does not mean asceticism or denial; rather it means that all actions should have meaning and purpose and one's behavior must be congruent with that.

I realized that there is truth in all religions, and that we must be at peace and one with Earth, our host. We are all sub-organisms of this great living planet.

Bringing food to a remote mountain village in Peru

Knowing that my life would never be the same, I then pondered my future. The Inner Voice gave me two inspirations. I have worked

> Children in Peruvian mountain village

full-time on them every day since then and will continue to do so for the rest of my days.

The first inspiration was about the health and nutrition crisis.

We have an obesity and healthcare crisis in America today primarily driven by preventable disease, where the underlying cause is poor nutrition and bad food. Its social and financial costs are unconscionable. Fake and bad foods are the primary causes of obesity, cancer, heart disease, and diabetes. The best cure is prevention and eating good food. I started a company called Beautifull, which makes prepared, fresh food that is tasty, healthy, and real. Our mission is to serve the world better food—the best you can eat.

RESTORING OUR CHILDREN'S BIRTHRIGHT: *THE REASON FOR THIS BOOK*

The second inspiration was about my children and their future, and that of every other young person on the planet. Once upon a time in America, everyone had access to the American dream. It was a birthright. I am living proof of it.

Today, however, I worry about the world my two children are inheriting. Their birthright of a world that is in better condition than the one their parents received has been violated. Further, all children should have the same opportunity to thrive, just as I did. Instead, we have a permanent underclass, and it is increasingly harder for the less fortunate to survive, much less succeed. Because we are all connected, inhabiting the same planetary biosphere, we must restore our children's future and birthright.

There are roughly 95 million youth living in the United States born between the years 1978 and 2000. Sometimes referred to as the Millennial generation, I call them "Generation We" because of the selflessness and devotion to the greater good that characterize them. By contrast, there are only about 78 million Baby Boomers, the generation that rules the country today. Generation We will be in power very shortly. The same is true on a global scale. Humanity's median age was 28 in 2005, and it is decreasing every year. This means more than half the people in the world are under 30 years of age.

Today, however, I worry about the world my two children are inheriting. Their birthright of a world that is in better condition than the one their parents received has been violated.

There are enough of them that today's youth could become a political force that could dominate all political factions and institutions if they are united and share beliefs and long-term planetary orientation. Youth at present do not have the sense of just how powerful they are, despite differences in race, religion, party affiliation, geography, and gender. Nor do they share an agenda, as the great institutions of power

I came to understand that we are all connected, as a species and as a planet. We are all related, genetically proven to be descendants of a single ancestral woman who lived in Africa some 140,000 years ago. Thus, there is no separateness of people from our Creator or each other. We are here to learn and evolve as souls, and this journey we call life is about having a higher purpose and meaning beyond satisfaction of our senses and accumulating possessions. Life is about working on behalf of others, taming our egos, and sharing our talents to make the planet a better place.

and the industries and media they control have prevented the unification of the youth around a common purpose.

AN AGENDA, NOT A PLAN

The Millennials are a special generation, potentially the greatest generation ever. They are not pessimistic or vengeful. Rather, they are sober in their view of the world. They believe in technology and know they can innovate themselves out of the mess they are inheriting. They believe in entrepreneurship and collective action, and that each person *can* make a difference. They are about plenitude, and they reject cruelty. They are spiritual, responsible, tolerant, and in many ways more mature than their predecessor generations. They reject punditry and bickering, because they are post-partisan, post-ideological, and post-political.

Most important, they believe in the greater good and are ready to dedicate themselves to achieving it.

> Summit of Mount Pachatusan in Peru, elevation 15,930 feet

We propose an agenda for Generation We, a slate of things to be done that serve the best interests of those who have a common need. An agenda is not a plan; it is shared intention. A plan must be inclusive and multipartisan, and it must have broad-based support with the political will to implement its mechanisms and ends.

There are enough Millennials that today's youth could become a political force that could dominate all political factions and institutions if they are united and share beliefs and long-term planetary orientation.

Youths have the common need of a future worth living, where they can enjoy, in the immortal words of the Declaration of Independence, "certain unalienable rights, that among these are Life, Liberty, and the Pursuit of Happiness." Remember that the majority of our Founding Fathers were only in their twenties and thirties at the time our great nation was created from the Revolution in 1776 to the implementation of the Constitution in 1789—not much older than the Millennial generation today. They shared an agenda and created the greatest nation and form of government that the world has ever seen.

PROTECTING OUR CONSTITUTION

I am a passionate believer in the American system—the concept of freedom under law, and a flexible, balanced government responsive to the will of the people as formulated by our Founders and delineated in the Constitution they wrote more than two centuries ago. It grieves me to see how that system has been abused and eroded in recent decades with the help of members of both major political parties. I am writing in hopes that my message will help mobilize millions of citizens—particularly Generation We—to reclaim their power under the constitutional system and return our government to its rightful role of serving the common good.

Politics today is mainly about spin—about twisting facts and ideas in support of a particular ideology, whether of right or left, and a particular party, whether Republican or Democratic. My message in this book should be about reason, not spin; about facts, not emotions; about common sense (as appealed to by the great Thomas Paine) rather than partisan passion.

All of the data we researched in writing the book—our extensive proprietary survey results, the transcripts of our focus groups, and a detailed research bibliography—are on the web at www.gen-we.com to be judged objectively by anyone interested. We are hiding nothing and not manipulating any facts. This is about truth and the start of a conversation that leads to a course of correction. Transparency is the way we choose to achieve that end.

A LABOR OF LOVE

Over the past two years, I've found a number of friends and allies who shared my worries about our world and bought into my vision of what to do about it. They have helped me transform my epiphany in the Amazon jungle into the germ of a planetary movement, beginning with this book. It has been quite literally a labor of love.

As I'll explain in more detail in just a few pages, I met talented social and political scientists who had already been studying the problems and opportunities confronting Generation We. I worked with these experts to sponsor the most detailed and probing research ever done into the Millennial generation, the better to understand their interests, values, strengths, and concerns.

I got to meet many members of Generation We as well. Of course, they are as varied as any other group of human beings. But I found that they include some of the smartest, most caring, and most spiritually grounded people I have ever met. I came away from these encounters more convinced than ever that today's youth have the capacity to change the world for the better, provided they have the knowledge and the will.

I also spoke with and read the writings of many of the world's leading experts on the major problems of our time, from our reliance on fossil fuels and our burgeoning burden of debt to the deepening crises affecting the environment, healthcare, and education. This research greatly enhanced my understanding of the world that the next generation will inherit as well as my sense of what they will need to do to reverse the destructive trends older people have set in motion.

Finally, in November 2007, I met Karl Weber, a talented writer who had previously worked on several books dealing with major social and political issues, including, most recently, *Creating a World Without*

"Until he extends his circle of compassion to include all living things, man will not himself find peace."

ALBERT SCHWEITZER

"The means by which we live have outdistanced the ends for which we live. Our scientific power has outrun our spiritual power. We have guided missiles and misguided men."

MARTIN LUTHER KING, JR.

Poverty by Muhammad Yunus, the Bangladeshi economist who pioneered microcredit and received the 2006 Nobel Peace Prize for his creative work helping some of the world's poorest people escape poverty. When I shared my ideas with Karl, he became very excited and quickly agreed to collaborate with me. We spent a lot of time together talking about my ideas, and Karl did extensive research and reading of his own to back up the concepts we developed.

The result of all these shared experiences and efforts is the book you are holding.

DENIAL IS NO LONGER AN OPTION

The problems of today will not go away if we just sweep them under the rug and ignore them. They will only get worse. We cannot rely on those bound by special interests or protecting their turf to enact great changes and create a new order of justice and fairness. We need the unjaded youth, with their energy, optimism, and sense of purpose, to lead the world out of the mess it is in and toward the full potential of mankind.

On January 6, 1941, Franklin D. Roosevelt gave a famous speech describing what he called "the Four Freedoms":

- **Freedom of speech and expression**
- **Freedom to worship**
- **Freedom from want**
- **Freedom from fear**

The Four Freedoms are still hugely important. But based on the progression of our society and technology, we need to accompany them with the Four Fundamental Rights:

- **Right to health—an unspoiled environment, good nutrition, and affordable healthcare**
- **Right to a good education**
- **Right to clean, affordable energy**
- **Right to information, including computing power and unfettered Internet access**

In the contemporary world, the Four Fundamental Rights are needed for people to have the opportunity to live life to the fullest and contribute to society to the best of their ability. Making them a reality for all should be part of the Millennial agenda.

THE AMERICAN BIRTHRIGHT

This book is for our future. The most powerful force that can make our future better than our past is the youth binding together on the outcome, resolve, and political will to achieve it, no matter how they may differ on details of implementation.

I'm not a member of Generation We, and I don't aspire to lead it. My hope in writing this book is that it will inspire a handful of great leaders like Dr. Martin Luther King, Jr., or Mahatma Gandhi to emerge and lead their peers.

I do know solutions are out there, waiting to be mobilized by the creative, entrepreneurial spirit of our people. And I have faith that with open, informed debate, Americans can use the system we inherited from the Founders to make the wisest long-term choices and get our country back on the track toward peace, prosperity, and freedom.

This, I believe, is our American birthright. And if my book has a single message, it is simply this: Now is the time to reclaim it.

Eric H. Greenberg
July 4, 2008

> In the Amazon Jungle, where the idea for this book originated

1 THIS MOMENT IN HISTORY

A Nation Adrift, a Planet at Risk

You don't have to look hard to find the bad news. It's everywhere—on the TV networks and the cable channels, on the radio talk shows, in our local newspapers, in every magazine, and all over the Internet. The economy is in the tank. Americans by the tens of thousands are losing their jobs.

In Iraq, a wasteful war of dubious necessity grinds on, while terrorists in other countries regroup and hatch fresh plans. Pollution poisons our environment and junk food poisons our bodies. Millions go without healthcare. Corporate plunderers and speculators grab an ever-growing share of profits while worker salaries dwindle. The price of oil skyrockets, making everyday necessities more and more costly. Millions lose their homes as a nationwide mortgage crisis spirals out of control. And the mountains of debt we're all carrying—government debt, credit-card debt, student loans—continue to grow, burying our hopes for a secure future.

Yes, the bad news is everywhere. We worry about it. We gripe about it. Bloggers rant about it. Jon Stewart and Stephen Colbert joke about it. Talking heads and politicians argue about it.

It's time we do something about it.

"The difference between what we do and what we are capable of doing would suffice to solve most of the world's problems."

MOHANDAS K. GANDHI

THE MOMENT IS COMING

Someone once said that history is "just one damn thing after another." Usually it is—just a parade of presidents elected, of wars fought, of bills passed, of economic booms and busts.

But standing out from the parade are the real turning points—the crucial moments, few and far between, when major changes occur that affect civilization and life on this planet for decades or centuries to come.

It's always easier to recognize those turning points after they've come and gone. But once in a while—once in a great while—you can sense when such a moment is coming. And right now, millions of us are aware, vaguely or vividly, that Something Big is in the air, that a crucial moment of opportunity has come when we can change the course of history for the better.

It's not about the arrival of a great leader—although crucial turning points in history often seem to conjure up the inspired leadership needed to make powerful changes happen (think about George Washington, Abraham Lincoln, Franklin D. Roosevelt, and Martin Luther King, Jr.). It's about deep-seated social, economic, and political forces that prepare the way for profound change.

And perhaps the greatest of those forces is the power of a generational shift.

THE MILLENNIALS ARE HERE

Great leaders play an important role in shaping history. But an even greater role is played by the generations of ordinary people from whom the great leaders arise. Without those millions of people, sharing a common vision and ready to shape the future together, even great leaders can accomplish little.

©AMERICAN SPIRIT IMAGES/UNLISTED IMAGES,INC.

Washington could never have led a successful revolution without millions of patriots ready to fight for their own independence. Lincoln could never have freed the slaves and reunited the nation without millions of Americans willing to put their lives on the line for that cause. Roosevelt could never have lifted the United States out of the Great Depression or spearheaded a victorious war against fascism without the heroism of what's now called "the Greatest Generation." King could never have aroused the conscience of white America without the voices of thousands of courageous supporters who made up the ground forces of the civil rights movement.

Today, a new generation is about to seize the reins of history. This book has been written about them and for them. They are a generation that appears to be unique in American and world history—a generation that is incredibly well prepared to tackle the huge challenges we all are facing. They are often known as the Millennial generation. Born between 1978 and 2000, the Millennials currently include 95 million young people up to 30 years of age—the biggest age cohort in the history of the nation.

In the last three years, the Millennial generation has begun to emerge as a powerful political and social force. They are smart, well educated, open-minded, and independent—politically, socially, and philosophically. They are also a caring generation, one that appears ready to put the greater good ahead of individual rewards. Hence our preferred name for them—Generation We. And they are already spearheading a period of sweeping change in America and around the world.

As this period of change unfolds, Generation We will follow (if possible), lead (if necessary). And because of their huge numbers and their unique new perspective, they will make dramatic changes happen, one way or another.

You probably already know a lot about the Millennials. You may be a Millennial yourself, or you may have read or heard about the Millennials in the media. During 2008, the Millennials have been getting a lot of buzz, thanks in part to the amazing rise of Barack Obama—the first presidential candidate to build a campaign largely on their support.

But few people realize how unique Generation We actually is, and even fewer have recognized the incredible opportunities they have to transform society for the better, both here in the United States and around the world.

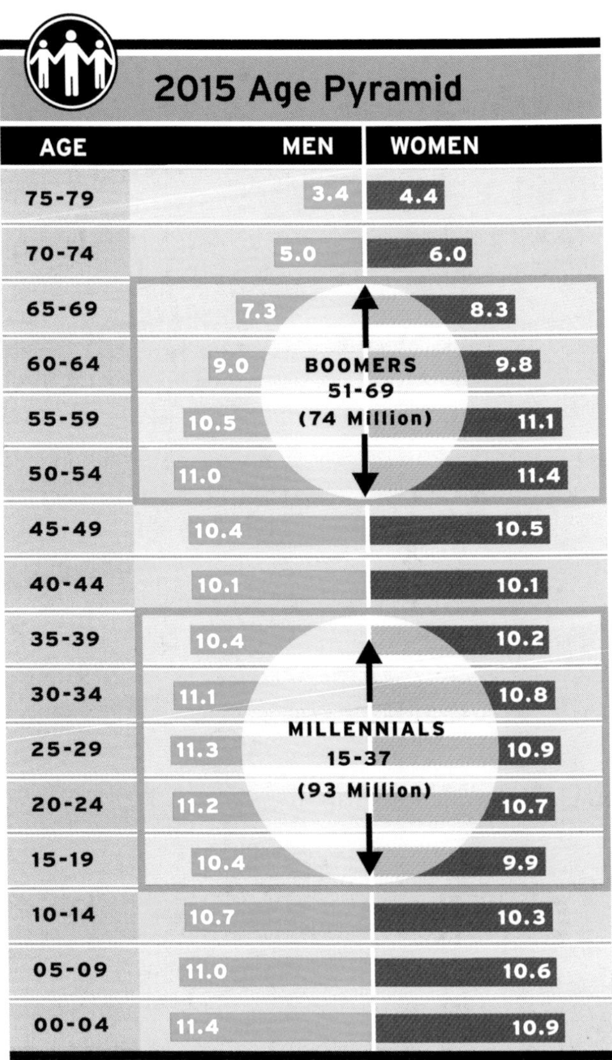

The first purpose of this book is to explore the emerging power of Generation We and to show how the Millennials (and their supporters from other generations) are poised to drive the next great turning point of history. And the second purpose is to propose an agenda and a road map—to provide Generation We with some ideas and a rallying cry around which, we hope, they can begin to mobilize.

It's time we do something about the bad news. Generation We can lead the way.

It's time we do something about the bad news. Generation We can lead the way.

A NOTE TO THE READER

If you are a member of the Millennial generation, this book is a call to action. Our goal is to help you fully grasp the remarkable opportunity that you and others of your age group have to make our world a better place, and to encourage you to seize that opportunity while you can.

The book begins with a chapter that describes in some detail the characteristics of Generation We. (For you, this may feel a bit like looking in a mirror—though we bet you'll learn some things about yourself and your age-mates you never fully realized before.) The rest of the book then explains how the special qualities of your generation have prepared you uniquely well to reshape our world, and suggests some of the ways you might go about doing that.

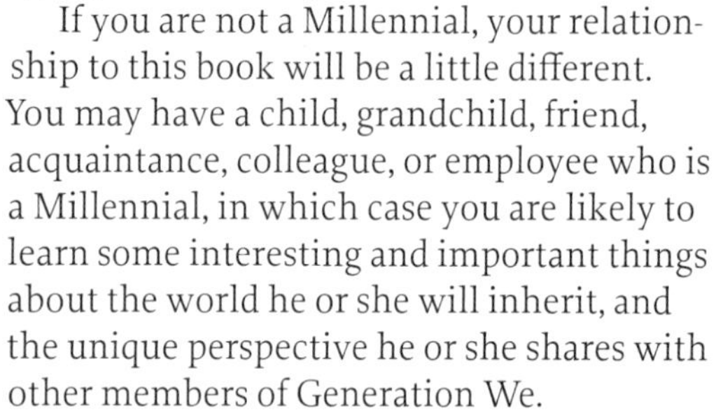

If you are not a Millennial, your relationship to this book will be a little different. You may have a child, grandchild, friend, acquaintance, colleague, or employee who is a Millennial, in which case you are likely to learn some interesting and important things about the world he or she will inherit, and the unique perspective he or she shares with other members of Generation We.

Most important, if you are a citizen of any age who is concerned about the direction in which our nation and our world are heading, this book is directed especially at you. It describes the coming revolution we believe Generation We is poised to lead. When that revolution begins, all of us will have a role to play. What will yours be? Will you support, encourage, guide, and defend the best efforts of Generation We to remake our social, political, and economic systems and to protect the deepest interests of every person on our planet? Or will you stand aside, remain uninvolved, or even put up roadblocks against the coming change?

The time to begin thinking about these questions and challenges is now.

Perceived Commonalities Among Millennials: Older Generations vs. Global Millennials

Do you agree or disagree that your generation shares specific beliefs, attitudes, and experiences that set you apart from generations that have come before you?	How much do you feel your generation of Americans under the age of 30 has in common with young adults of your generation in other countries?	Do you feel your generation of Americans under 30 has more in common with Americans of older generations or with young adults of your generation in other countries?
90% Total Agree	68% Great Deal/ Fair Amount	54% Total Young Adults Other Countries

SOURCE: GREENBERG MILLENNIAL STUDY 2007

"We are called to be architects of the future, not its victims."

R. BUCKMINSTER FULLER

Q5

Please tell us how important each of the following has been in shaping the attitudes and beliefs of your generation of Americans under the age of 30, on a scale of 0-10, where 10 means it has been extremely important in shaping your generation's attitudes and beliefs, and 0 means it has not been at all important.

A

You can choose any number between 0 and 10 - the higher the number, the more important that factor has been in shaping the attitudes and beliefs of your generation.

	M	10	8-10	6-10	0-5	DK-Ref
The terrorist attacks of 9/11	7.9	36	67	83	17	-
Global climate change	6.5	18	41	65	35	0
The growing racial and ethnic diversity of the U.S.	7.1	21	51	74	26	0
The rise of the Internet, cell phones, text messaging, e-mail, and other advances in personal technology	8.3	46	73	85	15	-
America's dependence on foreign oil	7.2	22	52	75	24	0
America's dependence on fossil fuels like coal, natural gas, and oil	7.2	22	53	76	24	0
Declining quality and rising inequality in America's public education system	7.2	23	52	75	25	0
Rapid shift of U.S. economy from manufacturing to services, information and technology	7.0	18	48	73	27	0
The war in Iraq	7.7	31	63	81	19	0
Corporate scandals such as Enron	5.7	10	27	52	47	1
The partisan divide in U.S. politics	6.2	11	32	60	40	0
Lack of long-term job and retirement security	7.1	22	51	74	26	0
Increase in obesity and chronic disease	7.0	19	49	74	26	-
The rising cost of health care and growing number of uninsured	7.2	23	50	74	25	0

SOURCE: GREENBERG MILLENNIAL STUDY 2007

Q19

Next, please tell us whether your generation of Americans under the age of 30 is more likely or less likely than earlier generations of Americans to be characterized by each of the following.

A

	Much More Lkly	Smwt More Lkly	No Diff	Smwt Less Lkly	Much Less Lkly	DK-Ref	Total More Lkly	Total Less Lkly	More - Less
Embrace innovation and new ideas	44	34	15	5	2	0	78	7	71
Start a new business	27	37	22	10	4	0	64	14	50
Make environmental protection a top priority	27	40	20	9	4	0	67	13	54
Express patriotic pride	15	23	28	26	8	0	38	34	3
Support those in the armed forces	22	26	28	18	6	0	48	24	24
Trust government and political leaders	5	12	20	36	27	0	17	63	-46
Believe government has a positive role to play	8	17	27	33	16	0	24	49	-25
Support working with other countries to achieve shared goals	19	42	24	11	4	0	60	15	45
Engage in volunteer activities or community service	12	33	29	20	6	0	45	26	20
Try to directly influence and communicate with elected officials	12	32	26	22	8	0	45	29	15
Engage in political activism	13	30	28	23	6	0	42	29	13
Join a church or other organized religious community	9	16	29	33	13	0	25	46	-21
Express personal spiritual beliefs outside of organized religion	24	31	22	16	6	0	56	22	33
Join an independent or issue-based political movement	16	33	27	18	6	1	49	23	25
Support an emerging third political party	18	38	25	12	6	0	56	18	38

SOURCE: GREENBERG MILLENNIAL STUDY 2007

Q2

We often look at history in terms of generations—groups of people of similar age and experiences who often share specific attitudes and priorities regarding the world around them—such as the Baby Boomers or Generation X. As you look at your own generation of young adults under the age of 30, do you agree or disagree that your generation shares specific beliefs, attitudes, and experiences, that set you apart from generations that have come before you?

A

Answer	%
Strongly agree	35
Somewhat agree	55
Somewhat disagree	7
Strongly disagree	2
(Don't know/refused)	1
TOTAL AGREE	90
TOTAL DISAGREE	9

Q3

How much do you feel your generation of Americans under the age of 30 has in commom—in terms of attitudes, beliefs, and priorities—with young adults of your generation in other countries?

A

Answer	%
A great deal	12
A fair amount	56
Just a little	28
Nothing at all	3
(Don't know/refused)	1
GREAT DEAL/FAIR AMT.	68
LITTLE/NOTHING	31

Q4

Do you feel your generation of Americans under the age of 30 has more in common—in terms of attitudes, beliefs, and priorities—with Americans of older generations or with young adults of your generation in other countries?

A

Answer	%
Much more with older Americans	8
Somewhat more with older Americans	36
Somewhat more with young adults in other countries	42
Much more with young adults in other countries	11
(Don't know/refused)	2
TOTAL OLDER AMERICANS	44
TOTAL YOUNG ADULTS IN OTHER COUNTRIES	54

SOURCE THIS PAGE: GREENBERG MILLENNIAL STUDY 2007

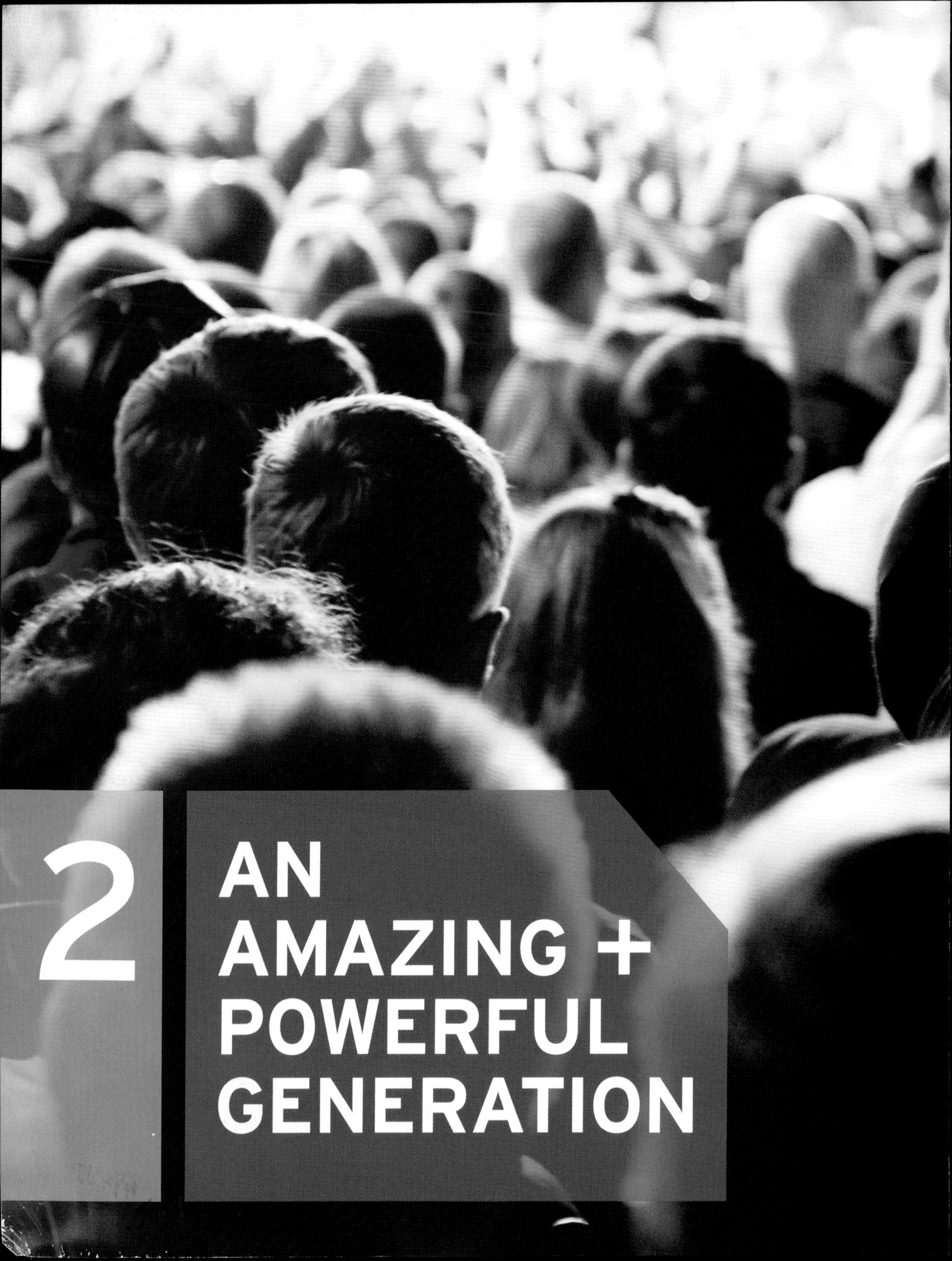

2 AN AMAZING + POWERFUL GENERATION

Who Are Generation We?

First, a few simple factual definitions. Generation We includes people born between 1978 and 2000. They follow two other well-known generations: the Baby Boomers (born 1946-1964), famous for their battles over sex, drugs, and rock 'n' roll, and currently holding most positions of power and influence in American society, and Generation X (born 1965-1977), a politically and socially conservative cohort that has struggled to define itself against the vast and dominant Boomer group it followed.

Of course, there is no absolute or objective definition of a generation. No one issues a decree from on high declaring "as of January 1, a new generation will begin." But the definition of Generation We we've adopted represents the emerging consensus among social commentators, statisticians, and demographers.

It would be simplistic to claim that everybody in a particular generation is the same or holds the same views. Of course they don't. Bill Clinton and Newt Gingrich are both Baby Boomers, and when they held political power, they fought tooth and nail over the best direction for the country. Being members of the same generation didn't give them identical perspectives on anything.

But members of a generation do have some things in common. Clinton and Gingrich, for example, were both members of the first generation to grow up after World War II, in an era of relative affluence. They were among the first Americans to watch and be shaped by TV, to dance to rock 'n' roll, to take geographic and social mobility for granted, and to participate in the sexual revolution. Maybe it's not an accident that they battled over issues from tax policy to healthcare: Baby Boomers have been fighting ideological and social battles with one another for almost 50 years.

So being part of a certain generation does have an influence on people, even if every generation has all the range of psychological, emotional, and personal variation human beings have always exhibited.

"We must use time wisely and forever realize that the time is always ripe to do right."

NELSON MANDELA

That's why the generation you belong to is genuinely meaningful and important—not a bit of fun but irrelevant trivia. Members of a generation tend to share a range of interests, beliefs, and values, as well as defining historical moments and cultural experiences that shape their point of view. It is these shared features that define a generation.

THE MILLENNIAL TIDAL WAVE

What, then, are the characteristics that make Generation We unique? One of the most important is their *huge numbers*. The Millennials are the largest generation in American history. Yes, you read that right—there are more Millennials than any other similar age group that has ever been born in this country.

Everyone has heard about the huge size and importance of the Baby Boom generation. (If you haven't, just ask any Boomer—most Boomers are endlessly fascinated by themselves and their special place in history.) American culture, business, politics, and society have all been transformed by the Baby Boom wave as it rolled through the history of the fifties, sixties, seventies, eighties, and nineties. Now, as they prepare to enter retirement, their vast numbers are about to seriously stress the nation's Social Security and Medicare systems.

There are 78 million Boomers—a larger number than any prior American generation, and more than the "baby bust" group that followed them, Generation X. But the Millennials are even more numerous—95 million strong, over 21 percent larger than the Baby Boom generation.

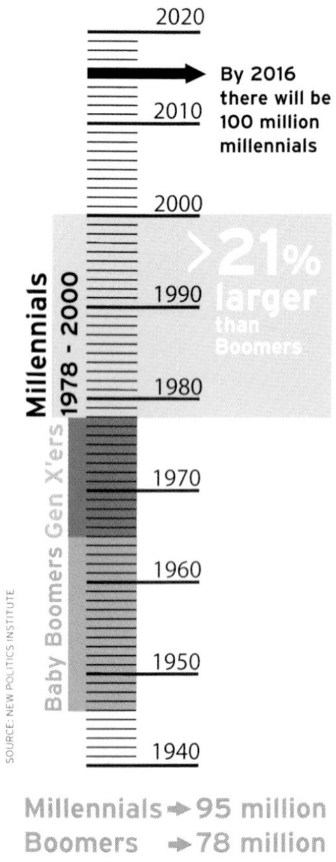

You might object that our definition of Generation We includes more birth years than we assigned to the Baby Boomers—maybe that's why the Millennials seem to be so numerous. Actually, it's not true. Even if you use a narrower definition of the Millennials, cutting off their birth years at 1996, they still outnumber the Boomers, 80 million to 78 million. (And note that other generations are routinely defined as including the larger number of birth years—for example, the group known as the Greatest Generation spans 22 years.) Sheer numbers mean that Generation We is going to have a gigantic impact on American society, and in turn, on the world.

Every life experience the Millennials pass through together will have a huge effect on the world. We already see this happening. Generation We includes the people who have made social networking (Facebook, MySpace, and so on) an important technological and societal trend. They live on instant messaging (IM), text each other continually, and have created entire new industries such as massive multiplayer online gaming. Through their vast numbers and economic power, they forced the music business to accept free downloading as a fact of life, and they appear poised to do the same to the TV and movie businesses. They've made the Internet the world's most important and fastest-growing medium for entertainment and information. And

2020
By 2016 there will be 100 million millennials
2010
2000
>21% larger than Boomers
1990
Millennials 1978 - 2000
1980
Gen X'ers
1970
1960
Baby Boomers
1950
1940
SOURCE: NEW POLITICS INSTITUTE

Millennials → 95 million
Boomers → 78 million

they've begun affecting the outcome of national elections, especially as participation rates by young voters climb steadily—a reflection, as we'll see, of the values of Generation We.

In years to come, the world will be changed by the shared life-cycle stages of Generation We. When large numbers of Millennials start buying houses and having children, it will affect industries such as real estate, education, and automobiles. When Millennials get older and more affluent, they will transform businesses like travel and the market for luxury goods. When Millennials reach their forties and fifties, they will take over positions of power in corporations, bringing with them their generational attitudes about consumerism, the environment, and society (all of which we'll discuss in a moment).

But think about their political impact. By 2016, there will be 100 million Millennials (taking immigration into account), and all will be old enough to vote. Even if Generation We follows past generations in voting at somewhat lower rates than older Americans, they will constitute some 30 percent of the electorate. On the other hand, if their rates of participation increase (as is already happening), their clout will be even greater. It will only increase over time, as the Millennials age and become a proportionately larger share of the voting-age population. For the first time, the youth could have *more* voting clout than their elders.

Generation We is about to rock the world. There are so many of them, they can't help doing it even if they wanted to.

A NEW FACE FOR AMERICA

Sheer numbers would make Generation We a powerful force for change even if they were basically similar to past American generations. But they're not. In many ways, the Millennials represent a brand-new America, transformed by demographic and cultural trends that have been building for decades.

Generation We is America's *most diverse* generation ever, with more Hispanics (18 percent), Blacks (14 percent), and Asians (five percent) than any previous cohort. This is due, in part, to the unprecedented numbers of immigrants to the United States over the past several decades.

They are also the *best-educated* generation in history, boasting a higher percentage of well-educated men and women than any other. Enrollment rates in postsecondary education are increasing; in 2004, the rate for 18- to 19-year-old Millennials was 64 percent. By comparison, the enrollment rate for Boomers of that age in 1970 was only 48 percent. Similarly, the enrollment rate for 20- to 24-year-olds was 35 percent in 2004, compared to just 22 percent in 1970.

According to 2005 Census data, about 28 percent of workers in their twenties had a B.A. degree or higher.[1] Generation We is also hanging out on college campuses longer than past generations. The median

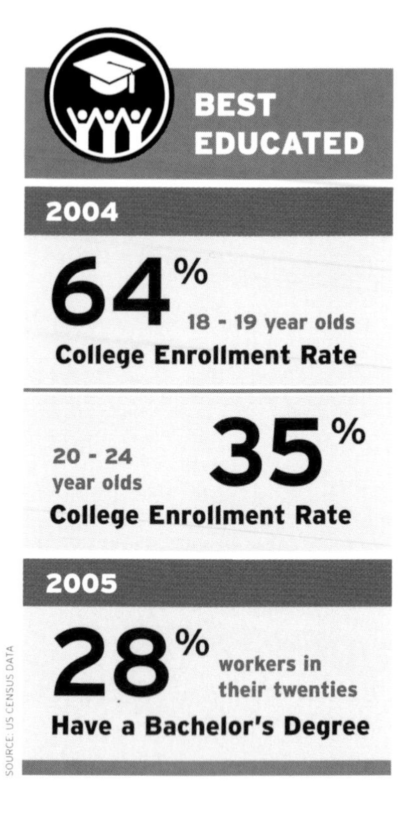

years taken for college completion went up from four to five years between 1970 and 2000. As a result, today 45 percent of college students are 21 or older, compared to just 25 percent in 1970.

THEY KNOW WHO THEY ARE

As we've seen, the demographic characteristics of Generation We are unique. But even more interesting and important are the attitudes and opinions of the Millennials. It is these qualities that tell us Generation We is poised to spearhead one of the decisive turning points in American history.

In the rest of this chapter, we'll be presenting the results of a major research study into the characteristics of the Millennial generation conducted especially for this book. It was sponsored by author Eric Greenberg and conducted by Gerstein | Agne Strategic Communications, one of the most respected research organizations in the United States, and included both extensive oral and written surveys and a series of in-depth focus groups. We'll refer to this study as the Greenberg Millennials Study (GMS). Detailed information about how this study was conducted, as well as a wealth of specific data, can be found in the appendix of this book.

From time to time, we'll also cite some other important studies of Generation We.[2] As you'll see—and as other commentators and analysts have observed—practically every study of the Millennials agrees on certain conclusions. The points we'll be making about the Millennials are about as well documented as any findings from social science can be.

One of the most significant basic findings of every study of Generation We is that they are a highly *self-aware* generation. They readily identify themselves as a unique age group with shared attitudes, experiences, and characteristics.

Findings from the GMS indicate that Millennials have a clear sense of generational identity. By 10 to 1 (90 percent to 9 percent) they agree that their generation "shares specific beliefs, attitudes, and experiences" that set them apart from generations that have come before them. By 68 to 31, they believe their generation has a great deal or a fair amount in common with young adults of their generation in other countries, rather than just a little or nothing at all. They even say, by 54 to 44, that they have more in common with young adults of their generation in other countries than they have with Americans of older generations.

> Generation We is poised to spearhead one of the decisive turning points in American history.

Note, however, that Millennials are not convinced that the needs and goals of their generation are necessarily *opposed* to that of older generations in their own country. Half believe that "[t]he needs and goals of my generation are similar to those of older generations, and our best course is to work together to advance common interests" rather than "[t]he needs and goals of my generation are fundamentally at odds with those of older generations, and accomplishing our goals will require removing those currently in power and replacing them with ourselves" (49 percent).

This tells us some important things about Generation We. They know who they are. They see themselves as a unique group, and identify strongly with others of the same age. Yet they *don't* define themselves in opposition to other generations—as the Baby Boomers did, for example. (Remember the Boomer slogan, "Don't trust anybody over 30"?) The Millennials are ready to work together with those who are older and younger than they. It's one of several qualities we'll point to that make Generation We especially well-positioned to serve as leaders for the revolutionary social changes we think are coming.

GENERATION WE AROUND THE WORLD

In this book, we'll focus primarily on Generation We in the United States. We have several reasons for choosing this focus: American youth are the Millennials about whom most is known. We, the authors, are Americans immersed in the political, social, and economic circumstances of our own country; and we view the United States as being at a crossroads in history, which Generation We is uniquely positioned to affect.

Since the United States is perhaps the most powerful nation on the planet—certainly in military terms, and arguably in cultural and economic terms as well—trends and changes driven by American Millennials are likely to have an enormous impact on the population of the whole world. But we live in an increasingly interdependent world, and American Millennials themselves believe that they are called to work with their counterparts from other nations and continents. We cannot—and must not—ignore the important role that youth from around the world will play in shaping the decades to come. Let's take a brief detour into the world of Millennials outside the United States. As you'll see, there are some notable similarities—as well as some striking differences.

First, whereas American Millennials are children of both the outsized Baby Boom generation and significant immigration from Latin America and Asia (which accounts, in large part, for their vast numbers), global Millennials are the offspring of a world in which fertility rates have generally been on the decline, especially in the developing world. Nonetheless, the number of young people around the world who are currently under the age of 30 is still huge, more than half of the world's population. In 2005, the median age of the world's population was 28 and falling. Current estimates suggest that the number

©IZABELA HABUR/ISTOCK INTERNATIONAL

©KEN SEET/CORBIS

©URIEL SINAI/GETTY IMAGES

of people in the world in their twenties (which does *not* include the youngest Millennials, now 18 and 19 years old) is over 1.1 billion, or nearly 17 percent of the total population.[3]

Second, in cultural and social terms, it seems likely that most non-U.S. Millennials are several years "younger" than their American counterparts. As generational scholars Neil Howe and William Strauss explain in their study *Millennials Rising*, this fits the differing historical circumstances they and their parents experienced in the post–World War II period. The affluence, security, and freedom that characterized life in the United States during the 1950s (and which shaped the world of the Baby Boomers) came later to Europe and Asia. Therefore, young people outside the United States are still catching up to Americans in terms of their social and cultural characteristics.

But they're catching up fast. Thanks to the Internet and other global communications technologies, youth culture is rapidly becoming a planetary rather than national or regional culture. As Howe and Strauss put it (at a time when Generation We was still mostly in its early teens), "Millennials are today forging a mind-set borrowed from bits and pieces of their countries of origin. The amalgam is part Ricky Martin, part Harry Potter, part Lego, part Kwanzaa, and part Pokémon."[4]

The crucial point is Generation We around the world is an incredible force, and one that sees itself as a single, closely linked generation with much more in common than dividing them. They all watch TV together, go online together, and swap ideas and information continually. As a result, they will make crucial social and political decisions within a framework that is multicultural and planetary rather than nationalistic, making their combined global power even greater.

A WIRED GENERATION

American Millennials share a remarkable number of personal and attitudinal traits regardless of geographic, gender, religious, and ethnic differences.

The first and most striking trait is this: *Generation We is incredibly smart about and driven by technology.* They are profoundly shaped by, and comfortable with, the new technologies that connect people around the world electronically, and they have already played a major role in creating and shaping some of those technologies (such as social networking).

The GMS asked Millennials to rate a series of events or trends for their importance in shaping the attitudes and beliefs of their generation. The clear leader was "the rise of the Internet, cell phones, text messaging, email, and similar advances in personal technology," with an average importance rating of 8.3 (where 10, the highest rating, represents extremely important, and 0, the lowest rating, represents not at all important). Moreover, 48 percent of Millennials gave this trend a perfect 10 rating for its effect on their generation. (The next most important influence was the terrorist attacks of 9/11, with an average 7.9 rating and 36 percent giving it a perfect 10.)

This impression is borne out by a wealth of other survey data. A survey of "Generation Next" by the respected Pew Research Center in January 2007, shows rates of Internet usage (86 percent) and email usage (77 percent) are high among Millennials (18–25-year-olds). And more than half of Millennials (54 percent) say they have used a social networking site such as Facebook or MySpace.

Even stronger results come from an April 2006 survey of 18- to 25-year-olds by Greenberg, Quinlan, Rosner Research (no relation to author Eric Greenberg). In that survey, respondents reported spending an average of 21.3 hours a week online, including time spent emailing and instant messaging (IM). In the June 2007 Democracy Corps survey, 18- to 29-year-old Millennials reported a lower average weekly time online of 15.1 hours.

Also in the April 2006 GQR survey, 86 percent reported using email every day; 56 percent said they read news online every day; 41 percent said they used MySpace, Facebook, or something similar every day; and 40 percent said they instant messaged every day. More than half (52 percent) said they had a personal page on MySpace and 34 percent said they had one on Facebook.

But perhaps the most striking and distinctive aspect of technology usage by Generation We is their embrace of mobile media. For example, in a March 2005 mKids World Study survey (reported in NPI's 2006 study, *Mobile Media in 21st Century Politics*), 28 percent of 18- to 24-year-olds reported text messaging regularly, compared to 16 percent of 25- to 34-year-olds and just 7 percent of 35- to 54-year-olds. Even more impressive, in the 2005 Pew Gen Next survey, a majority (51 percent) of 18- to 25-year-olds said they had sent or received a text message *in the past 24 hours*, compared to 22 percent of those 26 to 40 and 10 percent of those 41 to 60.

So Generation We is deeply involved in using new technologies. They also *like* the new technologies and feel good about their impact on the world.

Generation We is generally optimistic about the social and economic impact of new technologies. In the May 2006 Young Voter Strategies poll, 69 percent of Millennials believe new technologies (such as the Internet, cell phones, text messaging, IM, iPods, etc.) make people more efficient, 64 percent believe they make you closer to old friends and family, and 69 percent believe they make it easier to make new friends (the latter two figures are substantially higher than among older generations). On the other hand, 84 percent believe these

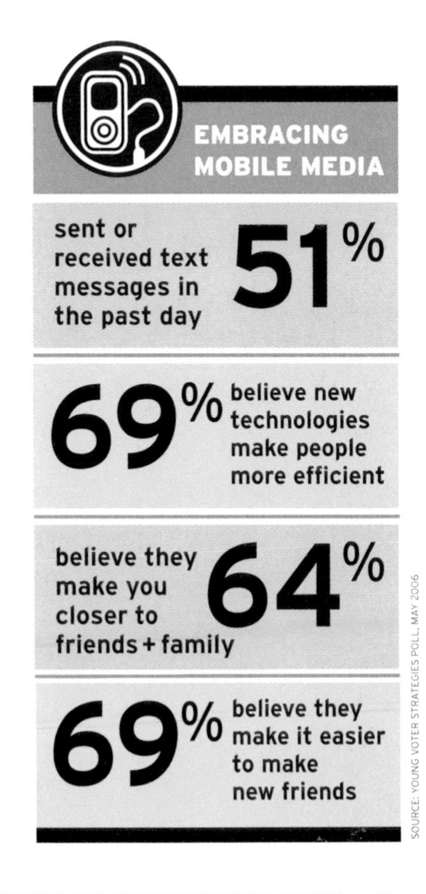

©VLADIMIR V. GEORGIEVSKIY/SHUTTERSTOCK IMAGES

new technologies make people lazier (more than any other age group), 67 percent believe they make people more isolated, and 68 percent believe they make people waste time.

In a June 2006 Pew survey, 18- to 25-year-old Millennials were more likely than any other age group to believe that email and new ways of communication have helped American workers (88 percent). They were also the only age group where a majority thought that the automation of jobs has helped American workers (54 percent). In an April 2006 GQR survey of 18- to 25–year-olds, 86 percent agreed that the benefits of the Internet far outweigh any dangers it presents.

The fact that the largest generation in history is also the first generation for whom technology is as basic as eating, drinking, and breathing will revolutionize economies around the world. Metcalfe's Law states that the value of a network expands logarithmically as its volume/usage doubles; in other words, as participation in the wired economy grows, the impact of that economy grows even faster. Look at how the Internet has transformed life in the last 15 years. The long-term effects of the technological innovations Generation We will spearhead will be even greater, impacting business, finance, communications, entertainment, education, government, and healthcare in ways we can't even conceive of today.

In short, we're living in the Millennials' world, part of a global economy and technological infrastructure that is in the midst of transformational change and whose future will be based on *their* behavior.

A HOPEFUL GENERATION

Generation We is optimistic. As a generation, they are generally convinced that today's children will grow up to be better off than people of today.

A June 2007 Democracy Corps survey of 18- to 29-year-old Millennials bears out this impression. In that poll, 79 percent thought "hopeful" described most people their age very well or well, 78 percent thought "independent" well-described their age group, and 77 percent thought "forward-looking" and "progressive" well-described their generation. When asked how well specific terms described themselves, 93 percent picked "forward-looking," and 90 percent, 91 percent, and 86 percent, respectively, felt that about the terms "hopeful," "independent," and "progressive."

What's more, according to the Pew Center's September 2006 Gen Next survey of today's 18- to 25-year-olds, 84 percent believe that, compared with young adults 20 years ago, they have better educational opportunities, 72 percent believe they have access to higher-paying jobs, 64 percent they believe they live in more exciting times, and 56 percent believe they have better opportunities to bring about social change.

In terms of their overall views, as measured in the same Gen Next survey, 50 percent thought it was better to be a young adult today than 20 years ago, compared to 45 percent who thought those 20 years ago had the better deal.

Another sign of optimism in the Gen Next survey among 18- to 25-year-olds was that, while most believe they currently do not have enough money "to lead the kind of life you want" (63 percent among those not employed and 70 percent among those who are employed), almost all of those individuals believe they *will* have enough money to do so in the future.

Other Pew surveys also show considerable optimism among members of Generation We. In a February 2006 survey, 18- to 29-year-olds (Millennials would include the 18- to 28-year-olds in this group) were the most optimistic age group in assessing whether today's children would grow up better or worse off than people are now (45 percent better/39 percent worse; other age groups were more negative than positive by margins of from 17–27 points). In a July 2006 survey, 18- to 29-year-olds were the most optimistic about whether they would move ahead in life (as measured by self-placement on a "ladder of life" going from 0 as lowest to 10 as highest) in the next five years. Seventy-two percent thought they would, compared to 13 percent who expected no change and 8 percent who thought things would get worse. They were also more likely to believe they had made progress in life in the last five years (58 percent thought so, while 20 percent thought they'd stayed the same and 18 percent thought they'd slipped).

...a generation that believes in the power of human ingenuity and creativity to develop solutions to the problems we face.

At the same time, despite their optimism in life, Generation We has a sober sense of reality and of the problems their generation faces. Many worry that, if current trends continue, the world will be worse off, and they understand the peril of not doing anything at all.

A plurality in the GMS (46 percent) believed that 20 years from now their generation will live in a country that is worse off than the one we live in today, compared to 34 percent who thought the country will be better off. In a June 2007 *New York Times*/CBS News/MTV survey of 17- to 29-year-old Millennials, almost half (48 percent) thought their generation will be worse off than their parents' generation, compared to 50 percent who thought their generation would be the same (25 percent) or better off (25 percent).

Certain aspects of the way things have changed in the last 20 to 30 years elicit clearly negative views from Generation We (though even here they tend to be less pessimistic than older generations about these changes). Pluralities or majorities of 18- to 29-year-olds believe

hopeful
optimistic
progressive
forward-thinking
independent

there is less job security for the average worker today than 20 to 30 years ago; there is more on-the-job stress; retirement benefits are worse; and people need to work harder to make a decent living.

Yet despite these concerns, Generation We is optimistic about their potential and believe that their destiny is in their own hands. Combine the Millennials' belief in technology with their fundamental optimism, and you get a generation that is strongly committed to the idea of *innovation*—a generation that believes in the power of human ingenuity and creativity to develop solutions to the problems we face.

Later, we'll be looking at some of the problems Generation We will face as they gradually take responsibility for the world they are inheriting. Those problems are serious—even frightening. Sobering statistics suggest that the Millennials may, in fact, be the first generation in American history to face tougher life prospects than their parents did. This makes their optimistic attitude toward the future all the more remarkable—and admirable.

A RESPONSIBLE GENERATION

Generation We is a responsible group. In comparison with other generations, they shy away from drugs, unsafe sex, and other high-risk behaviors that harmed the two preceding generations, the Baby Boomers and the Generation Xers.

The first Millennials entered their senior years in high school in 1996 and 1997. Those years generally marked the peak of drug use by twelfth graders (as measured by the National Institute on Drug Abuse's annual Monitoring the Future survey), which had been rising throughout the early 1990s, when the later Gen Xers were reaching that grade. Since then, drug use has been declining for almost all drugs tracked by the survey. For example, 42 percent of twelfth graders in 1996 said they had used some illicit drug in the last year, compared to 37 percent in 2006. Perhaps of even more significance is the fact that drug use is now being delayed by adolescents. In 1996, 24 percent of eighth graders said they had used an illicit drug in the last year; that's now down to 15 percent.

These levels are still higher than they were in the very early 1990s, before measured drug use started increasing. But if current trends continue, measured adolescent illicit drug use should fall below those levels in several more years.

Teens are also waiting longer to have sex. According to the Guttmacher Institute, some 13 percent of females and 15 percent of males ages 15 to 19 in 2002 had sex before they were 15; that's down from 19 and 21 percent, respectively, in 1995. In addition, currently 75 pregnancies occur every year among females age 15 to 19; that rate is down 36 percent since its peak in 1990. Births among this age group are also down by 31 percent over this time period.

Recent rates of juvenile crime have also declined dramatically. For example, in 1994, the rate of violent crime by juveniles was 40 percent above its average for the last several decades; the latest data show that rate is now 15 percent *below* its average. Also, between 1994 and 2002, the number of murders involving a juvenile offender fell 65 percent, to its lowest level since 1984.

Furthermore, as Millennials are shying away from dangerous or health-threatening behaviors, they are also enthusiastically taking up socially beneficial activities, including volunteerism, activism, charity, blogging on social issues, political organizing, and voting. The youth of Generation We care more deeply about the poor, the disenfranchised, and the vulnerable than past generations. They are especially concerned about the environment and the effects of our past bad stewardship over it, and as we'll show in later chapters, they are changing their behaviors to reflect these concerns. These are all impressive signs of responsibility, all the more remarkable in a generation that is still so young.

Many people, especially Baby Boomers, make the assumption that irresponsible behavior is just a natural part of being young. (President George W. Bush, himself a Boomer, responded to rumors of his substance abuse by saying, "When I was young and irresponsible, I was young and irresponsible.") But what was true of the Boomers isn't true of Generation We. They tend to take life and its responsibilities seriously—the kind of trait most of us like to see in a generation that will soon be helping to guide the fate of our nation and our world.

READY FOR CHANGE

Generation We is innovation-minded. They've adopted the pioneering American spirit and embraced it in the form of a profound belief in innovation—technological, social, political. This belief is the hallmark of their generation. Millennials do not see a world of limits but one of possibilities in which anything can be accomplished with enough creativity and determination.

Generation We is also comfortable with risk, as evidenced by their embrace of the ideal of entrepreneurship. In our focus groups, when we asked Millennials to name their personal heroes, they rarely mentioned politicians, athletes, or entertainers, choosing instead creative visionaries from the worlds of business, technology, and social innovation—people such as Bill Gates, Steve Jobs, Nelson Mandela, Muhammad Yunus, and even Oprah Winfrey (whom Millennials view not as a talk show host but as a pioneering female business leader and human rights advocate).

With their affinity for technology, Generation We is pursuing their belief in innovation personally. They are working in the world's top

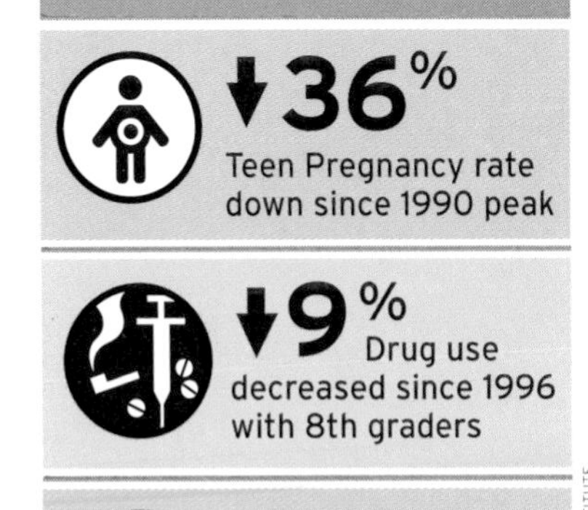

©SW PRODUCTIONS/BRANDX/CORBIS

university research labs, witnessing the laws of chemistry, physics, materials science, and electrical engineering being transformed by their own research. They know from personal experience that the future is in their hands, and their comfort with the latest technology along with their open-minded attitude makes them a more formidable force for innovation than any previous generation.

Survey results bear out these impressions. The GMS asked Millennials whether their generation was more likely or less likely than earlier generations of Americans to be characterized by various attitudes and behaviors. Topping the list was *embracing innovation and new ideas.* More than three-quarters (78 percent) thought Millennials were more likely than earlier generations to embrace innovation and new ideas, compared to a mere 7 percent who thought Millennials were less likely than earlier generations to do so, for a net score (more likely minus less likely) of +71. *This is by far the strongest result for any of the 14 characteristics we tested.*

charity
volunteerism
activism
entrepreneurship
political organizing

Consistent with this finding, another question in the GMS found 87 percent of Generation We agreeing with the statement, "Throughout our history, America's success has been built on innovation and entrepreneurship. As we confront the many challenges facing us today, it is that same spirit of innovation and entrepreneurship that is needed to maintain America's strength in the 21st century."

Equally important, *Generation We is noncynical and civic-minded.* They believe in the value of political engagement and are convinced that government can be a powerful force for good. What's more, there are many signs that Generation We is already acting on these beliefs, getting far more involved in social and political activism at a young age than other recent American generations.

One of the most significant findings from the GMS is Millennials' interest in and belief in collective social action. When asked about the best way to address the challenges facing the country, the leading choice by far was "through a collective social movement" (60 percent made that their first or second choice) over through individual action and entrepreneurship (35 percent), through the media and popular culture (33 percent), through government action (40 percent), or through international cooperation (30 percent). Note that the number choosing a collective social movement (38 percent) as their first choice was more than twice the number that chose any other option as their first choice.

Consistent with this belief in collective action, Generation We has a strong and activist sense of generational mission. The results of these four questions from the GMS show just how robust that sense of mission is:

> *In our country, each generation has a responsibility to wisely use the country's resources and power so that they can provide the next generation a secure, sustainable country that is stronger than the one they inherited* (91 percent agree, 53 percent strongly agree).
>
> *Young Americans must take action now to reverse the rapid decline of our country. If we wait until we are older, it will be too late* (89 percent agree, 48 percent strongly agree).
>
> *Life in the future in America will be much worse unless my generation of Americans takes the lead in pushing for change* (85 percent agree, 42 percent strongly agree).
>
> *My generation of Americans has better opportunities to make a difference and produce structural change than previous generations* (79 percent agree, 31 percent strongly agree).

Moreover, Generation We explicitly rejects the idea that individuals shouldn't step forward and try to make a difference. More than three-quarters (78 percent) say they are willing to make significant sacrifices in their own life "to address the major environmental, economic, and security challenges facing our country." By 4 to 1, Millennials say that *addressing the big issues facing my generation starts with individuals willing to take a stand and take action (80 percent) rather than individuals can't make a real difference in addressing the big issues facing my generation* (20 percent).

Consistent with these sentiments, volunteerism is unusually high among Millennials. According to UCLA's American Freshman survey—conducted for the past 40 years with several hundred thousand respondents each year—83 percent of entering freshman in 2005 volunteered at least occasionally during their high school senior year, the highest ever measured in this survey. Seventy-one percent said they volunteered on a weekly basis. (Some data sources indicate that rates of volunteering among Millennials may actually have been highest right after—and presumably in reaction to—9/11, but differences in question wording and population surveyed prevent a definitive judgment on this possibility.)

Millennials do not see a world of limits but one of possibilities in which anything can be accomplished with enough creativity and determination.

Generation We is deeply concerned about the common good. They also believe in social change—and they are ready, even eager,

Generation We is deeply concerned about the common good. They also believe in social change—and they are ready, even eager, to play their role in making positive changes happen.

to play their role in making positive changes happen. Committed to innovation, they are determined to leave the world better off (even if this means they must take on the difficult challenge of reversing decades of environmental, economic, and social damage), and they are prepared to work outside the traditional boundaries and institutions to drive change.

Combined with their technology-driven culture, this means the Millennials are ready to mobilize differently, more powerfully, more collaboratively, and more creatively than past generations. The results are likely to be astounding.

POLITICALLY ENGAGED

By comparison with past generations, *Generation We is highly politically engaged.* In the 2006 American Freshman survey, more freshman reported they discussed politics more frequently as high school seniors (34 percent) than at any other point in the 40 years covered by the survey. According to the December 2006 Pew Research Center Gen Next data, Millennials who are 18 to 25 today (birth years 1981–1988) are running about 10 points higher than Gen Xers at the same age on following what's going on in government and in level of interest in keeping up with national affairs. In a Greenberg Quinlan Rosner (GQR) April 2005 survey of 18- to 25-year-olds, respondents gave themselves an average of 7 on a 10-point scale as to how well "I read a lot about politics" describes them (higher even than the 5.6 they gave themselves on reading about technology).

More recently, in a January 2007 Pew Research Center survey, 77 percent of 18- to 29-year-olds said they are interested in local politics, up 28 points from 49 percent in 1999—the highest increase of any age group surveyed. The survey also found that 85 percent of 18- to 29-year-olds report they are "interested in keeping up with national affairs," a 14-point increase from 71 percent in 1999 and nearly the same level of interest as adults of all ages (89 percent).

Generation We also comes out well in measures of election-related political engagement. According to the University of Michigan's National Election Study (NES), 18- to 29-year-olds in 2004 (an age group dominated by Millennials who were 18–26 at the time), were either higher or matched previous highs on a wide range of political involvement indicators, when compared to 18- to 29-year-olds in previous elections. These indicators included level of interest in the election, caring a good deal who wins the election, trying to influence others' votes, displaying candidate buttons or stickers, attending political meetings, and watching TV programs about the campaign.

More detail on political engagement is provided by the Harvard Institute of Politics (IOP) November 2007 survey of 18–24-year-olds.

In that survey, 50 percent said they had signed an online petition, 28 percent had written an email or letter advocating a political position, 23 percent had contributed to an political discussion or blog advocating a political position, 21 percent had attended a political rally, 15 percent had donated money to a political campaign or cause, and 12 percent had volunteered on a political campaign for a candidate or issue. In addition, 60 percent said they closely followed news about national politics.

In the same survey, 63 percent also thought political engagement was an effective way of solving important issues facing the country, 66 percent thought such engagement was an effective way of solving important issues facing their local community; the analogous figures for community volunteerism were 61 and 80. The GMS found somewhat stronger results, with 69 percent saying political activism was a very or somewhat effective way of solving the major challenges facing our country and 73 percent saying community volunteerism was an effective way of solving those challenges.

Given Generation We's strong support for collective action, sense of generational mission, and high levels of activism and political interest, it is not surprising that Millennials' voter turnout so far has been exceptionally strong.

In the 2004 election, Census data indicate that the 18- to 24-year-old group, completely composed of Millennials, increased their turnout 11 points to 47 percent of citizens in that age group, while 18- to 29-year-olds—dominated for the first time by Millennials—increased their turnout 9 points to 49 percent. These increases were far higher than among any other age group.

Studies from 2006 also suggest that turnout went up even more in precincts where a special face-to-face, door-to-door effort was made to get young voters to the polls. CIRCLE's analysis of nonpartisan voter turnout efforts in student-dense precincts indicated that turnout, on average, doubled over 2002 in these precincts. Evidence continues to accumulate that direct contact (as opposed to phone-banking) turnout efforts are extraordinarily effective with Generation We voters.

The long-term trends at work here are huge and spell a steady increase in the influence of youthful voters. Pundits called the electoral shift of 2006 a mandate on the war in Iraq, but it reflected even more the rise in youth voting combined with their strongly progressive attitudes (as we'll explain in the next section).

Turnout among members of Generation We, even with these increases, still lags behind older cohorts—a long-standing pattern among American voters. But the gap has narrowed dramatically. If we take into account volunteerism and community activism levels that are already on a par in most respects with older cohorts, it is clear that Millennials are poised to make a big impact on society with their unusually high rates of civic participation, political involvement, and voting.

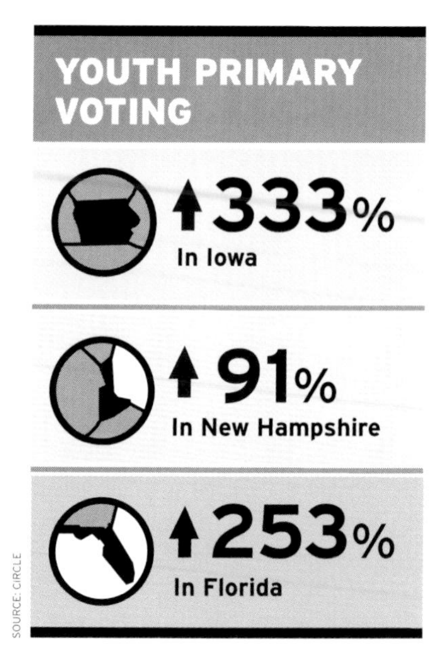

In the 2008 primaries, Generation We is continuing their trend toward increased voter participation in dramatic fashion. Here's a summary by CIRCLE of youth (18- to 29-year-olds—all Millennials) turnout in early primaries where comparison to previous elections was possible:

> [Y]outh turnout rose dramatically in Iowa, Florida, and New Hampshire. In Iowa, the youth turnout rate rose to 13 percent in 2008 from four percent in 2004 and three percent in 2000. Young voters expanded as a proportion of all caucus-goers, and the total number of Iowans who caucused grew, producing a three-fold increase in youth participation. Similarly, in New Hampshire, the youth turnout rate rose sharply to 43 percent in 2008 compared to 18 percent in 2004 and 28 percent in 2000. Young people increased their turnout more than the older voters. The youth turnout rate increased by 15 percentage points over 2000 while the turnout rate for those ages 30 and above increased by only six percentage points. In Florida, the youth voter turnout tripled compared to 2000 despite the fact that the Democratic primary was not fully contested.

These trends continued into Super Tuesday. The basic results in states that had previously participated in Super Tuesday were as follows: in California, youth turnout went up from 13 percent to 17 percent; in Connecticut, youth turnout went up from 7 to 12 percent; in Georgia, youth turnout tripled; in Massachusetts, youth turnout doubled; in Missouri, youth turnout tripled; in New York, youth turnout was steady while overall turnout fell; in Oklahoma, youth turnout tripled; and in Tennessee, youth turnout quadrupled. Granted these turnout increases are measured against a low base, but they are impressive nonetheless. And typically the percentage point increase in youth turnout exceeded the percentage point increase among voters as a whole.

Paradoxically, members of Generation We are not quick to claim for themselves the mantle of being particularly active or politically engaged, even though they are, in fact, among the most involved young people in history. In our focus groups, many Millennials criticized their own generation as being "apathetic" or "materialistic." There are a number of possible explanations for this paradox.

One is that the Millennials are measuring their and their generation's activism—actually high relative to earlier generations of young people—against the seriousness of the planetary problems they face and finding it wanting. They are worried that their generation has not yet launched the kind of social and political movement they see as necessary to address the major issues of our time. This attitude is a reflection of their strong sense of responsibility—and also a measure of their readiness to step forward when conditions are right and a clear agenda emerges for Millennials to rally around.

Negative media coverage of youth probably also plays a role. It is intriguing to note that although Millennials in the June 2007 Democracy Corps survey were overwhelmingly convinced (87 percent) that the word "materialistic" well-described people their own age, only 35 percent felt that term well-described themselves. Generation We as a group strongly condemns materialism even as they believe (or fear) it is rampant among their peers.

The fact is Generation We is ready to work for large-scale change and to support the kind of collective movement they consider necessary for such change to occur. Perhaps only such a movement—one that empowers individuals to become, in Gandhi's words, "the change they wish to see in the world"—can overcome the barriers Millennials see as holding them and their generation back.

We'd argue that a movement aimed at engaging and mobilizing Generation We must build on the distinctive aspects of the Millennial personality: a view that overcoming tradition and innovating to create a better future is both necessary and a central strength of their generation; a wish to embody in their lives and actions the kind of change they are seeking to make; an unabashed willingness to use their economic power as consumers; a deep embeddedness in social networks; a clear-eyed assessment of the difficulties of change, which leads them to seek not just action but plans for successful action; and of course, an appreciation of the potential of the new technologies that have done so much to shape this generation.

By comparison with past generations, Generation We is highly politically engaged.

In short, Generation We is becoming more active and increasingly ready to support a collective social movement that embraces both government and entrepreneurship focused on the greater good. Based on their numbers and their sense of urgency, once such a movement emerges it is certain to be large, powerful, and lasting.

THE PROGRESSIVE SHIFT

The political attitudes of Generation We reveal a distinct pattern that is markedly different from that of their immediate predecessors, the Gen Xers—the most politically conservative cohort in American history. *Thanks to their open-mindedness and their overwhelming embrace of the greater good, Generation We is developing strongly progressive views on a wide range of issues and is poised to lead the most dramatic leftward political shift in recent American history.*

On the political stage, Generation We is already beginning to make their influence felt. The oldest Millennials were eligible to vote for the first time in 1996. In their first few elections, Generation We has voted more heavily Democratic than other recent generations. For example, in 2002 (otherwise a terrible year for Democrats), Millennials (then 18- to 24-years old) voted Democratic by 49 to 47 percent. In 2004, Millennials age 18 to 24 favored Democrat John Kerry for president by 56 to 43 percent. (Polling data for the entire Millennial cohort aren't available.) If young people ruled America, Kerry would have been elected with a landslide victory of 372 electoral votes to 166 for Bush.[5] In 2006, Millennial voters (then 18- to 29-years old) favored Democrats for Congress by a margin of 60 to 38 percent. They were the swing vote role that delivered the Democratic takeover of Congress during that year's midterm elections.

GEN WE: Voting Heavily Democratic

Since 2002 there has been a steady increase in a progressive direction with Millennial voters.

In 2002 Millennials voted Democratic by a 49 to 47 margin. **2002**

2004 In 2004 Millennials voted Democratic by a 56 to 43 margin.

SOURCE: RUY TEIXEIRA, 2008

The Democratic leanings of Generation We extend beyond voting choices into party identification. According to the most recent survey by the Pew Research Center for the People and the Press (released in April, 2008), Americans age 18 to 29 identify themselves as Democrats (or "lean" Democratic) over Republicans by a 58 to 33 percent margin.

This is the largest progressive shift since the New Deal—the movement launched in the 1930s by Franklin D. Roosevelt that earned him four terms in the White House...

This is the largest progressive shift since the New Deal—the movement launched in the 1930s by Franklin D. Roosevelt that earned him four terms in the White House, a rewriting of the social contract between Americans and their government, and nearly a half-century of political dominance for the Democratic Party, buoyed by the loyalties of voters whose sensibilities were shaped by the politics of the New Deal. Thus, the progressive shift of Generation We isn't going to be an important trend for one or two years or even one or two elections. It's likely to shape American politics for several decades to come.

You might wonder whether the Democratic preferences of Generation We simply reflect their youth. After all, it's a common folk belief that young people are generally liberal and gradually become more conservative as they get older. But that's not the case. When we compare today's Generation We with their predecessors the Gen Xers, we see a huge crash in Republican support. Back in the 1990s, when the Gen Xers were the same age as Generation We is today, they identified with the Republicans at a 55 percent rate. Those same Gen Xers, now in their thirties, continue to be the most Republican generation today.

The fact is that party identification and other voting behaviors formed in a generation's twenties tend to persist for a lifetime, as demonstrated by many political science studies.[6] This is good news for the Democratic Party. On Election Day in 2006, the exit polls showed the

Democrats with a 12-point lead in party identification among 18- to 29-year-old voters. Polls taken since then typically give the Democrats even larger leads in party identification among this age group, as well as substantial leads in generic presidential and congressional voting intentions for 2008.

Of course, party preference is one thing—political attitudes are another. Does the Millennial leaning toward the Democratic party merely represent a swing in "brand preference" from one vaguely defined collection of positions to another—or does it reflect a real shift in attitudes?

Our research demonstrates that the latter is true. In fact, *Generation We is far more wedded to progressive political and social views than to the Democratic party.* On issue after issue, Generation We favors progressive positions, even as they resolutely *reject* familiar labels, party banners, and ideological straitjackets. For example, in the GMS, fully 70 percent of respondents agreed with this statement:

> *Democrats and Republicans alike are failing our country, putting partisanship ahead of our country's needs and offering voters no real solutions to our country's problems.*

And more Millennials surveyed described themselves as independents (39 percent) than either Democrats (36 percent) or Republicans (24 percent).

The fact is that the progressive shift of Generation We is not about party politics. It's about a belief in the future; about embracing possibility and hope (the themes that have driven Barack Obama's popularity among the young); and about rejecting the divisive rhetoric, penchant for social control, and protection of entrenched interests that young Americans identify with the conservative movement.

Members of Generation We see their friends coming home from war with permanent injuries; they find themselves unable to afford healthcare, to save for retirement, or to fill up their tanks with gas. They blame the right for these problems, and they see the obstinacy and narrow-mindedness of conservatives as being antithetical to their own optimism and spirit of innovation. So they reject the failed solutions of the right, even as they refuse to commit themselves wholeheartedly to any political party.

Q92

Generally speaking, do you think of yourself as a Democrat, a Republican or what?

	Total
Strong Democrat	16
Weak Democrat	20
Independent-lean Democrat	11
Independent	22
Independent-lean Republican	6
Weak Republican	14
Strong Republican	10
(Don't know/refused)	1
Strong Affiliation	**48**
Lean/Weak Affiliation	**50**
Democrat/Lean Democrat	**47**
Republican/Lean Republican	**30**

SOURCE: GREENBERG MILLENNIAL STUDY 2007

©COLORBLIND IMAGES/BLEND

A TOLERANT GENERATION

Generation We is remarkably open-minded and tolerant on social issues. They are more accepting of gender equality, gay rights, racial blending, and immigration than any other generation.

Gender equality is rapidly becoming a nonissue with Generation We. In the 2004 National Election study, respondents were asked to place themselves on a 7-point scale relative to the following statements: "Some people feel that women should have an equal role with men in running business, industry and government. Others feel that women's place is in the home," where 1 is the strongest support for women's equal role and 7 is the strongest support for women's place being in the home. Two-thirds of Millennials selected 1, the strongest support for women's equal role, and 88 percent of Millennials picked 1, 2, or 3—both figures that are higher than for any other generation.

In another NES question on whether government should see to it that women receive equal treatment on the job, Millennials (18- to 26-year-olds in their 2004 survey) were significantly stronger than other generations in the women's equality direction. Eighty-five percent of Millennials felt that government should do this, compared to 68 percent of Xers and 71 percent of Boomers.

To some extent, Generation We is just responding to the lived reality of their generation—for them, gender equality is a "fact on the ground." Indeed, women are not only equal in their experience but frequently taking the lead. For example, today girls tend to outperform boys in elementary and secondary school, getting higher grades, following more rigorous academic programs, and participating in advanced placement classes at higher rates. They also now outnumber boys in student government, in honor societies, on school newspapers, and in debating clubs. And more girls are attending college than boys: 56 percent of today's undergraduates are women, compared to 44 percent who are men. Reflecting this disparity, women now earn 170,000 more bachelor's degrees each year than men do. Finally, while in 1970 fewer than 10 percent of medical students and four percent of law students were women, today women are roughly half of the nation's law and medical students, not to mention 55 percent of the nation's professionals as a whole.

On race, too, there's strong trend among Generation We toward seeing race as fundamentally a nonissue. In 2003, almost all (89 percent) of white 18- to 25-year-old Millennials said they agreed that "it's all right for Blacks and Whites to date each other," including 64 percent who "completely" agreed. Back in 1987–1988, when the same question was posed to white 18- to 25-year-old Gen Xers, just 56 percent agreed with this statement.

Gallup data from a 2005 poll underscore these findings; 95 percent of 18- to 29-year-olds said they approve of Blacks and Whites dating, and 60 percent of this age group said they had dated someone of a different race. In addition, 82 percent of white 18- to 25-year-old Millennials in 2003 disagreed with the idea that they "don't have much in common with people of other races."

But it is their views on sexual preference issues that are perhaps the most strikingly liberal. On gays, the views of Generation We are far more liberal than that of their elders. For example, in a 2007 Pew survey, an outright majority (56 percent) of 18- to 29-year-olds supported allowing gays and lesbians to marry, while the public as a whole opposed gay marriage by a 55-to-37 majority.

Millennials are also concerned about political trends that put tolerance at risk. In an April 2005 GQR poll of 18- to 25-year-olds, 64 percent believed that religious conservatives had gone too far in invading people's personal lives, and 58 percent thought the country needs to work harder at accepting and tolerating gays, rather than work harder at upholding traditional values.

Sexual tolerance was not a big subject of the GMS focus group discussions. Nevertheless, it is striking just how much tolerance of diversity and difference defines this generation's perspective. In fact, they pride themselves on this tolerance and see it as distinctive to their generation. Consequently, they believe divisive social issues will have far less effect on their generation than on previous generations.

Generation We also has an open and positive attitude toward immigration, much more so than older generations. In the Pew Gen Next poll, 18- to 25-year-olds, by 52 to 38, said immigrants strengthen the country with their hard work and talent, rather than are a burden on the country because they take our jobs, housing, and healthcare, compared to very narrow pluralities in this direction among Gen Xers

64% BELIEVED that religious conservatives had gone too far in invading people's personal lives.

58% THOUGHT the country needs to work harder at accepting and tolerating gays, rather than work harder at upholding traditional values.

and Boomers and 50–30 sentiment in the other direction among those 61 and over. In a 2004 Pew survey, 67 percent of 18- to 25-year-old Millennials thought the growing number of immigrants strengthens American society and only 30 percent believed this trend threatens our customs and values—again, much stronger positive sentiment than among any other generation.

Generation We not only believes in the concept of "live and let live," they are prepared to act on it—and to vote by it. The "culture war" politics that were used effectively by right-wing politicians during the 1970s, 1980s, and 1990s appears to have little power over the tolerant, open-minded Millennial generation.

The socially tolerant attitudes of Generation We mirror and link to their openness to new ideas and approaches toward solving our problems. It also means that the Millennials are ready to consider themselves a part of a planetary humankind not divided by race, religion, or national boundaries, but ready to accept differences in beliefs and values in exchange for progress, peace, and a better life for all.

ENVIRONMENTAL URGENCY

74% Believe we must make major investments now in nonfossil fuel based energy solutions

94% Believe our country must take extreme measures to protect the environment now before it is too late

74% Believe our environmental situation is a "crisis that our country must address immediately"or it will be a major problem.

SOURCE: GREENBERG MILLENNIAL STUDY 2007

A GENERATION OF GREEN ACTIVISTS

Generation We is overwhelmingly pro-environment. Having grown up—unlike any previous generation—with the image on their computer monitors of Planet Earth as a precious, fragile blue sphere floating like an island of life in the darkness of space, the Millennials have a more profound environmental consciousness than earlier Americans. They can't even remember a time when they thought of themselves as disconnected from other peoples, nations, or continents, their behavior of no consequence to others. They've always understood the deep interdependence of all humans on one another and on the environment we share.

They worry about global warming and believe strongly that we need to move away from dependence on fossil fuels and embrace the need for major investments in new energy technologies. In fact, one of the strongest elements of Millennials' generational identity is making environmental protection a top priority—two-thirds said their generation is more likely than earlier generations to have this orientation.

Not only does Generation We embrace the cause of environmental protection and a new energy paradigm, they have a real sense of urgency about it. For example, in the GMS, 74 percent say, "We must make major investments now to innovate the next generation of nonfossil fuel based energy solutions," compared to just 26 percent who say, "We should continue on our current path, gradually shifting the mix of sources used to meet our energy needs." In addition, 94 percent agreed that "our country must take extreme measures now, before it is too late, to protect the environment and begin to reverse the damage we have done." Seventy-four percent say this situation is either a "crisis that our country must address immediately" or a major problem.

The sentiments underlying this sense of urgency are vividly highlighted by responses to three other GMS questions:

> *Our nation's continuing dependence on oil has weakened our economy and stifled innovation, left us dependent on foreign countries—some of whom sponsor terrorism against us—and dragged us into unnecessary wars* (93 percent agree; 79 percent say this situation is either "a crisis that our country must address immediately" or a major problem).

93% AGREE

Our nation's continuing dependence on oil has weakened our economy and, stifled innovation, left us dependent on foreign countries—some of whom sponsor terrorism against us—and dragged us into unnecessary wars.

> *Man-made causes are destroying our environment and the Earth's delicate ecosystem. As a result, we could see massive, irreversible damage to the Earth's landscape during our lifetimes* (91 percent agree; 74 percent say this situation is either "a crisis that our country must address immediately" or a major problem).

> *Our reliance on fossil fuels is a byproduct of the interests of those currently in power. We need to invest in and innovate new energy sources in order to protect our quality of life and prosperity* (96 percent agree; 76 percent say this situation is either "a crisis that our country must address immediately" or a major problem).

In light of these views, it should come as no surprise that Generation We is highly supportive of ambitious ideas for changing our paradigm on energy and the environment. (Such ambitious ideas also closely track their penchant for innovation, collective social movements, and optimism.) For example, the following proposed solution received an average effectiveness rating of 7, where 10, the highest rating, represents extremely effective in dealing with that challenge and 0, the lowest rating, represents not at all effective in dealing with that challenge. Moreover, 71 percent gave it a rating of between 6 and 10 and about half (49 percent) rated it between 8 and 10 on the effectiveness scale.

> *Launch a concerted national effort, similar to the Apollo Program that put a man on the moon, with the goal of moving America beyond fossil fuels and inventing the next generation of energy, based on new technologies such as hydrogen or fusion. This aggressive plan would require a huge national investment*

but would produce millions of new jobs, could dramatically reduce environmental damage, and free us from our dependence on fossil fuels and foreign oil.

Given the scale of the proposed solution, this is an impressive response to which national leaders must pay attention. (We'll have more to say about the energy issue and this proposed solution a little later in the book.)

Evidence from other surveys is consistent with the GMS findings. According to the Pew Gen Next survey, Generation We overwhelmingly believes that the country should do "whatever it takes" to protect the environment, that stricter environmental laws and regulations are worth the cost and that people should be willing to pay higher prices in order to protect the environment. They also, according to the Magid Associates 2006 survey of Millennials, were more likely than any other age group to favor environmental protection, even at the cost of economic growth.

Concern about global warming, as in the GMS, is also high. In the June 2007 Democracy Corps poll of Millennials, 61 percent thought that "global warming represents an immediate threat and we need to start taking action now," rather than "global warming represents a long-term threat and we need to study the problem before taking drastic action."

Generation We is also concerned about the possibility of large-scale environmental disasters and the ability of government to prevent them. In a GQR December 2005 survey of 18- to 25-year-olds, 71 percent thought it was very or somewhat likely that environment damage caused by global warming would happen in their lifetime, and 88 percent thought a natural disaster would wipe out another U.S. city, like what happened to New Orleans. Sixty and 49 percent, respectively, did not trust the government to deal with the problem.

The GMS focus groups confirmed the centrality of protecting the environment, promoting alternative energy and combating global warming to the Millennials' generational agenda. In particular, focus group participants fully endorsed the idea that reliance on fossil fuels, since it both threatens our national security and contributes to global warming, must be eliminated as rapidly as possible. They were willing to endorse very bold efforts to try to accomplish this goal.

A quest to develop the next generation of energy sources also seemed to engage the focus group participants more personally than most of the other big challenges presented to them. In keeping with the Millennials' view that innovation, entrepreneurship, collective action, and advanced technology are the best ways to solve our biggest problems, they saw energy as an area within which they could really

Not only does Generation We embrace the cause of environmental protection and a new energy paradigm, they have a real sense of urgency about it…74 percent say, "We must make major investments now to innovate the next generation of nonfossil fuel based energy solutions,"…94 percent agreed that "our country must take extreme measures now, before it is too late, to protect the environment and begin to reverse the damage we have done." Seventy-four percent say this situation is either a "crisis that our country must address immediately" or a major problem.

"Freedom is never more than one generation away from extinction. We didn't pass it to our children in the bloodstream. It must be fought for, protected, and handed on for them to do the same."

RONALD REAGAN

make a difference and where advancing American technology could potentially achieve something quite spectacular and alter the course of America's future.

ECONOMIC WORRIES

Generation We is deeply concerned about a host of large-scale economic problems affecting the country. They are worried particularly about healthcare, but also about education, inequality, the decline of middle-class jobs, and the national debt. What is most striking, though, is their understanding of the financial costs of social problems and how these will impact their future.

In the GMS, Millennials register high levels of concern about the U.S. healthcare system and endorse the need to fundamentally overhaul it. These views are highlighted by the following two statements:

> *With costs rising out of control and the quality of health coverage declining, the health care system in our country is broken, and we need to make fundamental change* (96 percent agree; 80 percent say this situation is either "a crisis that our country must address immediately" or a major problem).

> *The health of our country is collapsing under an epidemic of chronic, preventable diseases as we slowly poison our own bodies through environmental pollution, overmedication, and unhealthy diets* (93 percent agree; 71 percent say this situation is either a "a crisis that our country must address immediately" or a major problem).

It's worth noting that among the 15 situations tested, the first listed above elicited the highest levels of Millennials saying the situation was a crisis to be addressed immediately. It also had the highest levels saying it was either a crisis or a major problem.

The solution proposed below to the healthcare crisis also elicited the highest effectiveness rating from Millennials of the nine solutions tested. Generation We gave this solution an average effectiveness rating of 7.3, and 75 percent rated it between 6 and 10 on the 10-point effectiveness scale.

> *Provide quality health care and nutrition for all children in our country, regardless of their financial condition. Poor nutrition is creating an epidemic of preventable chronic diseases, including diabetes and obesity, that will cost our country billions of dollars and ruin the lives of millions of children.*

Consistent with this, in the June 2007 *New York Times*/CBS News/MTV survey of 17- to 29-year-olds, Generation We endorsed having one health insurance program administered by the government cover all Americans, rather than the current system, by a 62–32 margin. This contrasts with a 47–38 split among all adults in a February, 2007 survey that asked the same question.

Generation We also registers high level of concern about the educational system, as shown by the GMS question below.

> *We have an unequal education system in our country, where students in affluent areas enjoy better resources and learning environments while those in rural areas and inner cities too often receive an inferior education* (92 percent agree; 71 percent say it is "a crisis that our country must address immediately" or a major problem).

This translates into a desire to reform the educational system to mitigate this inequality and meet global challenges. The solution to educational system problems proposed below elicited the second-highest effectiveness rating from Millennials of the nine solutions tested. Millennials gave this solution an average effectiveness rating of 7.2, and 73 percent rated it between 6 and 10 on the 10-point effectiveness scale.

> *Provide equal funding for public education and learning resources for all children and all communities, regardless of economic class. This is a critical investment in the human potential of our country and its ability to compete in a global economy.*

Concern about inequality is generally high and goes far beyond the educational system, as shown by the question below (also from the GMS):

> *Hurricane Katrina revealed the extent to which our country is divided into two Americas, one of which lacks many basic needs and is largely ignored by our government. The growing gap between the wealthy and the rest of us must be addressed, because no democracy can survive without a large, vibrant middle class* (90 percent agree; 70 percent say this situation is either "a crisis that our country must address immediately" or a major problem).

Related to this, there are strong concerns that middle-class jobs and benefits are eroding drastically in today's economy:

> *The changing nature of America's economy, where we import most of our goods and export millions of jobs to developing countries, is threatening America's middle class* (92 percent agree;

©BRIAN NOLAN/ISTOCK INTERNATIONAL, INC

69 percent say this situation is either "a crisis that our country must address immediately" or a major problem).

Long-term jobs that provide comprehensive health benefits and retirement security are becoming a thing of the past, and individuals in our generation will have to provide for their own health care and retirement security (93 percent agree; 74 percent say this situation is either "a crisis that our country must address immediately" or a major problem).

An issue underlying all of these questions is that of equality of treatment and the claim of America to be a land of opportunity for all. The fairness issue is a major one for Generation We; their commitment to the greater good makes them intolerant of economic structures that benefit the few at the expense of the many.

Finally, the GMS also finds high levels of concern about the national debt and strong support for a serious effort to deal with it. The high level of concern is demonstrated by results from two GMS questions:

The growing burden placed on our country by our massive national debt is hurting our economy, stifling job growth and investment, and making it harder for American businesses and entrepreneurs to be competitive in the global marketplace (94 percent agree; 74 percent say this situation is either "a crisis that our country must address immediately" or a major problem).

The federal debt is exploding, with no end in sight, shifting a tremendous burden onto future generations to pay for the failed leadership of the current generation and weakening America's economic growth for decades to come (92 percent agree; 65 percent say this situation is either "a crisis that our country must address immediately" or a major problem).

Support for a bold solution is indicated by response to the proposal below. Millennials gave this proposal an average effectiveness rating of 6.8, with 69 percent rating it between 6 and 10 on the 10-point effectiveness scale.

Balance the federal budget, but also eliminate the 8 trillion dollars of national debt that have been built up over decades of irresponsible spending. This debt makes it impossible for our country to keep pace and leaves us indebted to other countries who are potential competitors.

Another budget-related proposal also received a positive response. The proposal below on fully funding Social Security and Medicare received an average effectiveness rating of 6.7, with 66 percent rating it between 6 and 10 on the 10-point effectiveness scale.

Fully fund Social Security, Medicare, and other social insurance commitments being passed on to future generations, which have doubled to over 40 trillion dollars just since 2000 and are increasing by several trillion every year. These commitments must be met by current generations because it would be morally wrong to pass on unfunded liabilities of this size to our own children.

Evidence from other surveys is consistent with findings from the GMS, particularly on inequality and jobs. In the 2004 NES, 84 percent of Millennials (18- to 26-year-olds) said the gap between rich and poor had grown in the last 20 years and 94 percent thought that the change in the gap between rich and poor was a bad thing. Also, despite their personal optimism about their own future, they do worry about how poorly the economy has been performing for ordinary people. In June 2005 Democracy Corps polling, 62 percent of 18- to 29-year-olds (Note: Only the 18- to 27-year-olds in this group qualify as Millennials.) believed the economy wasn't doing well and jobs were scarce, incomes stagnant, and benefits being cut back, compared to 35 percent who thought the economy was doing well, with rising incomes and home ownership.

The focus groups, consistent with the GMS, documented Generation We's deep feelings about the healthcare crisis and interest in large-scale change in this area. They see the healthcare crisis, including cost, quality, and coverage problems as not just a tragedy for the country but as a problem of catastrophic proportions for their own generation—a problem that makes the society they live in and are inheriting so much worse than it needs to be.

An issue underlying all of these questions is that of equality of treatment and the claim of America to be a land of opportunity for all.

They are also hugely concerned with the prevention aspects of the healthcare crisis and believe the country in general, and their generation in particular, is being encouraged to consume food and prescription drugs that worsen health, even as they enhance corporate profit margins. In their view, this is outrageous and should be combated by a new emphasis on healthy diet and lifestyles. They are less sure about how exactly to reform the healthcare system but clearly see

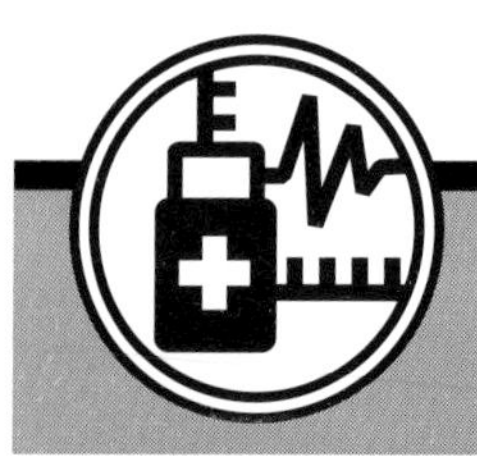

HEALTHCARE CONCERNS

96% AGREE With costs rising out of control and the quality of health coverage declining, the health care system in our country is broken, and we need to make fundamental change

93% AGREE The health of our country is collapsing under an epidemic of chronic, preventable diseases as we slowly poison our own bodies through environmental pollution, overmedication, and unhealthy diets

71% AGREE This situation is either a "a crisis that our country must address immediately"or a major problem

SOURCE: GREENBERG MILLENNIAL STUDY 2007

big change as necessary, leading to a system where universal access is combined with a far stronger emphasis on prevention.

Focus group participants were also concerned with the various aspects of economic insecurity that affect today's labor market and the jobs they hope to attain. And they definitely saw rising inequality as a problem that was having a deep effect on their society and themselves. They particularly worried about how inequality is entrenched in the educational system and is putting an unfair burden on many members of their generation who are not getting the education they need. They appeared willing to support aggressive action to address this problem, including diversion of tax revenue to areas that are educationally distressed. But focus group participants did not feel a comparable level of urgency about economic problems that were more distant from their day-to-day experiences and concerns—the primary example here being the national debt.

To summarize, members of Generation We tend to be hopeful and ready, as a group, to take collective action to solve problems. However, they see the national economy as having been badly mismanaged, and systems such as healthcare and education as broken and in need of repair. They're also more mature in their attitudes than earlier generations, and because of their belief in technology and innovation, they are impatient when it comes to demanding change.

This combination of attitudes offers fertile ground for a powerful response to these vexing national issues. Given the right leadership and inspiration, they will be ready to provide the political will that change agents can rely upon, much as Roosevelt's support helped galvanize the transformation of America in the New Deal era.

FOR A PEACEFUL WORLD

Generation We strongly believes in a cooperative, multilateral approach to foreign policy and solving global problems. The Millennials already see themselves as part of an interconnected planet linked by the Internet and other technologies that are integral parts of their lives. Tolerant and accepting of different cultures, they consider isolationism contrary to their social and political mores. Further, deeply influenced by what they perceive as a failed U.S. response to the terror attacks of 9/11 and a disastrous war in Iraq, they are ready to jettison the unilateral approach to world affairs that has characterized the far right, the neoconservatives, and the Bush Administration.

Generation We seems more oriented toward a multilateral and cooperative foreign policy than their elders. Pew Values data show that 18- to 25-year-old Millennials in 2002–03 were split down the middle on whether military strength is the best way to ensure peace, while older adults endorsed this idea 61 to 35.

In 2004 Pew data, only 29 percent of 18- to 25-year-old Millennials believed that "using overwhelming force is the best way to defeat terrorism," compared to 67 percent who thought "relying too much on military force leads to hatred and more terrorism." By contrast, those 26 and over were much more closely split (49–41). In addition, 62 percent of 18- to 25-year-olds believe the United States should take into account the interests of its allies even if it means making compromises with them, compared to 52 percent of their elders.

Furthermore, in November 2004 Democracy Corps polling, 57 percent of 18- to 29-year-olds (Note: Only the 18- to 26-year-olds in this group qualify as Millennials.) believed that America's security depends on building strong ties with other nations, compared to just 37 percent who believed that, "bottom line," America's security depends on its own military strength. This was the most pro-multilateralist sentiment of any age group.

Moreover, when the same question was asked of 18- to 29-year-olds in 2007 in the GMS, when all members of that age group were Millennials, sentiment was even stronger on the multilateral side. In that survey, 69 percent said that America's security depends on building strong ties with other nations, compared to only 30 percent who thought that America's security depends on its own military strength.

Generation We rejects dogma and propaganda that pits one race or nation against another.

Millennial 18- to 25-year-olds also tend to be less worried about terrorists attacking the United States. In 2004, 53 percent of this age group said they were very or somewhat worried about this, compared to 63 of those 26 and older. In addition, just 27 percent of these Millennials say they are more suspicious of those with Middle Eastern origins since 9/11.

They also take different lessons from 9/11. In an April 2005 GQR poll, 18- to 25-year-olds believed by 55 to 44 that the attack on 9/11 means America needs to be more connected to the world, rather than have more control over its borders. And in the 2004 NES, 57 percent of Millennials (18- to 26-year-olds) said that promoting human rights was a "very important" goal of U.S. foreign policy, a figure substantially higher than among any other generation.

Comments from our focus groups suggested that these reactions to 9/11 are widespread among Generation We. One participant made the following comment, to general agreement:

> 9/11 made our society paranoid. The security measures that are in place now are just ridiculous. You even have to justify where your money is going when you do a simple bank transaction. People overreact to a silly joke. And the media encourages us to be afraid of one another. Americans seem to believe everything scary they hear on TV.

©LUSHPIX/FOTOSEARCH

Millennial 18- to 25-year-olds are now most hostile to the war in Iraq and to George W. Bush's handling of it. In 2006 Pew polls, an average of 26 percent of this age group approved of Bush's handling of the Iraq war, compared to 69 percent who disapproved. In the 2006 exit polls, 62 percent of 18- to 29-year-old voters disapproved of Bush's handling of Iraq, including 43 percent who strongly disapproved. Sixty-five percent—more than any other age group—thought the United States should start withdrawing troops from Iraq. In addition, a majority of those voters did not think the Iraq war had improved the long-term security of the United States.

Similarly, in an April 2005 GQR poll of 18- to 25-year-olds, 63 percent of this age group thought the war in Iraq wasn't worth the costs and 64 percent thought the Iraq war wasn't part of the war on terrorism. In the June 2007 Democracy Corps poll of Millennials, 65 percent thought "the current course cannot bring stability [in Iraq] and we need to start reducing the number of U.S. troops in Iraq." Sixty-six percent thought "we should withdraw our troops from Iraq" rather than give the president's plan a chance. Finally, in the June 2007 *New York Times*/CBS News/MTV survey of 17- to 29-year-old Millennials, only 31 percent thought the war in Iraq had made the United States safer from terrorism, compared to 66 percent who thought it had either made no difference (47 percent) or made the country less safe (19 percent).

As for patriotism, Generation We members in the same poll gave themselves a 7.2 out of 10 on whether they consider themselves patriotic, higher than any other trait tested except for being a healthy person. But almost 70 percent say they would be unwilling to join the U.S. military.

Although this area was not one explored in any detail in the focus groups, two factors in Millennials' experience appeared to move them strongly toward a global mindset and orientation: 9/11 and the Internet. The former forced them to see their country as part of a global system that could not be ignored, and the latter has made it vastly easier to know about and interact with people in other parts of the world.

More than any other recent generation, Generation We rejects dogma and propaganda that pits one race or nation against another. Boundaries mean little to them, especially in comparison to their idealistic vision of a peaceful world. Having lived much of their lives in a nation at war, they yearn for a united planet in which the environment is being cleaned up and resources that might be squandered on arms and warfare are devoted instead to creating a prosperous, secure world. Generation We wants the same opportunity previous generations had to raise their families in peace, and given the opportunity they will vote, organize, and act in support of that objective.

IDEALISTIC ABOUT GOVERNMENT, YET FRUSTRATED

Generation We believes strongly in the potential of government to do good. They don't see government as a panacea for all problems and reject socialist doctrine as outdated and discredited. But they believe in the power of the collective—including government—to achieve the greater good for society as a whole. At the same time, they have serious reservations about the ability of today's politicians and political parties to realize that potential. They believe in our American system, but fear it is being hijacked by special interests and self-serving power elite.

Generation We endorses ambitious problem-solving goals for our nation on a scale that can only be achieved with government playing a large role. They are ready to embrace that role for government, provided individual action, private enterprise, and entrepreneurship are also given free rein to contribute.

Here's some specific supporting data. Millennials in the GMS strongly endorsed the idea that *government needs to do more to address the major challenges facing our country* (63 percent) rather than agreeing that *Government is already too involved in areas that are better left to individuals or the free marke*t (37 percent).

Similarly, Millennials in the GMS said that *Government has a responsibility to pursue policies that benefit all of society and balance the rights of the individual with the needs of the entire society* (63 percent) rather than *The primary responsibility of government is to protect the rights of the individual* (37 percent).

But Generation We's views about whether today's government, political leaders, and political parties are meeting these responsibilities are decidedly negative, consistent with their self-image as a generation less likely than earlier generations to "trust government and political leaders." Consider these results from two GMS questions about the current role of government:

Government is dominated by special interests and lobbyists,

Q95

How often do you talk about politics with your friends and co-workers?	A
Frequently	19
Sometimes	45
Hardly ever	26
Never	10
(Don't know/refused)	-
Frequently/sometimes	**64**
Hardly ever/never	**36**

SOURCE: GREENBERG MILLENNIAL STUDY 2007

> *who give millions of dollars in campaign contributions to politicians, who in turn give even more back to those special interests, while the rest of us are left holding the bag* (95 percent agree; 73 percent say this situation is either "a crisis that our country must address immediately" or a major problem).
>
> *From the failed response to Hurricane Katrina to persistent fraud, corruption, and abuse, our government has failed to meet its most basic responsibilities and violated the very taxpayers who fund it* (90 percent agree; 71 percent say this situation is either "a crisis that our country must address immediately" or a major problem).

Similarly, 82 percent of Millennials in the GMS agree (45 percent strongly) that "[o]ur current political and corporate leaders are abusing their power for selfish gains, wasting our nation's resources for their own short-term gain and threatening our long-term security."

As discussed earlier, Generation We tends to lean Democratic in elections and in party identification, probably because they consider Democrats more sympathetic to their progressive ideals and because they reject the conservative dogma that has controlled the Republican Party for the past 25 years. Despite these partisan leanings, however, both political parties and the two-party system in general tend to be regarded with considerable dissatisfaction by Millennials. For example, Millennials overwhelmingly say that *Democrats and Republicans alike are failing our country, putting partisanship ahead of our country's needs and offering voters no real solutions to our country's problems* (70 percent) rather than *The two-party political system in our country is working because it offers voters a clear choice between two different visions for our country's future* (29 percent).

Not surprisingly, given these sentiments, Generation We expresses some interest in the possibility of a third party that might offer an alternative to the Democrats and Republicans:

> *There should be a third political party in our country that fits between the Democrats and Republicans and offers a viable alternative to the two major parties* (76 percent agree, 35 percent strongly agree).

This is consistent with their generational self-image as a generation more likely than earlier generations to "support an emerging third political party." (As we'll discuss later, although we share the Millennials' frustration with the failures of the two leading political parties, we don't advocate a third party as a solution.)

Findings from other surveys are generally consistent with GMS findings on Millennials' positive view of government's potential role.

For example, in June 2005 Democracy Corps polling, 63 percent of 18- to 29-year-olds (Note: Only the 18- to 27-year-olds in this group qualify as Millennials.) believed the role of government should be to promote the principle of a strong community and policies that expand opportunity and promote prosperity for all not just a few, compared to 35 percent who thought the role of government should be to promote the principle of self-reliance and policies of limited government and low taxes. This split was by far the most pro-active government/strong community of all the age group; 30- to 39-year-old Xers, for example, were split 50 to 45 on this question.

Similarly, the 2006 CIRCLE Civic and Political Health of the Nation survey of 15- to 25-year-olds found strong endorsement among this age group of the idea that "government should do more to solve problems" (63 percent), rather than "government does too many things better left to businesses and individuals" (31 percent), a view that is essentially unchanged in that survey since 2002.

And in a June 2007 Democracy Corps poll of 18- to 29-year-olds, Millennials even declared themselves in favor of "a bigger government providing more services" (68 percent), rather than "a smaller government that provides fewer services" (28 percent).

In addition, the Harvard IOP October, 2006 survey of 18–24-year-olds found considerable evidence of a rejection of political cynicism among Generation We. Seventy-one percent disagreed that "politics is not relevant to my life right now"; 84 percent disagreed that "it really doesn't matter to me who the president is"; 55 percent disagreed that "people like me don't have any say about what the government does"; 59 percent disagreed that "political involvement rarely has any tangible results"; and 56 percent disagreed that "it is difficult to find ways to be involved in politics." In addition, 67 percent agreed that "running for office is an honorable thing to do"; the analogous figures for community service and getting involved in politics were 88 and 60.

The GMS focus groups strongly support the survey findings that, for Generation We, although government has much potential to do good and *should* be doing good, at this point, it is falling woefully short of that potential. Participants in our focus groups expressed considerable contempt for many current political leaders and the system that is producing them. Because of their disgust with the system, they tend to lump all political leaders together, seeing many of them as venal and self-serving, making little effort to deal with the challenges that are putting America and the world as a whole at risk. They are "fiddling as Rome burns," in the old phrase, and Generation We fears they will inherit the consequences.

They believe in our American system, but fear it is being hijacked by special interests and self-serving power elite.

Our focus group participants were particularly incensed at the influence of lobbyists and special interests on government and politicians. They believe that this breeds pervasive corruption that strongly impedes positive change. In their view, rooting out government pandering to special interests and the plundering it permits is critical to getting the country moving in the right direction again.

Given these views, it's not surprising that the focus group members found little satisfaction with the two parties as currently constituted. They may lean Democratic when they vote, but both Republicans *and* Democrats came in for withering criticism as institutions not up to the task of change and more responsive to the wishes of lobbyists than the needs of the country.

...eager to experiment with new solutions no matter where they may come from and no matter what political orientation they may be associated with.

That said, conservatives and the policies they have come to represent were a particular focus of Millennials' ire. They are seen as hopelessly out of touch and reactionary in the classic sense of the term. When asked to define "conservatism," most focus group participants referred not to political positions or ideological tenets (small government, low taxes, strong national defense) but rather to personal traits and qualities, and mostly negative ones: rigidity, close-mindedness, intolerance, moralism, and even hypocrisy.

This is a striking political development. It means that, for Generation We, the conservative movement has been fundamentally discredited. Having seen "conservatism" used to justify bigger government, limitation of free debate, and an economic free-for-all that serves the rich and powerful, they appear poised to reject this label decisively for the next 30 to 40 years.

But this doesn't mean the focus group participants were comfortable with the label of "liberal." *Generation We tends to reject conventional labels as not well representing their views and preferences.* They see extreme liberalism as being almost as flawed as conservatism, pointing toward large government programs that are self-justifying rather than tailored to serving human needs and that end up limiting rather than expanding the scope of human freedom.

Interestingly, though this was not a spontaneous form of self-identification, the word "progressive," when brought to their attention, did seem to capture much of the way they like to think about themselves. They see themselves as creators of the future, and the progressive word resonates with their sentiments. They believe in a government that does good things, but they do not want a socialist state that dictates how the economy works, nor do they desire a moralist state that tells them how they should think and live. They see the progressive label as representing a moderate approach that is focused on the important issues of the day rather than ideology.

Millennials' rejection of current political institutions also extends to institutions outside the government, especially dominant business interests. Perhaps the chief difference here with our focus groups participants was that they did not necessarily expect big business to act in a way that promoted the common good, while they had some expectation or hope that political institutions could act in this way. Much of the vitriol toward government and parties is, therefore, an expression of frustrated idealism as much as anything else.

Generation We believes that government can do a lot to help people, even though it is currently failing to live up to that responsibility. Rather than echoing the conservative mantra that "government should just get out of the way and let individuals solve their own problems," the Millennials expect government to play a positive role in helping people help themselves. They're ready to support a new effort to reform government along more responsive, responsible lines.

POST-IDEOLOGICAL, POST-PARTISAN, POST-POLITICAL

Determined to find their own solutions to the major problems we face, and convinced that their unprecedented levels of education and technological prowess will enable them to do so, Generation We shares a social orientation that might best be described in terms of what they have left behind. Speaking in broad terms, Generation We is post-ideological, post-partisan, and post-political.

They are post-ideological because they are uninterested in learning about and defending the "conservative" or "liberal" approaches to the problems our country faces. Instead, they are pragmatic, open-minded, and innovation-oriented, eager to experiment with new solutions no matter where they may come from and no matter what political orientation they may be associated with.

PHOTO: ERIC GREENBERG

They are post-partisan because, although they lean Democratic, they are disgusted with what they perceive as the narrowness, pettiness, and stagnation that often characterize both major parties. Though they are open to the possibility of a third party, the Millennials are far more interested in getting beyond party identification altogether and in focusing on cooperative efforts to make America and the world a better place.

They are post-political because they are fed up and bored with the interest-group conflicts, identity-based appeals, and power-seeking maneuvers they see as dominating the public arena. More tolerant and accepting than any previous generation, Generation We is ready to call a halt to "culture wars" that pit people of different religions, races, ethnicities, regions, cultures, values, and sexual orientations against one another for political gain. They believe that all of us—not only all Americans, but all humans around the planet—will ultimately share the same destiny, and therefore must find ways to work together for the common good. And they stand ready to lead the effort.

How can Americans build on the promise of Generation We to cre-

Q34

Please tell me whether the FIRST statement or the SECOND statement comes closer to your own views, even if neither is exactly right.

	1st Stmt Much	1st Stmt Smwt	2nd Stmt Much	2nd Stmt Smwt	DK-Ref	Total 1st Stmt	Total 2nd Stmt	1st - 2nd
America's security depends on building strong ties with other nations. **OR** Bottom line, America's security depends on its own military strength.	37	32	18	12	0	69	30	39
Addressing the big issues facing my generation starts with individuals willing to take a stand and take action. **OR** Individuals can't make a real difference in addressing the big issues facing my generation.	47	33	15	5	0	80	20	60
The two-party political system in our country is working because it offers voters a clear choice between two different visions for our country's future. **OR** Democrats and Republicans alike are failing our country, putting partisanship ahead of our country's needs and offering voters no real solutions to our country's problems.	12	18	31	39	0	29	70	-41
Businesses and corporate leaders have a responsibility to try to make the world a better place, not just make money. **OR** Businesses and corporate leaders' responsibility to their shareholders is to make money, not to worry about making the world a better place.	44	30	17	9	0	74	26	48
Government has a responsibility to pursue policies that benefit all of society and balance the rights of the individual with the needs of the entire society. **OR** The primary responsibility of government is to protect the rights of the individual.	27	35	23	14	0	63	37	25
The needs and goals of my generation are fundamen tally at odds with those of older generations, and accomplishing our goals will require removing those currently in power and replacing them with ourselves. **OR** The needs and goals of my generation are similar to those of older generations, and our best course is to work together to advance common interests.	19	30	34	16	1	40	50	-1
Government needs to do more to address the major challenges facing our country. **OR** Government is already too involved in areas that are better left to individuals or the free market.	34	29	22	15	0	63	37	26
I believe that spending money with companies that reflect my values and priorities is an effective way to express my values and to promote change through my daily life. **OR** My consumer choices are based on economics, not values, and I don't see my purchasing decisions as an effective way of expressing my values or promoting change.	23	31	29	16	0	55	45	10
We must make major investments now to innovate the next generation of non-fossil fuel based energy solutions. **OR** We should continue on our current path, gradually shifting the mix of sources used to meet our energy needs.	46	29	17	8	0	74	26	49

SOURCE: GREENBERG MILLENNIAL STUDY 2007

Q43

Please tell me whether you agree or disagree with the statement.

	Strng Agree	Smwt Agree	Smwt Dis Agree	Strng Dis Agree	DK-Ref	Total Agree	Total Dis Agree	Agree Dis
In our country, each generation has a responsibility to wisely use the country's resources and power so that they can provide the next generation a secure, sustainable country that is stronger than the one they inherited.	53	38	8	1	0	91	9	82
Our current political and corporate leaders are abusing their power for selfish gains, wasting our nation's resources for their own short-term gain and threatening our long-term security.	45	37	15	3	0	82	18	64
Young Americans must take action now to reverse the rapid decline of our country. If we wait until we are older, it will be too late.	48	41	9	1	0	89	11	78
Life in the future in America will be much worse unless my generation of Americans takes the lead in pushing for change.	42	43	13	2	0	85	15	70
I am willing to personally make significant sacrifices in my own life to address the major environmental, economic, and security challenges facing our country.	27	51	18	4	0	78	22	56
My generation of Americans has better opportunities to make a difference and produce structural change than previous generations.	31	48	17	3	0	79	20	59
Throughout our history, America's success has been built on innovation and entrepreneurship. As we confront the many challenges facing us today, it is that same spirit of innovation and entrepreneurship that is needed to maintain America's strength in the 21st century.	38	49	11	2	0	87	13	75
When something is run by the government, it is necessarily inefficient and wasteful.	14	40	36	9	0	54	45	9
There should be a third political party in our country that fits between the Democrats and Republicans and offers a viable alternative to the two major parties.	35	41	18	6	1	76	24	52

SOURCE: GREENBERG MILLENNIAL STUDY 2007

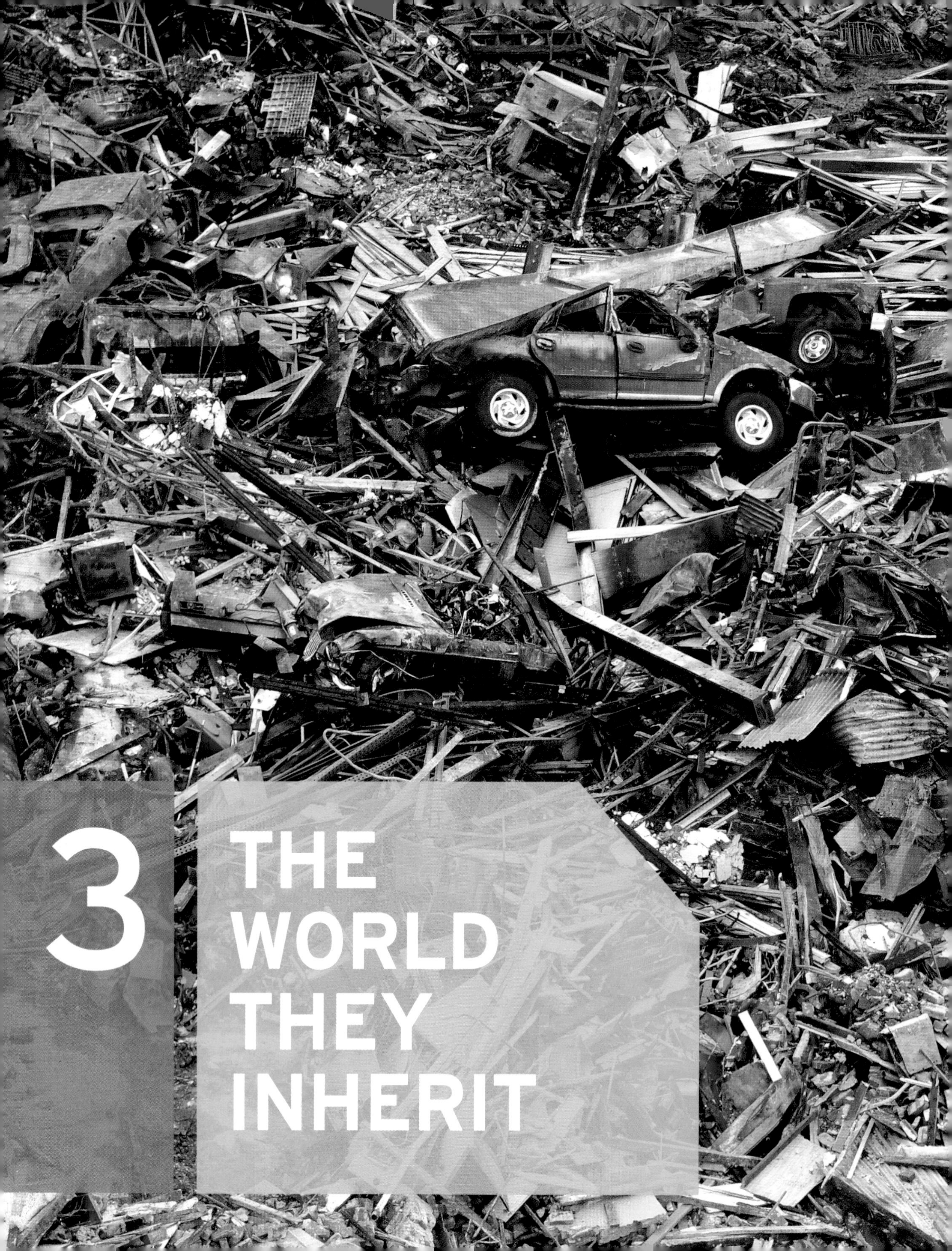

3 THE WORLD THEY INHERIT

A Road to Global Disaster

In these early years of the twenty-first century, humankind faces unprecedented dangers at the same time as it enjoys unique opportunities. The shifting patterns of history—demographic, technological, economic, and political—have brought us to a crossroads from which divergent paths lead in very different directions. As a result, we face a series of unprecedented dangers.

The world Generation We will inherit is a world shaped by the decisions (conscious and unconscious) of the Baby Boomers and the generations that came before them. Like every generation, the Boomers and their predecessors have had a responsibility to pass along a world that is at least as healthy, peaceful, and prosperous as the one they received from their ancestors. Unfortunately, despite the best efforts of the Boomers, they appear to be failing in that responsibility. Instead, they are bequeathing to the Millennials a world that may be heading down a catastrophic path, unless we start making smarter choices—and soon.

Let's examine the world Generation We is inheriting.

> "The most dangerous threat to our global environment may not be the strategic threats themselves but rather our perception of them, for most people do not yet accept the fact that this crisis is extremely grave."
>
> AL GORE

ENVIRONMENTAL COLLAPSE

Generation We inherits a world in which climate change and global pollution threaten an unprecedented environmental collapse—one that could even spell the end of human existence on this planet—because of unconstrained extraction and desecration of natural resources and reliance on carbon-spewing fossil fuels.

The so-called debate over global warming has long been settled—at least, to the satisfaction of the vast majority of scientists who have studied the issue. There are still a few stragglers who deny the reality of global warming, pooh-pooh its importance, or dispute the role of human behavior in causing it. Most of these self-proclaimed "climate skeptics," however, are either on the payroll of OPEC countries or corporate interests whose primary goal is to fend off action that will reduce their profits, or doctrinaire conservatives who pander to big business and whose ideology prevents them from admitting that free-market principles can ever produce less-than-ideal results.

Obstructionists and shills aside, the overwhelming consensus among scientists is that the world's climate has been changing and is continuing to change at a rate that appears to be unprecedented in history. There is also agreement that the accumulation of greenhouse gases in the atmosphere is an important contributing factor in this change, and that human activity—in particular the burning of fossil fuels such as oil, gas, and coal—has played a major role in the creation and build-up of these gases. Even most conservative Republicans (who long denied the reality of global warming or the fact that human beings are contributing to it) and business leaders (whose companies will be dramatically impacted by any effort to reverse the dangerous warming trend) have largely come to accept these realities.

The questions now are: What are the likely impacts from the climate change processes that are already underway? What can be done, if anything, to avert a possible environmental catastrophe?

Because the current climate change is of a kind that has not happened since the end of the last ice age, and because massive climatic change inevitably includes complex side effects that cannot be fully understood or precisely anticipated with our current technology, scientists can't fully predict the nature and extent of the damage or what it means to humans. There are signs that even forecasts made in the last decade may already be outdated. For example, the observed acceleration in summer melting of the Arctic icecap is occurring at a markedly faster rate than climate scientists had predicted. It is conceivable, by some models, that the icecap over Greenland could melt almost entirely in the next 50 years, releasing an amount of water so large it would cause ocean levels to rise more than 20 feet and submerge many developed coastal regions worldwide. No natural disaster or act of God in human history comes close to the sheer suffering, loss, and displacement that would result from such a crisis.

The notion that trends accelerate as they mature is even more sobering. As the melting of glaciers, permafrost, and poles continues, it systemically assists in furthering planetary warming so that an accelerator effect takes place. Take permafrost in the Arctic regions as an example. Once the ground melts, the frozen carbon-based elements in the soil start to decompose, emitting massive amounts of carbon in the process and multiplying the effect of the warming. The scariest part is that nobody can model or measure how profound the effect will be.

Here are some of the latest findings from the 2007 report of the authoritative Intergovernmental Panel on Climate Change (IPCC):

- Eleven of the 12 warmest years on record have occurred since 1995. Between 1950 and 2000, average temperatures in the Northern Hemisphere appear to have been the highest in at least the last 1,300 years. The likelihood that these trends were caused mainly by human activities is greater than 90 percent.

- If current trends continue, the impact on climate during the twenty-first century will likely be greater than that experienced during the twentieth century.

- Among the effects to be expected are rising sea levels, more severe and frequent storms and droughts, global deforestation, and dramatically shifting patterns of rainfall.

- Human populations will suffer deaths—perhaps in the millions—due to increases in malnutrition, heat waves, drought, infectious diseases, and air pollution.[1]

As for what can be done, we shift here from the area of science into that of public policy, involving government, industry, consumer behavior, and almost every other element of human society. In a later chapter, we'll look at possible solutions to the climate change problem, focusing particularly on the leadership role Generation We will be called upon to play. But for now, let's consider how our actions are contributing to the slow-motion ecological disaster we now see unfolding on our planet.

The single most dangerous fact about the American economy as it currently operates is our profound reliance on fossil fuels, in particular oil and coal. Our nation consumes roughly 24 percent of global oil production, by far the largest share of any country on the planet. (China currently is in second place, with oil consumption running at 9 percent of the total; Japan is third, at 6 percent.) Measure our consumption on a per-capita basis, and the discrepancy is still large: The average American uses about 2.8 gallons of gasoline per day, versus 1.8

©FRANK VAN HAALEN/ISTOCK INTERNATIONAL

gallons used by the typical Japanese consumer (in second place).

Coal is close behind oil as a source of energy in this country. More than half the electricity generated in the United States comes from coal, most of it from "dirty" power plants that are between 30 and 50 years old and lack modern pollution controls.[2]

This dependence on fossil fuels has enormous economic, political, and military effects on our country, which we'll consider later. But the environmental impact alone is significant. The burning of oil creates 44 percent of our nation's carbon-dioxide emissions—over 1.5 tons' worth of carbon injected into the atmosphere per car, per year. These emissions are a major cause of the greenhouse effect that is driving global climate change. Coal-burning power plants, second only to automobiles as a source of carbon-dioxide emissions, produce other forms of pollution, including sulfur dioxide, nitrogen oxides, and toxic mercury contaminants. (As an unexpected side effect, coal emissions that drift over the oceans are causing the mercury poisoning of seafood, making much of it unfit for human consumption.)

The average American uses about 2.8 gallons of gasoline per day, versus 1.8 gallons used by the typical Japanese consumer (in second place).

Currently, the industrialized nations of the Western world—especially North America, Europe, and Japan—produce the vast bulk of the greenhouse gas emissions that threaten our environment. But that is changing. Large portions of the developing world, especially the two Asian giants, China and India, are rapidly industrializing. Factories and even entire cities are springing up overnight, often constructed hastily and with little consideration of environmental and safety concerns.

The economic rise of "Chindia" is, in many ways, great news for the world. It is bringing tens of millions of people out of poverty and creating a huge new middle class that is already becoming part of the global marketplace. These newly empowered citizens will eventually also press their governments for democratic reforms and an end to the corruption that is rampant in their countries.

But the rapid development of Chindia also worsens the environmental threat we face. Tens of millions of newly middle-class people will mean tens of millions of new cars on the roads, all spewing the same greenhouse gases that have already brought our planet to the brink of disaster. Coal-fired power plants without any meaningful environmental regulation or cleanliness standards, which use "dirty" coal with high moisture content and impure combustible matter, are popping up by the hundreds every year in Chindia and producing gigantic quantities of air pollution at rates that even exceed those found in the Western world. (Whereas coal is responsible for just over 50 percent of the electricity produced in the United States, it is the source of 69 percent of India's electric power and 78 percent of China's.)[3]

The individuals building the plants are not thinking about the long-term or planetary consequences. They are thinking about their countries' need for energy to fuel their rapid growth. It's understandable—and a recipe for disaster.

We in the rich nations of the West can't simply demand that the developing nations of Chindia halt their economic development or do without the luxuries—such as private cars—we've long enjoyed. But our planet can't afford a new round of industrialization as heedless as the one Europe and North America experienced in the nineteenth and twentieth centuries—not with potentially catastrophic climate change as a possible consequence.

Americans have much in common with the people of Chindia. Our countries need to collaborate on inventing and deploying new energy technologies, cleaning our existing power-generation capability, and applying strict pollution standards to automobiles.

Global warming is not the only environmental danger our species currently faces. There are a host of others, including irresponsible extraction and squandering of resources, from minerals to timber; overfishing of the world's waters, threatening collapse of the planet's last reliable source of wild protein; pollution of the seas by petrochemically derived plastics that take generations to degrade and are helping to create vast dead zones in the world's oceans; and air pollution that is helping to cause acid rain, deforestation, and epidemics of lung disease and cancer in both the developed world and the developing nations of Asia and Latin America.

The most serious environmental problem of all is the coming shortage of clean water for human consumption and agriculture. This is the hidden crisis nobody likes to talk about. It is not by coincidence that much of the water rights in the western United States have been purchased by oil families and hedge funds. The coming water shortages will cause conflicts even fiercer than any oil war. Energy wars are about money, but a water war is about day-to-day survival.

Although our planet is mostly covered by water, only about 2.5 percent of the total is freshwater useable for drinking and cooking, and much of that amount is either seriously polluted or locked up in glaciers and permafrost. Right now, approximately 20 percent of the world's population has insufficient clean water. That's a billion people who, according to UN experts, are drinking polluted, disease-carrying water every day. Ailments ranging from diarrhea (often fatal in developing countries) to schistosomiasis, malaria, scabies, cholera, and trachoma are associated with contaminated water supplies.[4] William Cosgrove, vice president of the World Water Council, says lack of safe water leads to the deaths of at least 2 million children every year.[5]

Over time, the problem is getting much worse. Deserts are spread-

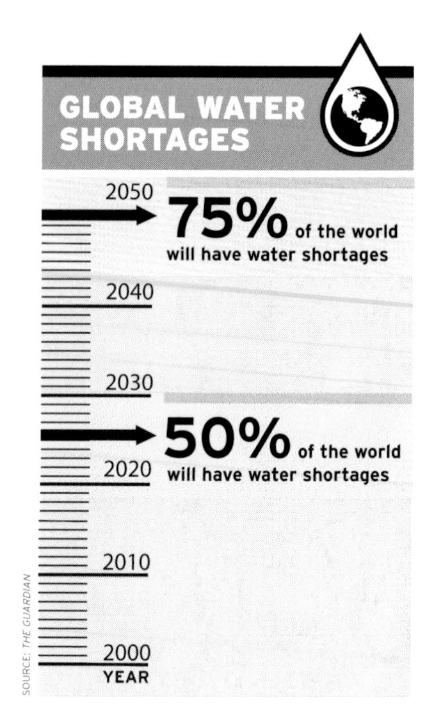

That's a billion people who, according to UN experts, are drinking polluted, disease-carrying water every day.

ing, and with them starvation and misery on an unprecedented scale. By 2025, climate scientists are warning that 50 percent of the world can expect to suffer severe water shortages, with the percentage rising to 75 percent by 2050—well within the life expectancy of the Millennials. By that same mid-century date, half of the world's currently arable land may no longer be suitable for agriculture—again, as a result of the deepening water crisis.[6]

In the United States today, we already have severe drought in once-fertile agricultural regions, and wildfires are burning the West at historically unseen levels. Climate change, irresponsible agriculture, and uncontrolled consumption are altering our ecosystem. We've built oasis-like cities in the desert; they're beautiful, but the water that fills those fountains and waters those gardens has to come from somewhere. It typically comes from a fragile ecosystem which is being plundered unchecked by any political power, since nobody understands the inevitable consequences.

Perhaps surprisingly, the water issue and the energy issue are related. There is an unlimited supply of water available in the oceans, but desalination is a costly, energy-intensive process. A cheap new source of clean energy would permit desalinization on a massive scale, eliminate starvation, and permit the replanting of our deserts and forests, which in turn would produce rainfall, climate cooling, and the absorption of carbon by plant life. The vicious cycle in which we're currently stuck could be replaced by a virtuous one.

We must innovate our way out of this complex set of problems, discovering and implementing solutions that will work on a global scale—and we need to do it soon.

HEALTH CATASTROPHE

In the developed world, the twentieth century was a time of steady advancements in human health. Food became cheap and plentiful, improved sanitary conditions slowed and stopped the spread of many infectious diseases, and antibiotics dramatically reduced infections, once the leading cause of death. As a result, life expectancies greatly increased, mortality rates declined, and millions of additional people got the chance to live long, productive lives.

Today, unfortunately, much of that progress is threatened.

The Millennials' world is threatened by epidemics of chronic disease and infectious diseases. These problems are made worse by an increasingly overburdened, ineffective, and unequal health system, as well as by environmental, nutritional, agricultural, and industrial practices that serve financial and political power interests rather than human needs.

It now appears that the emergence and rapid global spread of AIDS in the 1970s, abetted by the failure of authorities in the United States and around the world to take the threat seriously and invest in the systems needed to uncover, analyze, track, and treat the disease, may be merely a harbinger of even more deadly health threats to come.

Diseases of which most Americans are only vaguely aware, such as bovine spongiform encephalopathy ("mad cow disease"), SARS (which infected 8,400 people in 2003 and produced estimated losses of 60 billion dollars to the world economy), Nipah virus, and potentially pandemic avian influenza ("bird flu"), have the potential to spread worldwide and cause thousands or even millions of deaths. So do other diseases that are better-known but equally dangerous, including new drug-resistant strains of tuberculosis and the resurgent polio virus.

Does this sound overstated? Listen to how Margaret Chan, M.D., the highly-respected director-general of the UN's World Health Organization, summarizes the current situation in WHO's 2007 World Health Report (for emphasis, we've highlighted selected sentences that might otherwise be overlooked in the flow of Dr. Chan's sober prose):

Insufficient Clean Water

20% Approximately 20% of the world's population has insufficient clean water

Ailments associated with contaminated water supplies		
Diarrhea	Scabies	Schistosomiasis
Trachoma	Malaria	Cholera

SOURCE: UNESCO

> The disease situation is anything but stable. Population growth, incursion into previously uninhabited areas, rapid urbanization, intensive farming practices, environmental degradation, and the misuse of antimicrobials have disrupted the equilibrium of the microbial world. *New diseases are emerging at the historically unprecedented rate of one per year.* Airlines now carry more than 2 billion passengers annually, vastly increasing opportunities for the rapid international spread of infectious agents and their vectors.
>
> Dependence on chemicals has increased, as has awareness of the potential hazards for health and the environment. Industrialization of food production and processing, and globalization of marketing and distribution mean that a single tainted ingredient can lead to the recall of tons of food items from scores of countries. *In a particularly ominous trend, mainstay antimicrobials are failing at a rate that outpaces the development of replacement drugs.*
>
> These threats have become a much larger menace in a world characterized by high mobility, economic interdependence and electronic interconnectedness. Traditional defenses at national borders cannot protect against the invasion of a disease or vector. Real time news allows panic to spread with equal ease. Shocks to health reverberate as shocks to economies and business continuity in areas well beyond the affected site. *Vulnerability is universal.*[7]

Life-threatening infectious diseases aren't the only health problem we face, of course. We are already living through an epidemic of preventable chronic disease. An estimated 133 million Americans—45 percent of the population—suffer from a chronic illness such as asthma, diabetes, or heart disease. These illnesses kill millions of Americans every year and absorb an estimated 75 percent of total healthcare costs. If current trends continue, fully one-third of all the children born in 2000 will develop diabetes during their lifetimes.[8]

The sad fact is that this epidemic could be largely prevented through proper nutrition, a cleaner environment, and preventive medicine. We are sickening ourselves while insurers and pharmaceutical companies rake in record profits treating symptoms rather than curing people.

Even more insidious is the practice by hospitals of setting up diabetes treatment centers as loss leaders to attract patients for amputations and treatment of congestive heart failure, two common results of diabetes that also happen to be highly profitable. It's a perverse form of customer acquisition that serves the hospitals, not their patients.

Flawed incentives create destructive practices by insurance companies as well. High rates of patient churn make it natural for insurance companies to be basically unconcerned with the long-term health of their clients and to focus instead on immediate financial gain. Driven by short-term considerations—annual profits, quarterly results, share prices—they have no reason to reimburse customers for the cost of preventive care. Instead, they focus on denying care and treat only acute cases they cannot avoid. The inevitable long-term result is a population that is steadily getting sicker.

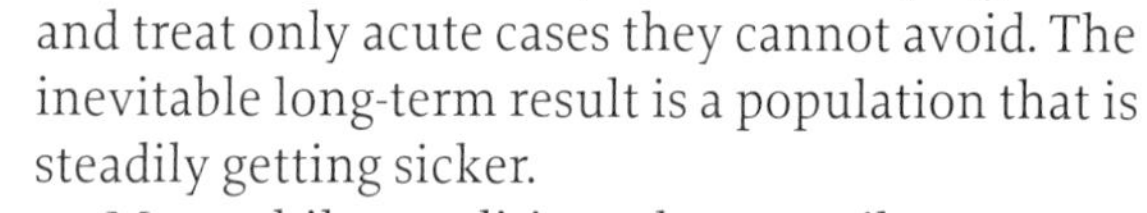

©MARK RICHARDS/CORBIS

Meanwhile, conditions that contribute to chronic illness, such as childhood obesity and exposure to toxic chemicals, are growing steadily more prevalent and serious, encouraged by corporate purveyors of junk foods, dangerous chemicals, and other products that exacerbate the problems. Today more than 15 percent of kids are obese, as compared with fewer than 5 percent in the 1960s and 1970s.[9] Millions are being raised on processed, fake, and junk foods that lack fiber and other nutrients, filling up instead on sugar, corn syrup, steroids, hormones, and the residues of chemical herbicides and fungicides, as well as artificial colors, flavors, and preservatives whose long-term effects are largely unknown.

Today one American in five will suffer from prostate or breast cancer, with younger and younger people being diagnosed every year. Some in the for-profit medical world blame genetics (though it seems odd that human genetics would change so dramatically in 20 to 40 years). What about the possible role of steroids and hormones in the meat, poultry, and dairy we eat, in causing these hormonal cancers? Agribusiness cattle-raisers use these substances to make a nine-month-old calf reach the one-ton weight that would normally take two years to achieve. When a human drinks the milk, the steroids and hormones are still in the cells. Paid experts claim it's safe (the same claim they once made about smoking), but there have been no real studies into the long-term effects of animal hormones and steroids on humans.

Today more than 15 percent of kids are obese, as compared with fewer than 5 percent in the 1960s and 1970s.

Yet despite the seriousness of these issues, many of the health-related problems threatening our world could be addressed by medical technologies that are currently available. Our failure to do so must be blamed on economic and political factors. Simply put, we aren't addressing the healthcare needs of humankind—either around the world or in our own country—because the powers-that-be have little incentive to do so.

The litany of problems with the U.S. healthcare system has become a familiar one. It begins with costs. Here's how one recent study summarizes the situation:

> Already, more and more middle-class Americans find themselves priced out of the health care market. Since 2000 the cost of health insurance has spiraled by 73 percent. Over the same span, the number of uninsured Americans climbed by more than 6 million. As of 2005, nearly 48 million Americans were "going naked," in insurance industry parlance—and not all were poor. Roughly one in three uninsured households earned more than $50,000 a year....
>
> And it is not only the uninsured who are vulnerable to being blindsided by the levitating cost of essential care. These days, more and more families who think they are covered are discovering that the blanket is short.... In 2005 nearly two-thirds of all families struggling to pay medical bills *had insurance*, according to a survey conducted by *USA Today*, the Kaiser Family Foundation, and the Harvard School of Public Health.
>
> At the same time, health care inflation has become a pervasive economic problem for American businesses, affecting labor negotiations, jobs, pensions, and the nation's ability to compete internationally.[10]

The amount the United States spends on healthcare is staggering. In 2007, healthcare spending in the United States amounted to 2.3 trillion dollars, more than 16 percent of the nation's gross domestic product (GDP). If present trends continue, the figures in 2016 will be 4.2 trillion dollars and 20 percent of GDP. Even more alarming, if the current growth rates persist, health expenditure requirements by the gov-

NOT ALL UNINSURED ARE POOR

One in three uninsured households earned more than $50,000 a year.

↑73% Increase in healthcare costs since 2000

48 MILLION As of 2005, nearly 48 million Americans were unsinsured

6 MILLION The number of additional uninsured Americans since 2000

SOURCE: MAHAR, *MONEY-DRIVEN MEDICINE*

ernment will be equal to *all* government receipts by 2060, when the Millennial generation is retired. What this means, in plain terms, is crushing taxation, severe rationing of healthcare, or just letting people die.

By contrast, healthcare spending in 2007 accounted for just 10.9 percent of the GDP in Switzerland, 10.7 percent in Germany, 9.7 percent in Canada, and 9.5 percent in France, according to the Organization for Economic Cooperation and Development. And in all those countries, *everyone* is covered by a national healthcare program, unlike the United States, which leaves tens of millions out in the cold.[11]

We Americans might not resent spending more on healthcare than other countries if the quality of the care we were receiving reflected the high cost. Unfortunately, the opposite is true. One study after another confirms that the healthcare received by Americans seriously lags both what is needed and what citizens of other developed countries enjoy.

Consider, for example, a few lowlights from a 2006 study of 13,000 Americans from a wide range of socio-economic circumstances conducted by the RAND Corporation (a government-sponsored think tank):

- Overall, participants in the study received about *half* the level of care recommended by physicians for such common clinical conditions as asthma, breast cancer, depression, diabetes, hypertension, and osteoarthritis.

- Serious gaps in care are found among citizens in cities across America and of every sex, age, race, and income level. As summarized by the RAND researchers, *"The bottom line: all adults in the United States are at risk for receiving poor health care, no matter where they live; why, where, and from whom they seek care; or what their race, gender, or financial status is."*

- Do these gaps in care matter? Absolutely. The RAND study found, for example, that diabetes sufferers received only 45 percent of the care they needed—a shortfall associated with kidney failure, blindness, and loss of limbs. Only 45 percent of heart attack patients received beta blockers, and 61 percent got aspirin—two forms of treatment that can reduce the risk of death by over 20 percent.[12]

Today one American in five will suffer from prostate or breast cancer, with younger and younger people being diagnosed every year.

Or consider these facts from a similar national study, also conducted in 2006, under the auspices of the Commonwealth Fund

Commission on a High Performance Health System, which compared the U.S. system to those of other countries across 37 key indicators, such as infant mortality, life expectancy at age 60, availability of treatment for mental illness, and appropriate care for chronic diseases:

- The United States lags behind the leading nations of the world by one-third in mortality from conditions "amenable to health care"—that is, preventable deaths.
- The U.S. infant mortality rate is 7.0 deaths per 1,000 live births, compared with 2.7 in the top three countries.
- Gaps in treatment for diabetes and blood pressure lead to an estimated 20,000 to 40,000 needless deaths annually, along with $1 billion to $2 billion in avoidable medical costs.
- Seventeen percent of U.S. doctors have access to electronic medical records, as compared to 80 percent in the top three countries.
- Thirty-four percent of American patients experience errors in treatment, medication, or testing, as compared to 22 percent in the top six countries.[13]

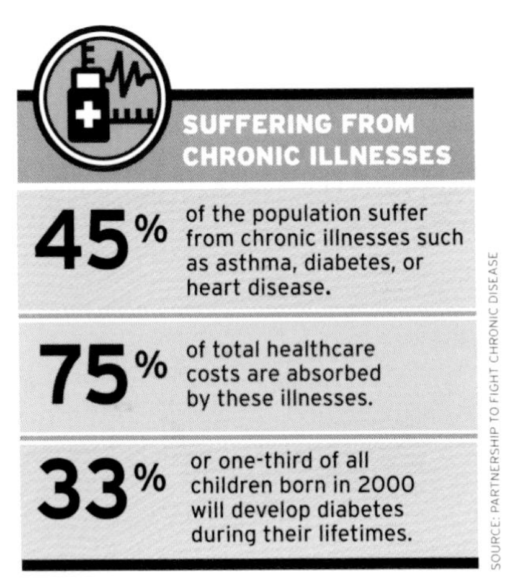

In the countries of the developing world, persistent poverty is the main culprit behind the lack of good healthcare. But in the United States, poverty can't be blamed for the failure of the healthcare system. Somehow we can't manage to provide decent-quality healthcare to millions of our citizens, despite the billions we throw at the problem. Why not?

Many thoughtful analysts have examined the problem, studying the history of healthcare in the United States and comparing our jerry-rigged "system" to the delivery programs provided in most other countries of the developed world. Most objective observers point to the same root problem: our profit-driven medical system, which channels a huge percentage of healthcare expenditures to insurance companies, for-profit hospital chains, giant pharmaceutical firms, and other businesses, while shamefully neglecting "unprofitable" services and patients.

As a result, an estimated one-third of U.S. healthcare expenditures are wasted on "ineffective, sometimes unwanted, and often unproven procedures" (according to Jack Wennberg, M.D., director of the Center for the Evaluative Clinical Sciences at Dartmouth Medical School)—simply because that's where the profits are.[14]

An even more shameful waste is the third of healthcare spending that goes to administration and overhead—filing of insurance claims, the back-and-forth of denial and adjudication, bureaucracy, red-tape, and supporting redundant parts of the medical infrastructure. Hence, only one of every three healthcare dollars is being spent wisely, a waste of almost 500 dollars per year per person in the United States.

American members of Generation We inherit a world of technological marvels and a nation with resources unmatched in human history. Yet thanks to decades of greed, mismanagement, plundering, and leadership distorted by rigid ideology, they also inherit a health system that is simply broken—one that may prove unable to treat them for the man-made diseases inflicted upon them or to protect them when the predictable next wave of diseases strikes some time in the next decade or two. There's a real and frightening danger that the healthcare enjoyed by recent generations of Americans may disappear by the time Generation We reaches old age.

A FAILING EDUCATIONAL SYSTEM

The American social contract has been based on equality of opportunity, and central to that is a good education. But today quality education is a matter of economic and social class rather than being a basic right for every citizen of the United States.

Inner cities and rural areas are the hardest hit. Lacking the large tax base of affluent areas, schools there lack the resources needed to pay for teachers, information technology, and other facilities. In 1999, the Department of Education reported that 127 billion dollars was needed to bring "the nation's school facilities into good overall condition."[15] In the years since then, conditions have steadily worsened. No wonder our students are failing to learn. How can they learn when they sit in classrooms with leaky roofs, work in science labs with outdated or broken equipment, and often have to do without such simple essentials as art and music studios, auditoriums, gyms, and libraries?

PHOTO: VEER IMAGES

As the best teachers flee these decrepit facilities, morale, discipline, and learning plummet. Many schools turn into breeding grounds for violence and drug use. Gangs proliferate, and the pressure to rebel against teachers, learning, and society is almost irresistible. With the current war spending, disastrous economic trends, and skyrocketing energy costs, public expenditures on education are being further squeezed.

As a result, students who are not among the lucky, gifted few are being left with an inferior education that affects them and successive generations. We are creating a permanent underclass of people suited only to the most trivial of labors and lacking the training and work ethic that enables lifelong progress. The existence of this underclass means less income earned, less home ownership, lower economic growth, poorer health, higher crime, higher criminal justice costs, lower tax receipts, and greater demands on government-funded social services.

Lack of investment in education also makes our country vulnerable to overseas economic competition. Here the problems go beyond inner-city and rural schools to include lagging performance by the entire educational system. Every three years, the Program for International Student Assessment (PISA) conducts what is widely regarded as the definitive study of student performance in schools from around the world. PISA focuses especially on science and math skills, since these are both comparable across cultures and languages and among the most important skills students will need to compete in today's technologically-advanced, global economy.

The latest PISA results are dismaying. Of the 30 nations in the Organization for Economic Cooperation and Development (roughly equivalent to "the developed world"), American students in 2006 ranked seventeenth in science, twenty-fourth in math. Students from Canada, Korea, Hong Kong, and Taiwan all scored higher than those from the United States, as did Poland (which raised its scores significantly in the last three years). The U.S. results are virtually identical to the last time the PISA tests were administered (2003), suggesting that President Bush's vaunted "No Child Left Behind" reforms have not yet had any noticeable impact on student achievement in science and math.[16]

Lack of investment in education also makes our country vulnerable to overseas economic competition.

The long-term implications of this problem are serious. In a 2008 study led by economists Eric A. Hanushek of Stanford University and Ludger Woessmann of the University of Munich, economic growth rates of 50 nations over 40 years (1960–2000) were compared with math and science skills like those measured by PISA. The results: Countries ranked among the leaders in those skills can expect a GDP growth rate that is noticeably higher than that experienced by laggards such as the United States. If the United States had managed to join the world leaders in math and science by 2000, for example, today's GDP would likely by some 2 percent higher than it is—a difference of 300 billion dollars in national income. A similar improvement projected into the future would project to a 4.5 percent boost to GDP by 2015, producing extra income sufficient to pay for *the entire country's primary and secondary school educational system in that year.*[17]

It's no secret that the American educational system is failing our students and our society. Practically everyone agrees on the nature of the problem, but nobody is doing much about it. Attempts to reform public schools have failed in part because entrenched union interests have prevented performance-based measures such as merit pay and competency standards from being implemented. The youth are being hit from two sides—a public apathetic to their needs and an entrenched bureaucracy that protects its own interests.

Some believe that charter schools or educational vouchers for parents to spend on private or faith-based schools can solve the problem. Although these ideas deserve more study, both have gotten caught up in cultural battles between left and right, and both ignore the vast majority of children. Rather than merely providing life rafts for a relative handful of students, the entire education system must be fixed.

"It is incumbent on every generation to pay its own debts as it goes. A principle which if acted on would save one-half the wars of the world"

THOMAS JEFFERSON

ECONOMIC DISASTER

Generation We inherits a nation rife with economic peril and injustice. It's a world in which a privileged few are reaping nearly all the economic benefits from recent technological breakthroughs and productivity improvements, while the average American family is struggling not to slip backward.

It's also a world riddled with economic weaknesses—a world in which economic failure, possibly even resulting in collapse, could occur at almost any time because of uncontrolled debt, unknown financial exposure from derivatives and monetary engineering, unregulated speculators driving oil and food prices to unsustainable levels, insolvent entitlement programs, a massive trade imbalance, and lack of worker security.

From time to time, signs of the system's underlying weaknesses break through to the surface. For example, there's the current mortgage crisis, which has already led to more than one million home foreclosures. This number is projected by the Secretary of the Treasury (July 2008) to mushroom to more than 2.5 million in 2009. This crisis was triggered by lax, predatory lending standards invented to feed the market and value of complex derivative securities. These markets were created by and for speculators and produced a level of risk exposure no one could accurately estimate. As a result of the inevitable crisis, home ownership, once a foundation of American prosperity, is now becoming inaccessible to average Americans.

Even worse was the enticing of working-class and middle-class home owners into taking out unaffordable second mortgages and rolling up huge levels of credit-card debt to pay for consumption. Banks were selling debt like televisions. But instead of holding the debt themselves as they'd always done, the banks packaged the debt into pools that would be sold by speculators to speculators, with profits earned at every turn. Then the banks, hedge funds, and investment banks made money insuring each other against losses in arcane transactions called derivative swaps. Now the large banks have tens of trillions of dollars of financial exposure they can't control or even measure. Ultimately, the government—and the middle-class taxpayer—will have to pick up the tab.

Another cause of our economic weakness is the current run-up in the price of oil, which is boosting the cost of practically every product we purchase and which has been driven, in large part, by the impact of speculators who can trade oil futures electronically and with no regulation or oversight thanks to the so-called "Enron loophole" passed by Congress in 2000 as a favor to the financial industry. Oil was priced at 23 dollars per barrel prior to the Iraqi war. In mid-2008, it soared past 140 dollars per barrel, making a few speculators very happy. But millions of people can't afford to commute to work, some schools are shutting down one day a week, and some businesses are laying off employees—all because of rising energy bills. With no end in sight, government officials are talking about plans that *may* reduce our dependence on fossil fuels—20 years or more from now.

The fuel crisis has caused much of the world's corn production to be applied to making ethanol. This has reduced the production of beef, pork, and poultry, and increased their prices. Poor families are substituting sugary drinks for more-expensive milk. Rising prices of rice, grain, and other foodstuffs are causing rioting in some parts of the world—mostly under the radar of the mainstream media.

Generation We is also inheriting financial burdens greater than those of any other generation in American history, thanks to the irresponsible behavior of their predecessors in generating massive deficit spending.

Most people are at least vaguely aware of the staggering statistics related to our national indebtedness, but here are a few of the frightening lowlights:[18]

- The U.S. national debt, which has been rising by about 1.4 billion dollars a day, will surpass the 10-trillion-dollar mark early in 2009. That amounts to about 30,000 dollars in debt for every man, woman, and child in the country, and equals around 65 percent of the GDP.

- About 44 percent of the publicly-held U.S. debt—some 2.23 trillion dollars—is owned by foreign governments and investors. Japan leads the way, followed by China, Britain, Saudi Arabia, and other countries from the Organization of Petroleum-Exporting Countries (OPEC). These holdings put our nation's economy at the mercy of foreign leaders, threatening our national security. (How does one say *no* to one's bankers in a time of crisis?) In the past, America could use its financial leverage as the weapon against its enemies; now our potential enemies can wield the same weapon against us.

- Interest on the national debt represents the third-largest item in the U.S. government budget, sucking up 430 billion dollars in 2007. Sums poured down this black hole could instead be invested in our nation's future through education, healthcare, energy and environmental research, infrastructure rebuilding, and other constructive programs.

Generation We is also inheriting financial burdens greater than those of any other generation in American history...

Even the government's own auditors have been trying to warn us that our current economic path is leading us toward disaster. Here is just a part of what Comptroller General David M. Walker wrote in his report on the national budget, dated 1 December 2006 (emphases added):

> Despite improvement in both the fiscal year 2006 reported net operating cost and the cash-based budget deficit, the U.S. government's total reported liabilities, net social insurance commitments [i.e., Social Security and Medicare], and other fiscal exposures continue to grow and now total approximately *$50 trillion, representing approximately four times the nation's total output (GDP) in fiscal year 2006*, up from about $20 trillion, or two times GDP in fiscal year 2000. As this long-term fiscal imbalance continues to grow, the retirement of the "baby boom" generation is closer to becoming a reality with the first wave of boomers eligible for early retirement under Social Security in 2008. Given these and other factors, *it seems clear that the nation's current fiscal path is unsustainable* and that tough choices by the President and the Congress are necessary in order to address the nation's large and growing long-term fiscal imbalance.[19]

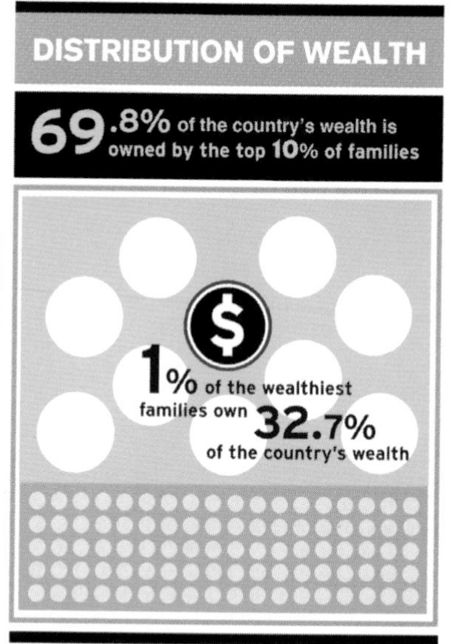

...the average American is actually earning less today than his or her counterpart of a generation ago.

Thanks in part to our staggering national debt, vital social needs are simply going unmet. We've already mentioned how essential school repairs are being neglected due to financial shortfalls. But schools aren't the only pieces of our nation's infrastructure that are crumbling. A 2005 report by the American Society of Civil Engineers declared that we are "failing to maintain even substandard conditions" in our highway system, draining more than 120 billion dollars from our economy in needless car repairs, lost productivity, and wasted fuel. The same report described the national power grid as "in urgent need of modernization," with annual maintenance spending having declined one percent per year since 1992 even as demand has grown steadily.[20] If blackouts, brownouts, and power failures seem to be more frequent in recent years, you're not imagining it. As a nation, we've simply ignored the basic, urgent need to take care of the systems upon which we rely.

As individuals, Americans are faring no better than their national government. Even as the economy—along with many corporations—continues to grow (albeit slowly), the working men and women who fuel that growth aren't receiving their fair share of the rewards. Statistics from the U.S. Department of Labor show that, while the productivity of labor has grown enormously since 1985, wages have failed to keep pace, creating a large and growing gap between industrial output per hour and real (inflation-adjusted) hourly compensation.[21] In fact, the average American is actually earning less today than his or her counterpart of a generation ago—the first time in our nation's history that this has been true.

For example, as shown in Census Bureau data, during the first quarter-century of post-war growth (1947–1973), real (inflation-adjusted) family income growth was almost the same, in percentage terms, across the entire spectrum of Americans. During that period, the income of the lowest quintile grew by 116 percent, while the highest quintile enjoyed income growth of about 85 percent.

By contrast, during the period from 1974 to 2004, real family income growth was heavily stacked in favor of the wealthiest Americans. The income of the lowest quintile grew by just 2.8 percent; that of the second lowest, by 12.9 percent; of the middle quintile, by 23.3 percent; of the second highest, by 34.9 percent; and of the highest quintile, by 63.6 percent. Notably, *no* quintile performed as well during the last quarter of the twentieth century as all Americans did three decades earlier; but those who were already wealthy enjoyed at least reasonable growth, while those at the bottom of the ladder found themselves falling further and further behind.[22]

Even more disturbing are the trends in household wealth, which represent the level of assets owned by the typical individual or family and therefore reflect their long-term economic health even better, perhaps, than annual income. In recent years, the concentration of wealth in relatively few hands has accelerated. As of 2000, the top 10 percent of American families controlled no less than 69.8 percent of the national wealth—and almost half of that (32.7 percent) was actually in the hands of the top 1 percent of families. By contrast, the *bottom* 50 percent held only 2.8 percent of the national wealth, a pitifully small share that bodes ill for their future prospects.[23] More recent statistics suggest that this distribution has, if anything, worsened in the past eight years.

©RHIENNA CUTLER/ISTOCK INTERNATIONAL

Generation We is well aware from painful personal experience that the national economy and their own financial prospects are on shaky ground. In an era when higher education is a prerequisite for most jobs with any career potential, many Millennials are finding it a painful financial struggle just to get through college. As tuition and related costs have mushroomed, financial-aid programs have shrunken and part-time job opportunities have dwindled.

The maximum Pell Grant, which covered 77 percent of the average cost of attending a public college in 1980, now covers just 33 percent

PHOTO: VEER IMAGES

of the same cost. As a result, getting a college education is becoming more and more difficult for young people who are not members of the economic elite.

Activist and journalist Paul Rogat Loeb has captured the typical human cost in a vivid personal anecdote:

> The encounter that crystallized the shift [for me] happened a few years ago, when I met a student who lived on the same Brooklyn block where I had lived while attending college in the early seventies. I'd worked my way through school as a bartender, making $5 an hour for twenty hours a week. I paid my tuition at a private university with costs as high as any in the nation, paid my food, rent, and books, and had money left over to go out on the weekends. Twenty-five years later, this student was working 30 hours a week for $6 an hour, a fraction in real dollars of what I'd been making. He commuted an hour and a half each way to the City College of New York, a public school with tuition far higher proportionate to his earnings than my private college tuition was to me. He kept dropping out and working fulltime to try to avoid getting too deep in debt, but would still owe $15,000 or more when and if he graduated. Though he was working harder than I had, the rules had changed to make his passage vastly more difficult.[24]

Things don't get better after graduation. As the Millennials grow up, graduate, and take their places in the work force, new sources of economic stress and dissatisfaction emerge. After adjustment for inflation, salaries paid to new college graduates have fallen by 8.5 percent since 2000. The average college grad now starts life carrying 20,000 dollars in student loan debt. [25]

No wonder Millennials share a general impression that they live in a more challenging economic environment than the ones their grandparents, parents, or even their older siblings faced. In our focus groups, they talked about having to work long hours—sometimes at two or more jobs—just to manage rent, food, and student loan payments. They worried about being stuck in dead-end jobs, and they were vociferous in their complaints about uncaring employers who provide little or no healthcare coverage, pension plans, and other safety-net programs.

News stories about predatory speculators and corporate malfeasance at firms like Enron only heighten the cynical attitude of Generation We toward big business. Most seem ready to agree that corporate leaders are only interested in lining their own pockets, and the idea of a "social contract" for the mutual benefit of workers and companies seems a distant dream.

The Generation We members we spoke to are also ready to acknowledge that their own behavior contributes to the economic problems we face, as individuals and as a society. In our focus groups, many spoke about the "mindless consumerism" encouraged by the mass media, and confessed to being influenced by commercials and peer pressure into buying "meaningless products," even to the extent of being driven deeper into debt.

Of course, this is both bad news and good news. The bad news is that, in the words of Walt Kelly's Pogo, "We have met the enemy and he is us." The good news is that, to a large extent, we have the power to resist the system and to improve our individual economic circumstances—if we choose to exercise it responsibly. Generation We understands this and appears ready to take the appropriate steps to restructure the financial system and its governance, provided the right leadership comes along to help educate and guide them.

CREEPING TOTALITARIANISM

Generation We inherits an America whose greatest political traditions, as embodied in the Declaration of Independence, the Constitution, and the Bill of Rights, are being slowly sapped. They are witnessing the gradual weakening of American democracy through erosion of human rights, media manipulation, and citizen apathy, and the concentration of excessive power in the hands of special interests.

In her powerful book *The End of America: Letter of Warning to a Young Patriot*, Naomi Wolf writes of 10 changes that have historically characterized nations that slip from democracy into dictatorship. Among the country examples she studies are Mussolini's Italy, Hitler's Germany, and Stalin's Russia. As she shows, each of the 10 changes—steps toward totalitarianism—can be seen and documented in the United States today.

The 10 steps include, for example, the invocation of an external and internal threat as an excuse for a crackdown on civil liberties—something the Bush administration hasn't been shy about doing since 9/11; the establishment of secret prisons—which we've seen happen at Guantánamo Bay as well as at other sites around the world, to which terror suspects have been sent for abusive questioning, and in some cases, torture; the branding of political dissent as "treason"—rhetorical labeling used frequently in recent years by conservative politicians, pundits, and outlets like Fox News; and the subversion of the rule of law—as illustrated by, among other scandals, the firing of Justice Department officials apparently for refusing to cooperate with politically-motivated prosecutions.[26]

Wolf's book, consciously modeled on the revolutionary-era writings of such freedom-loving patriots as Thomas Paine, is written in the form of a letter to a friend named Christopher Le, a Millennial youth. We would echo Wolf's call to young Americans to recognize the danger of creeping totalitarianism and stand up against it.

Does it seem exaggerated to compare the situation in the United States today with the early stages of totalitarianism under Hitler or Stalin? If you think so, we urge you to read Wolf's book and examine the parallels she documents.

Or consider just one example of the kinds of extraordinary, illegal, and unconstitutional powers the U.S. government now routinely claims—the right to engage in "extraordinary renditions" of people (potentially including U.S. citizens) it considers, sometimes without evidence, to be an "enemy combatant," "security threat," or "possible terrorist," all of which are ill-defined terms whose vagueness gives government officials excessive power they can use as they see fit.

An extraordinary rendition occurs when a person is seized by U.S. government authorities—including by law any one of thousands in the executive branch given that authority—and "rendered" to officials in another country, usually without any involvement by courts either here or abroad. In many cases, such renditions are used by the CIA and other intelligence organizations to get suspects into the hands of countries that are known to use torture as a way of gaining information. For example, since 9/11, the Bush administration has rendered terrorism suspects to countries such as Egypt, Jordan, Syria, Morocco, and Uzbekistan, where their custody receives no judicial oversight and where they may be held indefinitely for no reason at all.[27]

...each of the 10 changes—steps toward totalitarianism—can be seen and documented in the United States today.

Perhaps this doesn't sound so bad. After all, if someone is a suspected terrorist, isn't it reasonable for the government to take extraordinary steps to prevent this person from doing harm and to learn whatever secret plans he or she may be hatching? Maybe—except that the government contends it has no obligation to demonstrate to a court of law that those it has arrested are, in fact, terrorists, which means that completely innocent people are almost certain to be included among those who are seized and tortured. At least one investigative journalist has already found that "dozens," and "perhaps hundreds," of innocent men have been caught up in the anti-terror frenzy.[28]

What's more, the victims don't include only foreign nationals

...our diminishing liberties may be the most serious of all the problems the Millennials face.

©PHOTO: JEHAD NGA/CORBIS

picked up on battlefields in Afghanistan or Iraq. They include people like Maher Arar, a Canadian citizen who works as a software consultant and apparently suffered from a case of mistaken identity when he was detained at Kennedy Airport by U.S. officials in 2002. Arar was rendered to Syria, where he was imprisoned for a year and repeatedly beaten with a heavy metal cable. After a two-year investigation, the Canadian government concluded that Arar had no ties to terrorism and his arrest had been an unfortunate error.

Similarly, Army Chaplain James Yee—a Muslim who made the mistake of speaking up to request better treatment for detainees at Guantánamo Bay—was arrested on charges of "espionage and possibly treason," and held in solitary confinement in a U.S. Navy brig. Six months later, the government dropped all its accusations against Yee and released him, with the proviso that he never offer any public complaint about his mistreatment.[29]

If solid citizens with no history of any offenses, such as Arar and Yee, can be arbitrarily imprisoned and mistreated without recourse, how can we be sure future administrations won't use these powers to stifle dissent, intimidate political adversaries, and discourage criticism? It's not as though such outrages against human rights have never happened in America; just look at the use of violence, up to and including lynching, to terrorize and intimidate African-Americans in the South until well into the twentieth century; the wholesale incarceration of Japanese-Americans during World War II purely on the basis of race; and the stifling of political dissent through legal threats, public humiliation, and job loss during the McCarthy era of the 1950s.

Could the next Martin Luther King, Jr., or Susan B. Anthony be rendered, imprisoned, tortured, or even killed by the government for daring to dissent?

In those historic episodes, other excuses were used, ranging from the need to preserve "racial purity" to bogus claims of "threats to national security." Today, the "war on terror" is the all-embracing justification. But the abuses remain intolerable—and today, the government's claims of powers untouchable by any court are bolder and more dangerous than ever.

The gradual erosion of Americans' rights is being facilitated by a mainstream media that have largely abdicated their traditional role as watchdogs of democracy. Investigative journalism that probes the failings and misdeeds of our most powerful institutions, as in the days of Watergate, is almost extinct, replaced by a mindless media focus on scandal and sensation. And government repression encourages the cowardice of journalists. Look, for example, at what happened when Bush administration officials criminally leaked the identity of covert CIA agent Valerie Plame for political purposes: The only person to spend a day in jail was not one of the officials responsible, but a journalist who covered the story, Judith Miller of the *New York Times*.

We see this abdication in the media's failure to scrutinize and objectively evaluate the actions of the Bush administration, especially in the wake of the 9/11 attacks. The anti-democratic provisions in the USA PATRIOT Act—commonly referred to as the Patriot Act—received scanty coverage on the television networks or on cable news. The horrific photos from the Abu Ghraib torture scandal were shown on TV, but those in positions of authority—Defense Secretary Donald Rumsfeld, for example—were not held accountable. The administration was permitted to blame the outrages on "a few bad apples," even after a handful of intrepid reporters uncovered evidence that higher-ups sanctioned the abuse.

The disastrous Iraq war itself was facilitated by a docile and compliant news media. Numerous accounts have shown how a series of lies—largely unchallenged by the mainstream press—allowed the Bush administration to convince Americans that war was necessary and inevitable. From the fake "Niger yellowcake" story, based on forged documents, which Bush himself retailed in his 2003 State of the Union Address, and the false claims about mobile biological and chemical weapons labs, to the unsupported insinuations that Iraq was somehow involved in planning the 9/11 attacks, the media allowed the administration to create a public atmosphere of fear and hysteria that overwhelmed rational analysis.

In the months leading up to the war, the media everywhere endlessly replayed the famous sound bite, "Do you want the smoking gun to be a mushroom cloud?" in which Condoleezza Rice threatened Americans with death from Saddam Hussein's nonexistent nuclear weapons. The media then sensationalized the propaganda presenting false intelligence delivered by Secretary of State Colin Powell to the United Nations, helping to convince members of Congress to give broad war powers to the president and persuading the nation to go to war under false pretenses.

Once the war began, the administration mounted a massive public relations effort to manipulate the public into supporting it, again abetted by a complaisant news media, using supposedly independent "military analysts" as undisclosed shills for Pentagon talking points. As David Barstow of the *New York Times* has reported:

> Hidden behind that appearance of objectivity, though, is a Pentagon information apparatus that has used those analysts in a campaign to generate favorable news coverage of the administration's wartime performance...
>
> The effort, which began with the buildup to the Iraq war and continues to this day, has sought to exploit ideological and military allegiances, and also a powerful financial dynamic: Most of the analysts have ties to military contractors vested in the very war policies they are asked to assess on air.
>
> Those business relationships are hardly ever disclosed to the viewers, and sometimes not even to the networks themselves. But collectively, the men on the plane and several dozen other military analysts represent more than 150 military contractors either as lobbyists, senior executives, board members or consultants. The companies include defense heavyweights, but also scores of smaller companies, all part of a vast assemblage of contractors scrambling for hundreds of billions in military business generated by the administration's war on terror.[30]

Disturbing ownership trends in the U.S. media help to explain some of the failure of the media to stand up for the rights and interests of American citizens.

The *Times* story was an all-too-rare example of independent investigative reporting that dared to challenge government manipulation of the news. But relatively few Americans have heard about it. Barstow's expose was greeted with almost total silence by the broadcast and cable news networks whose malfeasance it described. Howard Kurtz, media critic for the *Washington Post* and *CNN*, called their response to the story "pathetic," and added, "If there has been any coverage of this on CBS, NBC, ABC, MSNBC or Fox, I've missed it. The story makes the networks look bad—and their response, by and large, has been to ignore it." [31]

This story is just one example of how our understanding of the wars in Iraq and Afghanistan has been impeded by a spineless media.

Think about it: When was the last time you saw combat footage from those countries on the TV news—let alone a picture of a fallen U.S. serviceman or civilian killed in the fighting? Discouraged by government restrictions on access as well as pressure from pro-administration advertisers and corporate chieftains, the news media have given far less daily coverage to our current wars than the Vietnam conflict received 40 years ago.

Imagine if the government had had the power to impose a similar blackout on coverage of Hurricane Katrina! Is it a stretch to infer that the "conditions on the ground" in Iraq and Afghanistan may be as bad as those experienced in New Orleans' Ninth Ward?

Disturbing ownership trends in the U.S. media help to explain some of the failure of the media to stand up for the rights and interests of American citizens. Content and distribution of media are now owned and controlled by the same corporate interests. Before Reagan deregulated media ownership and media concentration laws were gradually eroded, companies that created editorial content for electronic media had to be owned independently from the regulated distribution companies. Now that this separation is gone, those who need to rely on freedom of speech and the press—for example, TV news departments—are beholden to government regulators with a clear interest in controlling them because their satellite, broadcast, and transmission licenses can be revoked, thereby destroying their corporate earnings.

It's easy to see how this kind of intimidation could work. Suppose NBC or MSNBC—both owned by General Electric, a major defense contractor—were to violate a formal or informal "decree of silence" about some topic issued by the executive branch. The parent company might find itself losing defense contracts, satellite and spectrum licenses, and television station concessions. This would affect earnings, share prices, and job prospects of the corporate officers. How much easier for the news producers to quietly go along with the government mandate, and leave the public in the dark.

Think this is farfetched? At least one network owner has already admitted being influenced politically by his business interests. In the 2004 presidential election, Sumner Redstone of Viacom, owner of CBS, endorsed President Bush, saying, "It is in the best interests of my shareholders." (Redstone had been a life-long Democrat.) If you were a news producer for CBS, how eager would you have been to run stories critical of Bush or favorable to the opposition?

Some of the specific ownership links now prevalent in the world of media are even more troubling. For example, 10 percent of News Corporation, the parent company of Fox News, is owned by Prince Al-Walid bin Talal, a Saudi prince who has actually bragged about getting the network to alter news coverage he considered biased against Muslims.[32] (Al-Walid is also the largest single shareowner of the giant financial institution Citigroup, and in fact, the largest foreign investor in the U.S. economy.[33]) Without Al-Walid's support, Fox might well become a takeover target, threatening the entire media empire of Rupert Murdoch. Is it a stretch to think that the prince has profited handsomely from the increase in oil prices since the start of the Iraq war? If so, how might this further impact the supposedly "fair and balanced" coverage provided by Fox News.

Millennials should also be aware that the same corporation that owns Fox—News Corp—also owns the social-networking company many Millennials think of as "theirs": MySpace.

The nature of interlocking share ownership and large company interdependency means that our media is controlled by governmental and corporate interests that are run by members of older generations who are in thrall to the oligopolists, the plunderers, the petrodollar billionaires, and the propaganda network of the far right—people whose interests directly conflict with those of the Millennials (as well as the vast majority of Americans).

The idea of an independent news media prepared to challenge the powers-that-be on behalf of the people is almost dead. Today's mass media are effectively an instrument of mass consumerization. Commercials and editorial content both serve the same purpose: to brainwash viewers into choosing violent toys, processed food, fast food, and other poor lifestyle choices. They program us to spend our lives in front of a TV screen, video-game console, or computer monitor, where built-in tools for marketing, promotion, and habit influencing can work on us continually, making us sedentary, obese, diabetic, weak, and dependent on artificial stimulants. This then affects our cognitive ability and locks in spending, time, and consumption patterns. Before we know it, they own us. And if we are different and dissent, they marginalize us and ostracize us from society, abandoning us to lives of hopelessness, voicelessness, and poverty.

Thankfully, the brainwashing being practiced by the news and entertainment conglomerates is neither foolproof nor complete. The members of Generation We themselves are acutely aware of the effects their destructive media environment is having on them and their peers. In our focus groups, they spoke a lot about their dissatisfaction with the media—about the trivialization of news, the pro-corporate and pro-government slant of most media, and the sense that vital information is being withheld, distorted, or buried in an avalanche of irrelevant details. Generation We loves the Internet, and the power it brings to tap into myriad sources of information. But they also wonder, "How are we supposed to sort out what's true from what's false?" Many are searching for answers.

Some people might feel that the erosion of human rights and the corruption of the communications media by pro-government and pro-corporate interests are less significant problems for the average

You may be tempted to think that abstract principles like human rights and freedom of the press are "none of your business." In truth, they're the business of every citizen—which is why our ancestors fought and died to defend those rights. Generation We must treat this challenge as seriously as our Founders did.

person than the environmental, health, and economic challenges we've described. "After all," they may say, "I'm not a journalist, a political activist, or a human rights lawyer. So issues like Constitutional rights and media freedom don't directly concern me."

This may be true. Yet in a broader sense, our diminishing liberties may be the most serious of all the problems the Millennials face. After all, finding solutions to all the other issues we are struggling with depends on the existence of the freedoms we take for granted—freedom of speech, freedom of the press, freedom to assemble and petition for redress of grievances, freedom to demand the truth from our elected officials, and so on. If we allow corporate interests to completely take over our government and our news media, how will the needs of average Americans even get a hearing on Capitol Hill or on the TV news? How will dissenters get their voices heard by their fellow citizens? How will candidates who advocate genuine change have a chance to win power at the polls?

You may be tempted to think that abstract principles like human rights and freedom of the press are "none of your business." In truth, they're the business of every citizen—which is why our ancestors fought and died to defend those rights. Generation We must treat this challenge as seriously as our Founders did.

A WORLD RAVAGED BY WAR

Finally, the challenges faced by Generation We are not domestic problems alone. As citizens of the most powerful nation on the planet, they bear a major responsibility for redirecting the course of a world in which warfare of unprecedented destructiveness is a looming threat. Terrorism, sectarian hatred, and violence abetted by spreading availability of weapons of mass destruction are the all-too-likely results of the mismanagement of international relations by previous generations, both in the United States and around the world.

It's important to note that there are powerful interconnections among the global dysfunctions we've listed in this chapter. For example, the dependence of the United States, and the rest of the developed world, on fossil fuels is not only an environmental and economic problem; it is also a major cause of political unrest, upheaval, violence, and warfare.

In a tragic accident of fate, the world's largest remaining known oil reserves happen to be located in a part of the planet where cultures and religions have clashed for centuries—the Middle East. Our need to keep the oil flowing has inevitably embroiled us in these ancient rivalries, distorting our foreign policy and helping to make the world a more dangerous place. Making matters worse, other oil-exporting countries elsewhere in the world also pose political threats of their own, further complicating efforts to maintain global peace.

The geopolitical effects of our reliance on foreign oil include:

- U.S. military and economic support for some of the world's most backward totalitarian regimes, including countries such as Saudi Arabia, Nigeria, Kazakhstan, and Libya, undermining our nation's traditional and avowed support for democratic reform. By propping up these regimes we are indirectly fostering anti-Semitism, oppression of women and gays, and suppression of political dissent.

- Continuing American military presence in the Middle East, driven not by the need to protect our ally Israel but by our need to ensure the free flow of oil supplies.

- Consequent resentment of American influence in the Middle East by those who feel oppressed or neglected by their nations' autocratic regimes, leading to support for terrorist and Islamist groups.

- Acceptance of totalitarian dictatorships devoid of human rights and free markets as acceptable allies, where malfeasance and evil are swept under the rug to feed our energy appetite.

- Ability of oil-exporting regimes in the Middle East and elsewhere that are actively or potentially hostile to U.S. interests—including Iran, Nigeria, Libya, and Venezuela—to blackmail the United States by threatening to "play the oil card" by withholding their oil supplies and thereby driving world prices through the roof.

By allowing our economy to become so heavily dependent on foreign oil, we've made the United States vulnerable to economic assaults—intentional or unintentional—from a wide array of sources, and created an interlocking global system in which turbulence in one part of the globe can trigger economic problems and even warfare half a world away.

Oil isn't the only vital resource that is likely to be a source of military conflict and violence in the decades to come. As global warming intensifies and produces disastrous environmental changes around the world, one probable result will be spreading desertification and deepening water shortages on one continent after another. China, southeast Asia, southwestern North America, North Africa, South Asia, and the Middle East are all overpopulated, prone to water scarcity, and likely sites where social and even military struggles for control of water could occur in the near future.

There are already signs that "water wars" have begun to break out over control of this absolute vital resource:

healthcare
education energy
social security
infrastructure

> Egypt, a powerful downstream riparian [that is, a river-based society], has several times threatened to go to war over Nile water; only the fact that both Sudan and Ethiopia have been wracked by civil war and are too poor to develop "their" water resources has so far prevented conflict. In the Euphrates Basin, Turkey is militarily more potent than Syria, but that hasn't stopped the Syrians from threatening violence [over water rights]. And there are endless examples of powers that are similar in military might, but have threatened war [over water]: along the Mekong River, along the Paraná, and other places. In the Senegal Valley of West Africa, water shortages contributed to recent violent skirmishes between Mauritania and Senegal, complicated by the ethnic conflict between the black Africans and the paler-skinned Moors who control Mauritania. On the other side of the country, desperate Mauritanians wrecked a Malian village after cattle herders refused to let them cross the border to water their cattle at a well.[34]

Oil, water, and other vital resources (such as strategic minerals, access to ports, fertile farmland, and sheer living space) have always been causes of war, though as population pressures and environmental degradation increase, it seems likely that tensions over resources are likely to grow in the years to come. But war has other, even less acceptable causes, including the urge to power and the desire for profits of arms manufacturers and other military contractors.

War spending has grotesquely distorted the economies of both the United States and the entire world. Consider the fact that, since 1996, even with no rival superpower threatening our country, U.S. military spending has increased by 50 percent (160 billion dollars), and now totals over 711 billion dollars—nearly half the total military spending of the entire world. American military spending dwarfs that of any conceivable rival power. For example, China (which has the world's third-largest military budget, after the United States and Europe), spends "only" 122 billion dollars on the military, less than one-fifth the U.S. total. American military spending is greater than that of the next 45 countries—combined. It amounts to fully 43 percent of federal spending, crowding out desperately needed funds for Social Security, healthcare, education, infrastructure, energy research, and dozens of other important priorities.

Actually, the situation is *far worse* than even these statistics suggest, since the declared military budget *does not include* costs such as ongoing combat missions, veterans care, maintenance of nuclear weapons, and secret operations. The wars in Iraq and Afghanistan are expected to cost taxpayers at least 170 billion dollars in additional funds during fiscal 2009 alone.

Driven by American military spending, world spending on arms and armies has also grown dramatically in recent years. As of 2006, it is estimated to be over 1.2 trillion dollars—this in a world where alleviating global poverty, eradicating infectious diseases, educating all children, and providing clean water and sanitation for everyone are deemed to be "too expensive." [35]

Military spending profoundly distorts the world's wealth. It drains money that could be more usefully spent on projects to benefit humankind; it channels huge sums of money into the pockets of arms contractors and service providers like Halliburton, Blackwater, and KBR; and it provides an artificial stimulus to the economy, becoming a primary driver of growth (at the expense of human lives) that governments find it increasingly difficult to do without. (It is no coincidence that the current administration is talking about troop cuts that coincide directly with its exit from office. They have an election coming up, and the effects of a war slowdown on the economy prior to that would be bad politics.)

The direct effects of war itself are even more appalling. In modern warfare, which targets not just uniformed combatants but entire societies, there are no winners. War cripples economies, ravages the environment, shatters infrastructures, and destroys countless lives—not just the lives of soldiers but those of their families and of millions of helpless civilian victims killed by bombing, landmines, wanton attacks, and the famine, drought, disease, and dislocation inevitably produced by war. The fact that governments around the world—including preeminently the government of the United States—devote the lion's share of their discretionary spending to preparing for war and waging war is unforgivable.

The wars in Iraq and Afghanistan are expected to cost taxpayers at least 170 billion dollars in additional funds during fiscal 2009 alone.

And, of course, it is the youth of the world who bear the heaviest burden of war. The conflicts of the coming decades will be fought by Millennials—young people conscripted and forced by older generations to kill one another and perpetuate cycles of violence that have never solved any problem or improved anyone's life.

The saddest challenge Generation We faces is tens of thousands of their brethren coming home from war mutilated, dependent on prostheses, and suffering from record levels of post-traumatic stress disorder. The improvements in battlefield medicine have admirably reduced the number of mortalities, but the country is ill-prepared to support a generation that includes tens of thousands of veterans suffering from grievous long-term injuries. This is an incredible generational tragedy.

In particular, it is the poor and underprivileged who do most of the fighting and dying. Unlike in past wars, members of America's elite and powerful families aren't serving in Iraq or Afghanistan. Only a handful of members of Congress, for example, have children or other relatives in the uniformed services. Instead, kids from rural, poor, and working-class families are being enticed, and aggressively recruited, to serve. As the wars drag on, the military has been forced to lower standards for recruits' educational, criminal, health, and psychological status in order to fill their stretched ranks. Fairness? Equality of sacrifice? Those concepts aren't even slogans any more; they've simply been forgotten.

Generation We and all other citizens of conscience must have the courage and strength to stand up and say "Enough!" to the purveyors of war.

MILLENNIAL PERIL, MILLENNIAL OPPORTUNITY

Simply put, Generation We inherits a planet in peril, in which plunderers who treat the world as their private property are exploiting institutions of government, society, and business to control resources, manipulate media and markets, and sell out the long-term interests of their nation and the world for personal short-term gain.

These hostile trends aren't accidental, nor are they unconnected. They form a pattern by which plunderers and speculators seek to manipulate society so as to maintain and expand their own power and wealth. A former president and first lady used to speak about "a vast right-wing conspiracy." Here, if anywhere, is the real conspiracy—collusion among business and governmental leaders, media moguls, educators, and religious leaders who have contrived national and international systems that serve to keep the people weak, fearful, helpless, and under control. The goal of this conspiracy is not to impose ideological or political doctrine but simply to control the world's power and wealth.

©KAREN KASMAUSKI/CORBIS

These systems keep people sick and drained of energy through food that is nonnutritive, healthcare that is unaffordable, and an environment that is toxic. They keep people ignorant through an educational system that stifles dissent, stultifies creativity, and deadens the mind. They keep people physically and psychologically dependent through reliance on illegal drugs, pharmaceuticals, other addictive substances such as nicotine, caffeine, and alcohol, and addictive behaviors such as gambling,

Here, if anywhere, is the real conspiracy—collusion among business and governmental leaders, media moguls, educators, and religious leaders who have contrived national and international systems that serve to keep the people weak, fearful, helpless, and under control. The goal of this conspiracy is not to impose ideological or political doctrine but simply to control the world's power and wealth.

electronic games, and mindless entertainment. They prosecute and convict record numbers of youth, especially minorities, to keep them from exercising the power of their numbers in the political system. They keep people frightened through constant drum-beating for war, exaggerated threats of terrorism, and media-created bogeymen (from Islamist extremists to illegal immigrants). And they keep people helpless through out-of-control debt, brain-numbing work, and financial dependency.

...systems that serve to keep the people weak, fearful, helpless, and under control.

Their goal: to create a world in which the majority of the population are like high-paid serfs, unable or unwilling to organize, protest, or assert themselves and capable only of serving their corporate masters.

Journalist and television commentator Bill Moyers has written eloquently about the decline in social and economic equality even as an ideal in American society:

> Equality is not an objective that can be achieved but it is a goal worth fighting for. A more equal society would bring us closer to the "self-evident truth" of our common humanity. I remember the early 1960s, when for a season one could imagine progress among the races, a nation finally accepting immigrants for their value not only to the economy but to our collective identity, a people sniffing the prospect of progress. One could look at the person who is different in some particular way—skin color, language, religion—without feeling fear. America, so long the exploiter of the black, red, brown, and yellow, was feeling its oats; we were on our way to becoming the land of opportunity, at last. Now inequality—especially between wealth and worker—has opened like an unbridgeable chasm.
>
> Ronald Reagan once described a particular man he knew who was good steward of resources in the biblical sense. "This is a man," Reagan said, "who in his own business, before he entered politics, instituted a profit-sharing plan, before unions had ever thought of it. He put in health and medical insurance for all his employees. He took 50 percent of the profits before taxes and set up a retirement program, a pension plan for all his employees. He sent checks for life to an employee who was ill and couldn't work. He provided nursing care for the children of mothers who worked in the stores."
>
> That man was Barry Goldwater, a businessman before he entered politics. It's incredible how far we have deviated from even the most conservative understanding of social responsibility. For a generation now Goldwater's children [i.e., leaders of the modern conservative movement founded

They keep people ignorant through an educational system that stifles dissent, stultifies creativity, and deadens the mind. They keep people physically and psychologically dependent through reliance on illegal drugs, pharmaceuticals, other addictive substances such as nicotine, caffeine, and alcohol, and addictive behaviors such as gambling, electronic games, and mindless entertainment. They prosecute and convict record numbers of youth, especially minorities, to keep them from exercising the power of their numbers in the political system.

interaction, eye-to-eye contact, and public assembly.

Generation We needs to translate its social consciousness into real-life action. Happily, there are many signs they are beginning to do just that.

THE GLOBAL SPREAD OF KNOWLEDGE

Generation We is acutely aware of the gradually spreading availability of higher education, both within the United States and around the world, and they view this as a trend with potentially enormous beneficial impact. It's something they see at work in their own lives. In fact, many participants in our focus groups spoke with pride about how they've enjoyed greater educational opportunities than their parents or grandparents could have dreamed of, and how this has opened doors in terms of lifestyle and career that otherwise would have remained forever shut.

In a broader sense, Generation We is benefiting from an emerging sense of unity among the world's peoples as cultures around the planet become shared and linked. It's something they can see, hear, and feel happening all around them. They see "world music" as *their* music. Problems of poverty, disease, and hunger in Africa and Asia are *their* problems. Opportunities for women in traditional societies to finally control their own destinies and for children to receive the nutrition, healthcare, and schooling they need to live full lives are *their* concerns.

This movement toward planetary integration can have either a negative or a positive impact. If it is controlled by plunderers, financial speculators, arms makers, megamedia, or energy companies for their own benefit, its overall impact will be negative, resulting in a world where individuality and indigenous cultures are homogenized or replaced by corporate-controlled replicas and where the wealth of local economies is channeled for purely private gain. But if the peoples of the world, especially the youth, insist that it be used for the benefit of all, its impact will be incredibly positive.

ENVIRONMENTAL AWARENESS AND HOLISTIC THINKING

Because Generation We has been raised from infancy in the midst of a reawakening awareness of the fragility of the environment and an appreciation for its value, they are uniquely positioned to consider the long-term environmental impacts of everything they do. This is a natural remedy for the short-term thinking that has dominated most human behavior and that has helped to create our current dilemmas.

What's more, the heightened environmental awareness of Generation We encourages them to take a *holistic* approach to the problems they face. They are accustomed to thinking about the world as a set of interlocking systems that have profound, complex effects on one another, and they are acutely aware—perhaps more so than previous generations—of how the law of unintended consequences can produce devastating results when interactions aren't considered and planned for.

Millennials are inclined to extend this holistic mode of thinking beyond the natural world and into the social, economic, and political realms. When discussing problems in our focus groups, the Millennials routinely brushed aside the boundaries between the government, business, non-profit, academic, and civic worlds. They are impatient with dogmatic or ideological "rules" about the proper spheres of action for various kinds of organizations, and instead are accustomed to thinking pragmatically about how social groups and institutions can cooperate in search of solutions that serve society as a whole.

Former Vice President Al Gore said it well:

> There is an African proverb that says, "If you want to go quickly, go alone. If you want to go far, go together." We need to go far, quickly.
>
> We must abandon the conceit that individual, isolated, private actions are the answer. They can and do help. But they will not take us far enough without collective action.[37]

Generation We has embraced Gore's insight. Whether the most effective answer to a global problem can come from a government agency, or a for-profit business, or a university researcher, or a volunteer group, Generation We is happy to embrace it. For them, this is one world, and the combined efforts of everyone are required to make and keep it healthy.

Q53

Please tell us whether you agree or disagree with the statement. (IF AGREE) Does this situation represent a crisis that our country must address immediately, a major problem that must be addressed soon, or a minor problem that should be addressed eventually?

	Agree Crisis	Agree Major Prob.	Agree Minor Prob.	Dis-Agree	DK/ Ref	Total Agree
Our nation's continuing dependence on oil has weakened our economy and stifled innovation, left us dependent on foreign countries - some of whom sponsor terrorism against us - and dragged us into unnecessary wars.	37	42	15	6	1	93
With costs rising out of control and the quality of health coverage declining, the healthcare system in our country is broken, and we need to make fundamental changes.	38	42	15	6	1	93
The growing burden placed on our country by our massive national debt is hurting our economy, stifling job growth and investment and making it harder for American businesses and entrepeneurs to be competitive in the global marketplace.	22	43	27	8	0	92
The health of our country is collapsing under an epidemic of chronic, preventable diseases as we slowly poison our own bodies through environmental pollution, overmedication, and unhealthy diets.	28	43	22	7	0	93
We have an unequal education system in our country, where students in affluent areas enjoy better resources and learning environments while those in rural areas and inner cities too often receive and inferior education.	31	40	21	8	0	92
Man-made causes are destroying our environment and the Earth's delicate ecosystem. As a result, we could see massive, irreversible damage to the Earth's landscape during our lifetimes.	35	39	18	9	0	91
Our country must take extreme measures now, before it is too late, to protect the environment and begin to reverse the damage we have done.	33	41	20	6	-	94
The federal debt is exploding, with no end in sight, shifting a tremendous burden onto future generations to pay for the failed leadership of the current generation and weakening America's economic growth for decades to come.	30	44	21	5	0	94
The changing nature of America's economy, where we import most of our goods and export millions of jobs to developing countries, is threatening America's middle class.	26	43	24	7	0	92
Long-term jobs that provide comprehensive health benefits and retirement security are becoming a thing of the past, and individuals in our generation will have to provide for their own health care and retirement security.	32	42	18	7	0	93
Americans' basic civil rights are being undermined more every day. Government and business have compromised our privacy, the corporate media tells us what they want us to hear rather than the facts, and justice is for sale to anyone who can afford the right lawyers.	31	38	24	7	0	92

SOURCE: GREENBERG MILLENNIAL SURVEY 2007

continues on next page...

Q53 (continued)

	Agree Crisis	Agree Major Prob.	Agree Minor Prob.	Dis-Agree	DK/ Ref	Total Agree
From the failed response to Huricane Katrina to persistent fraud, corruption, and abuse, our government has failed to meet its most basic responsibilities and violated the very taxpayers who fund it.	30	41	20	9	0	90
Government is dominated by special interests and lobyists, who give millions of dollars in campaign contributions to politicians, who in turn give even more back to those special interests, while the rest of us are left holding the bag.	31	42	21	5	0	95
Hurricane Katrina revealed the extent to which our country is divided into two Americas, one of which lacks many basic needs and is largely ignored by our government. The growing gap between the wealthy and the rest of us must be addressed, because no democracy can survive without a large, vibrant middle class.	30	40	20	9	0	90
Our reliance on fossil fuels is a by-product of the interests of those currently in power. We need to invest in and innovate new energy sources in order to protect our quality of life and prosperity.	33	43	19	4	0	96

4 A CLEAR VISION

BEYOND THE RED PILL AND THE BLUE PILL

Getting Past Dogma

Thanks to the positive forces we've described and the expanding world of possibilities in the minds of the young, workable solutions to the threats we face are possible—especially if the people of the world's most dynamic and powerful society, the United States, take the lead. But there is a major psychological stumbling block we must first overcome.

For the past generation, Americans have been divided and distracted by bogus issues and false divisions—among ideologies (blue states versus red states, conservatives versus liberals), ethnicities (white versus black versus latino), genders (male versus female), and religious groups (fundamentalist Christians versus secular humanists versus Jews, Muslims, and what-have-you).

Over the past three decades, we've been increasingly focused on two and only two alternatives: the *"Red Pill"* offered by the Republican Party (culture wars, religious dogmatism, social intolerance, destruction of the social contract, and thoughtless militarism) and the *"Blue Pill"* of the Democratic Party (old-fashioned liberalism, pandering to unions and trial lawyers, reflexive anti-corporatism, and the politics of interest groups and ethnic identity). And throughout that period, these two choices have both been growing increasingly irrelevant and unhelpful.

The problem is that of dogma. Two opposing forces, which are driven by extremists in their ranks, have transformed politics from problem-solving into ideological warfare. Extremists tend to dominate the parties by voting in larger numbers in primary elections and by using their passion and organizational zeal to push specific agenda items and policy platforms. As a result, the extremes of the two parties drive candidates to pander to their narrow view of the world.

Because of their vast numbers and shared values, Generation We can sweep away the extremists and their phony issues and unite around a new approach to national politics. Having to choose between a Red Pill or a Blue Pill has caused the diseased state of our politics today.

©ILJA MAŠÍK/SHUTTERSTOCK IMAGES

We say, don't take either pill. Pills only obscure your vision and weaken your ability to get anything done for the greater good.

By taking no pills, one gets to the real solution: an unobscured Clear Vision that goes beyond the ideological constraints of the existing parties. The Clear Vision focuses on solving the problems that face all Americans and the planet rather than pandering to special interests, fringe groups, and far-right or far-left dogmatism.

The Clear Vision can unify our nation through the rebirth and revival of our brilliantly designed political system. Alexander Hamilton, in *The Federalist Papers* (number 51), explains eloquently how the system of checks and balances he and the other Founders created can prevent any narrow group from seizing control of our country and ensure that the greater good will eventually triumph:

> In order to lay a due foundation for that separate and distinct exercise of the different powers of government, which to a certain extent is admitted on all hands to be essential to the preservation of liberty, it is evident that each department should have a will of its own; and consequently should be so constituted that the members of each should have as little agency as possible in the appointment of the members of the others...
>
> But the great security against a gradual concentration of the several powers in the same department, consists in giving to those who administer each department the necessary constitutional means and personal motives to resist encroachments of the others. The provision for defense must in this, as in all other cases, be made commensurate to the danger of attack.
>
> Ambition must be made to counteract ambition. The interest of the man must be connected with the constitutional rights of the place. It may be a reflection on human nature, that such devices should be necessary to control the abuses of government. But what is government itself, but the greatest of all reflections on human nature? If men were angels, no government would be necessary. If angels were to govern men, neither external nor internal controls on government would be necessary.
>
> In framing a government which is to be administered by men over men, the great difficulty lies in this: you must first enable the government to control the governed; and in the next place oblige it to control itself. A dependence on the people is, no doubt, the primary control on the government; but experience has taught mankind the necessity of auxiliary precautions.

As a result, the extremes of the two parties drive candidates to pander to their narrow view of the world.

We need to return to the belief in the greater good shared by our nation's Founders and expressed in that magnificent document of nation-building, the U.S. Constitution.

"Politics hates a vacuum. If it isn't filled with hope, someone will fill it with fear."

NAOMI KLEIN

> This policy of supplying, by opposite and rival interests, the defect of better motives, might be traced through the whole system of human affairs, private as well as public. We see it particularly displayed in all the subordinate distributions of power, where the constant aim is to divide and arrange the several offices in such a manner as that each may be a check on the other—that the private interest of every individual may be a sentinel over the public rights. These inventions of prudence cannot be less requisite in the distribution of the supreme powers of the State.

We need to return to the belief in the greater good shared by our nation's Founders and expressed in that magnificent document of nation-building, the U.S. Constitution.

THE PROBLEM WITH A THIRD PARTY

How can this happen in practical, political terms? It *could* mean the creation of a new party. We've become so conditioned to see politics in terms of a black-and-white, either/or, Democratic/Republican divide, we almost forget that there is nothing sacrosanct or preordained about the existence of two and only two political parties. Many democracies in Europe and elsewhere have three or more viable parties, which increases the number of ideas in circulation, and promotes a healthy competition for voter support.

The two parties that have dominated the American system since the 1860s do not enjoy any sort of permanent mandate but are merely human creations arising from the accidents of history, like most other institutions. The Democratic Party as we know it today was founded in 1828 through the organizational efforts of Martin Van Buren, in support of the presidential candidacy of Andrew Jackson.

The Republican Party originated in 1854 as a third-party alternative to the then-dominant Democratic and Whig Parties; it rose to power behind the candidacy of Abraham Lincoln at the time of our country's greatest crisis. (In fact, the slavery crisis was so serious, it actually destroyed the two-party system as it then existed, leading to an 1860 election that featured no fewer than four serious parties—the Democrats, the Republicans, the Southern Democratic Party, and the Constitutional Union Party. The latter two parties soon disappeared.)

In theory, there's no reason why a new party could not be formed in today's time of crisis. It's even conceivable that a party driven mainly by members of Generation We, focused on the issues they are concerned with and reflecting their unique generational perspective, could become a major contender alongside the two traditional parties.

However, history shows that third-party efforts in the United States rarely succeed. Dozens of parties have been launched over the

Q89

How effective do you think political activism is a means of solving the major challenges facing our country?

	A
Very	18
Somewhat	51
A little	25
Not at all	6
(Don't know/refused)	1
Very/somewhat	**69**
Little/not	**31**

SOURCE: GREENBERG MILLENNIAL SURVEY 2007

decades, most of which quickly faded after having little impact. Even those that attracted support from significant shares of the electorate—such as the Populist Party, which won 8 percent of the vote in 1892, and the Progressive Party, which tallied more than 16 percent in 1924—never came close to winning the White House or any major presence in the U.S. Congress. Structural barriers, including the Electoral College, the winner-take-all voting system, and the complex hurdle system involved in 50 separate state ballot access laws, make it almost impossible for a third party to challenge the Democrats and the Republicans successfully on a national basis.

Thus, the idea of a Millennial Party or even a new Progressive Party aimed mainly at members of Generation We is probably not a practical one, nor is it one we support. A more plausible idea is a new social and political movement based on honesty, responsibility, and innovative thinking—a movement with the potential to influence, infiltrate, and take over one of the existing parties, or to form a grand alliance of shared goals that changes the agenda of *both* parties and uses the existing system to produce a positive revolution.

If a Millennial movement ended up transforming one of our major political parties, it would *not* be an unprecedented event in history. There are several examples of outside movements that have profoundly shaped, and in some cases eventually controlled, one of the traditional political parties. The Populist Party of the 1890s advocated a number of policies that eventually were adopted by the Democrats, and in more recent years, right-wing movements such as the Christian Coalition have had a powerful impact on the positions of the Republican Party.

In the wake of the 2008 election, which experts and analysts of every persuasion are already labeling as one of the great tidal shifts of American history, there is a huge opportunity for whichever party steps up to the Millennial challenge and offers the younger generation the fresh vision they are seeking. Such a party—whichever it is—has the potential to lead a sweeping realignment, and dominate national politics for the next 40 years.

The Clear Vision, unobscured by extremist dogma, breaks away from the trends of the last generation. Rather than an extrapolation from current ideas or opinions, it represents a glimpse of timeless wisdom that transcends the processes in which we've been trapped.

It's a vision of hope rather than one of despair; of higher purpose rather than selfishness; of a restored sense of fairness and justice for all people, rather than for a privileged few.

It's a vision of shared prosperity, of global security and peace, and of innovation and progress in the service of all humankind.

It's a vision in which government, business, education, and other social institutions will be run by leaders who are committed to integrity and honesty; in which secrecy and hidden agenda will be replaced

honesty
shared goals
innovative responsibility
thinking

by transparency and authenticity.

It's a vision in which exploitation of the world and its natural resources is replaced by an attitude of responsible, loving stewardship, and in which human beings treat creation with caring and kindness rather than cruelty.

And finally, it's a vision of a world without boundaries—a living planet glimpsed as if from outer space (a vision with which Generation We, unlike previous generations, grew up).

This is not an "end times" vision like the one some religious and political groups seek to foster. No one in his or her right mind wants to see apocalypse in their time. Yet some irresponsible spiritual and secular leaders are encouraging end-times thinking among their followers. The fact that some right-wing religious demagogues believe their job is to accelerate the end of history makes them enemies of the young. No wonder they are conscripting the young into their wars—to use them and ultimately to kill them.

Apocalyptic thinking in a less-extreme but ultimately also deadly form has infected the so-called mainstream of political thinking as well. The unsustainable debt rolled up by our political leaders in the last decade is a vivid example. Other examples include the plundering of our economy by financial and corporate leaders; the destruction of the environment by businesses that are seemingly incapable of thinking beyond the next quarter; and the depletion of resources like oil, gas, clean water, clean air, and the rain forests. An entire cadre of international leaders has chosen to run the planet as if there will be no tomorrow—or as if some magical breakthrough will happen all by itself to rescue their children from the death spiral in which they find themselves.

There is no magic. If a breakthrough is to occur, it will have to come from millions of young people saying, "Enough!"

The young need to reject the deathly vision in favor of the natural vision of life all healthy beings share—a vision of growing up, having fun, falling in love, raising families, traveling the world, and helping to build a better future.

If we love our planet and hope to live happily on it for generations to come, we need to act like it. Remember, actions speak louder than words. Now is the time to put up or shut up. This philosophy needs to be at the heart of the Millennial vision.

"The dogmas of the quiet past are inadequate to the stormy present. The occasion is piled high with difficulty, and we must rise with the occasion. As our case is new, so we must think anew and act anew."

ABRAHAM LINCOLN

Q68

Thinking about the many challenges facing our country, do you feel the best way to address these challenges is...through individual action and entrepreneurship, through a collective social movement, through the media and popular culture, through government action, or through international cooperation? And what do you feel is the second best way to address these challenges?

SOURCE: GREENBERG MILLENNIAL SURVEY 2007

A

	Comb	1st	2nd
A collective social movement	60	38	22
Government action	40	16	24
Individual action and entrepreneurship	35	16	19
Media and popular culture	33	16	17
International cooperation	30	12	18
(Don't know/refused)	1	1	1

5 THE EMERGENCE OF GENERATION WE

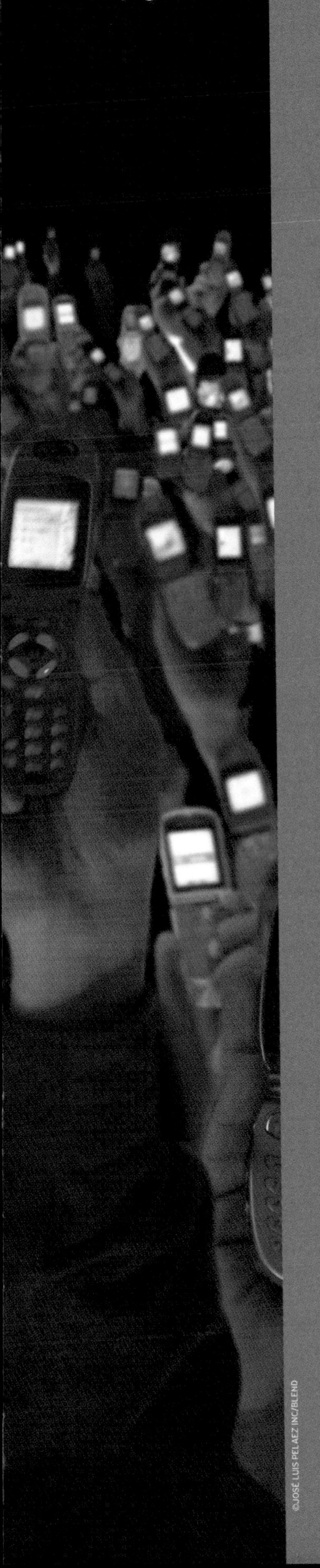

Images of Hope

We live in a cynical world. Many of those reading these pages are already immersed in doubt and despair. They're ready to dismiss the vision we're trying to evoke by calling it "naive," "unrealistic," or "utopian." They're eager to deny the potential for greatness contained in Generation We and to condemn today's youth to living out their lives in the same quagmire of quiet desperation their parents have experienced.

Life is tough, and the challenges Generation We will face are profoundly difficult. We know that. But we also know that the resources the Millennials will bring to the struggle are impressive. What's more, there are already signs the Millennials are beginning to rise to the challenge.

Deeply affected by the terror attacks of 9/11, the disastrous Iraq War, the horror of Hurricane Katrina, and the cynical dishonesty of the Bush administration, Generation We is already responding with their unique brand of social and political awareness. Using data from the GMS and other studies, as well as evidence from news stories and emerging trends that are popping up around us on an almost daily basis, we can see how the Millennials are beginning to shape their world, giving a foretaste of the changes to come.

As we've already mentioned, Generation We is history's most active volunteering generation. They are looking for—and finding—ways to change the world, redefining the boundary lines between work, education, government, charity, and politics through social entrepreneurship and creative new forms of business. They are also forming international bonds, combining their unprecedented opportunities to see the world with new planetary perspective on the issues and problems faced by humankind.

"A small body of determined spirits fired by an unquenchable faith in their mission can alter the course of history."

MOHANDAS K. GANDHI

Generation We is also using the power of the purse to influence business, shaping their consuming activities to influence the behavior of major corporations. For example, the widespread outrage that brought down the Boomer-beloved radio shock jock Don Imus in 2007 was initially sparked by a Millennial activist, Ryan Chiachiere. Working for the website Media Matters for America, the 26-year-old Chiachiere found the offensive video clip of Imus using racial and sexual stereotypes to slur the members of the Rutgers women's basketball team. He circulated the clip using one of Generation We's favorite technologies—YouTube. The resulting furor led to Imus's firing by CBS and his ultimate relegation to a far less influential radio slot on a different network.[1]

The buying power of the Millennials is now poised to be a driving force behind the growing "green revolution."

ALWAYS CONNECTED, AND WIELDING TECHNOLOGY TO CHANGE THE WORLD

As we've discussed—and as both our survey results and our Millennial focus groups brought home in a vivid way—new technologies for generating, communicating, and sharing information have been crucial in shaping the identity of Generation We. Now they are using these new technologies to shape the world—often in ways the developers of those technologies never intended.

One of the earliest and most dramatic examples of the power of technology in the hands of Millennials has been their use of peer-to-peer file-sharing to transform the entertainment industry.

For decades, record companies had controlled the production and distribution of recorded music, charging prices that many consumers viewed as excessive and forcing them to buy the same music in multiple formats—vinyl albums, cassettes, eight-track tapes, CDs—as delivery systems evolved. The creation of the broadband-enabled Internet and peer-to-peer (P2P) file-sharing technology opened the door for an entirely new, noncentralized system for distributing music. As implemented by companies such as Napster (founded in May 1999), P2P technology lets computer users exchange files—including files of digitized music—quickly and easily via the Internet. Within months, songs by the billion were being traded cost-free through cyberspace, and CD sales began a decline that has still not halted.

The record companies struggled to respond. Some tried to launch their own systems for downloading digital music files, but these were costly, had limited offerings, and attracted few customers. Finally, in exasperation, the record industry launched a series of copyright violation lawsuits against both the P2P service providers and the music-sharers themselves, even suing teenagers who'd swapped songs with online friends. (Notably, they sued only relatively poor and powerless

NEW TECHNOLOGIES

86% 18-25 year olds use email everyday

18-25 year olds read their news online everyday **56%**

41% 18-25 year olds use MySpace or Facebook everyday

Respondents reported spending an average of 21.3 hours a week online **21.3**

SOURCE: GQR SURVEY, APRIL 2006

individuals, as if to emphasize the fact that the real purpose of the suits was intimidation.)

©POLKA DOT IMAGES/FOTOSEARCH
©IMAGE SOURCE/BLEND

Although the record companies won some of their lawsuits, the industry's decline has continued. The ease and power of digital file-sharing is simply too great to be controlled through legal prohibitions. Only Steve Jobs and Apple Computer understood the sentiment of the generation and the power of the download. The emergence of the iTunes legal download store as a way to protect the industry has actually brought Apple and its proprietary iPod to the center of industry control. Apple now controls a large percentage of media content distribution and monetization because they recognized the changing forces and came up with a solution tailored to the behavior.

Perhaps the most important effects of the legal battle between record companies and music fans have been on the social and political attitudes of Generation We. As aptly stated by Morley Winograd and Michael D. Hais in their book *Millennial Makeover*:

> The effect of this legal war was to create a permanent mindset on the part of the Millennial generation that entrenched special interests would stop at nothing to prevent them from sharing information on the Net that was, or at least ought to be, inherently "free." Along the way, the struggle helped make Millennials suspicious of all elites attempting to control what they were allowed to know, whether it was the latest Indie band or the real story behind a political debate.

This dual theme—the tremendous power of the Internet to make information of every kind readily available to those who are technologically savvy, coupled with the sense of suspicion and resentment directed toward those in business and government who would control and limit the flow of that information for their own selfish objectives—is one we heard repeatedly in our Millennial focus groups. Today's young people *know* they have the power to uncover and master the truth about their world, and they are determined not to let the powers-that-be manipulate them into abandoning that power.

The power of file-sharing technologies to shape social and political change was illustrated in a dramatic way by an emblematic and game-changing incident in the 2006 election campaign. In August, U.S. Senator George Allen was seemingly cruising to reelection in Virginia against his Democratic challenger, former U.S. Navy Secretary Jim Webb. With his down-home style, populist credentials, and conserva-

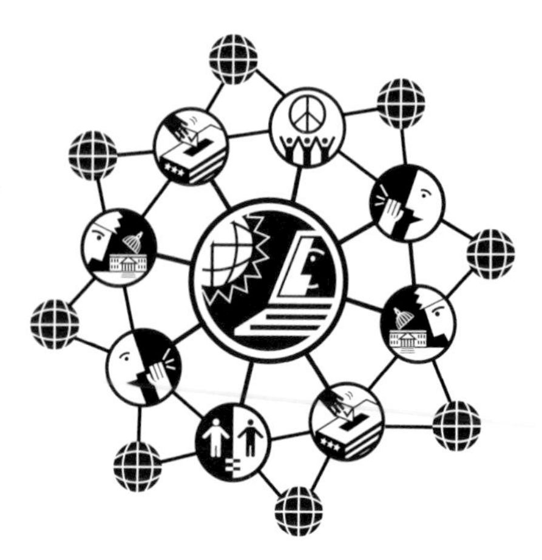

tive views, Allen was regarded by many as one of the front runners for the 2008 Republican presidential nomination.

All of that changed thanks to a bit of video footage captured by a volunteer for the Webb campaign. At an informal outdoor event, Allen singled out the young volunteer with the camera, an American of Indian descent named S. R. Sidarth (a member of Generation We, born in 1985). In a mocking tone, Allen called Sidarth *macaca* and sarcastically told him, "Welcome to America and the real world of Virginia."

It was a bit of casual bigotry—stupid and mean-spirited—that in past elections would likely have caused some short-lived embarrassment for the Allen campaign. But the Webb campaign posted the video clip on YouTube. When word got around, millions of people visited the site to watch the amazing gaffe. And Allen's blunder led to further embarrassments. Reporters investigating the origin of the strange ethnic slur *"macaca"* discovered that Allen's mother was a Jewish immigrant from Algeria (where the term is commonly used)—a previously unknown fact about Allen's background. Rather than responding with pride, Allen acted ashamed, denying his Jewish heritage with lame jokes about his mother serving him ham sandwiches—jokes that also wound up being circulated via YouTube.

It was a perfect storm of anti-Millennial gaffes: an ethnic insult (anathema to the ultra-tolerant Millennial generation) directed against a Millennial, and captured and distributed using the Millennials' favorite electronic technology, streaming file-shared video. Candidate Allen paid a heavy price. Within two weeks, his support among young voters had fallen by 40 points.[3] In November, voter turnout reached record levels for a midterm election in Virginia, led by huge numbers in the university towns dominated by Generation We. Despite outspending his opponent nearly three to one, Allen lost to Jim Webb and saw his presidential dreams go down the drain.[4]

It's not an accident that the Republican Allen was one of the most prominent victims of Millennials' new brand of electronic politicking in 2006. The progressive orientation of Generation We is reflected in the social networking they are practicing. In 2007, when a 26-year-old Facebook member launched a web page for supporters of Barack Obama's presidential campaign, he had more than 278,000 members signed up within months.[5] Relying on the Internet to reach out to small donors, Obama has set one fundraising record after another throughout the 2007–2008 campaign season.

Generation We played a key role in creating social networking, potentially the most significant social innovation driven by the Internet. According to one estimate, half of all Millennials are members of Facebook, and almost two-thirds have pages on MySpace.[6] Now these and other social networks are changing how products get launched, ideas get spread, and causes get traction.

The emergence of Generation We as a powerful voting bloc supporting progressive causes and candidates isn't happening by accident or purely as a result of broad social trends. It is also being spurred by a generation of activists, mostly themselves of Millennial age, who are building political organizations to educate, empower, and mobilize young people over the long term.

VOTER STRENGTH

Voter turnout among 18-24 year-olds

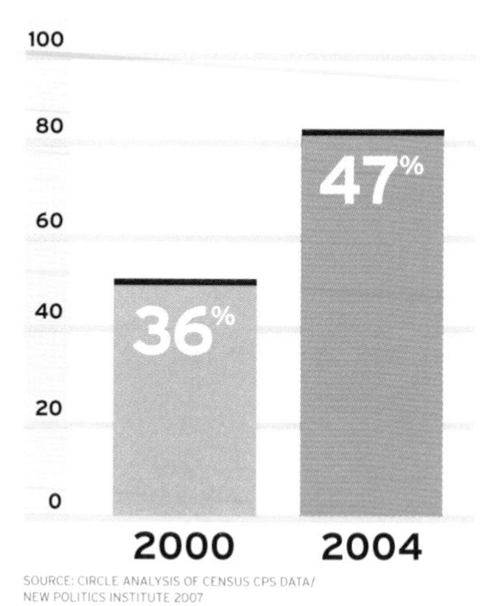

SOURCE: CIRCLE ANALYSIS OF CENSUS CPS DATA/ NEW POLITICS INSTITUTE 2007

Journalist Ben Adler discovered many groups on Facebook dedicated to reform of the American healthcare system. When he looked more closely, he found that these groups tilt decidedly toward the progressive side of the debate: A "perusal of Facebook groups," he wrote, "most with hundreds or more than a thousand members, on the health-care issue shows more than 20 that advocate some form of expanded government provisioning of coverage. But only three groups that actually oppose universal health care exist, all of them with just 100 members at the time of this writing."[7]

SWINGING ELECTIONS

Generation We is voting and participating in politics far more than past youthful cohorts. As a result, they've already influenced three national elections. They made the 2004 presidential race far closer than it otherwise would have been, and they tipped the 2006 Congressional elections firmly into the laps of the Democrats. The national party included improved college access for all as a part of their 2006 agenda, and once they won the majority, they passed laws providing for increased Pell grants and reductions in the interest rates paid by students on educational loans.

There are a number of specific Congressional elections we can point to as having been determined by Millennial voters. For example, in Connecticut's Second District, Democrat Joe Courtney ran on a platform that promised to make affordability of college a topic of legislative priority. Turnout at the University of Connecticut (located in the Second District) increased sharply, and Courtney unseated Republican Rob Simmons by a margin of just over 100 votes. Courtney followed through on his promise by sponsoring a bill to help low-income students attend college.

Similarly, an analysis by the Harvard Institute of Politics concluded that two Democratic victories in the Senate—those of Jim Webb in Virginia and Jon Tester in Montana—could be attributed to increased turnout among voters age 18 to 24.[8]

As we write, Generation We is helping to shape the outcome of the bellwether 2008 presidential election. Shortly after the primary elections ended in June

©BETH CONANT/ACCLAIM

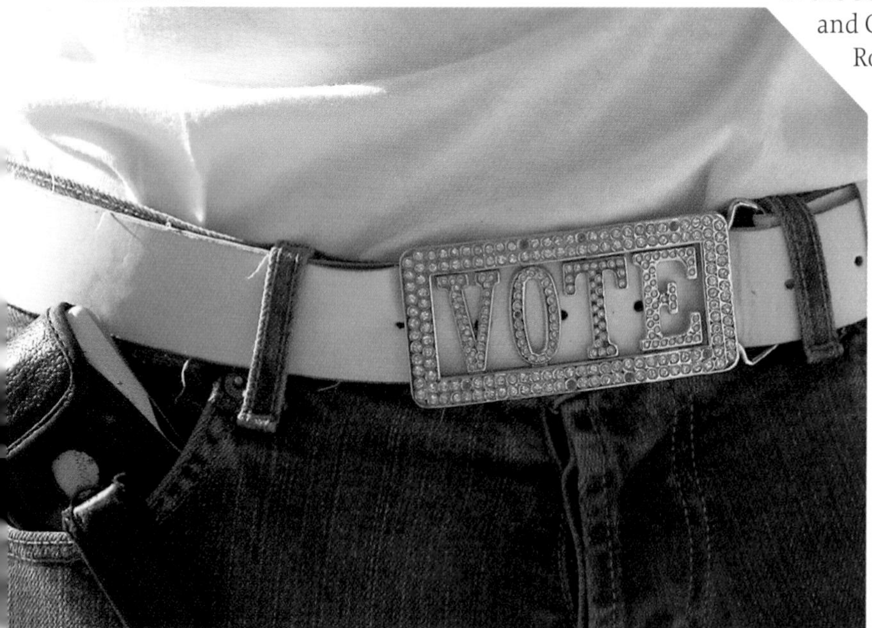

2008, Declare Yourself, a national nonpartisan youth voting initiative, completed its analysis of voting by young people. It found that voters age 18 to 29 turned out in record numbers in 2008, casting more than 6 million ballots in the Democratic and Republican races. Of those, about 4.9 million voted for Democrats. The youth turnout was more than *double* that of the 2000 and 2004 primaries and made up 14.5 percent of the total electorate, compared with 9.4 percent in 2004.[9]

Among political pros, conventional wisdom has long held that "Young people don't vote," which means that their positions on issues can be safely ignored. (By contrast, old people *do* vote, which helps to explain why Social Security, Medicare, and other programs tailored to help the elderly have always been treated as *"the third rail"* of politics, to be touched by politicians only at their peril.) The conventional wisdom is now being overturned. Young people—at least in their new Millennial incarnation—do indeed vote, and politicians are going to have to learn to pay attention to their concerns. It's about time.

The emergence of Generation We as a powerful voting bloc supporting progressive causes and candidates isn't happening by accident or purely as a result of broad social trends. It is also being spurred by a generation of activists, mostly themselves of Millennial age, who are building political organizations to educate, empower, and mobilize young people over the long term. Just as an earlier generation of activists with a very different agenda created the network of right-wing groups on campus, in local communities, in the business world, and in the media that helped to produce the conservative ascendancy of the 1980s, 1990s, and early 2000s, this new generation is determined to create a powerful base for progressive activism that will help shape the political landscape for decades to come.

Young people—at least in their new Millennial incarnation—do indeed vote, and politicians are going to have to learn to pay attention to their concerns. It's about time.

The emergence and growth of this Millennial political infrastructure is a rapidly changing story. One good recent survey of the current scene is the book *Youth to Power* by blogger and activist Michael Connery, himself the cofounder of one of the organizations he describes (Music for America, a youth-oriented get-out-the-vote operation mobilized for the 2004 presidential election). Among the organizations Connery describes:

- **The Young Elected Officials Network (YEO)**, founded by 2005 by 25-year-old Andrew Gillum, the youngest elected city commissioner in the history of Tallahassee, Florida. Devoted to the needs of the 4.8 percent of elected officials who are younger than 35, YEO holds national conferences in which its members are trained in electoral politics and meet with one another on policy and program topics. YEO also provides mentoring and conducts regular teleconferences on emerging issues, helping to build a national net-

PHOTOS: SANDRA KELCH

work of young leaders interested in pursuing a Millennial agenda. The initial YEO membership of 60 has grown to 318 in 2007.[10]

- **Campus Progress**, which is working to build a progressive presence in America's colleges and universities by launching publications and providing a roster of speakers who can counter the near-ubiquity of right-wing pundits like Michelle Malkin and Ann Coulter. Founded not by a Millennial but by Gen Xer David Halperin (a former Clinton staffer now in his mid-forties), Campus Progress supports 47 campus magazines and newspapers, maintains its own online magazine which draws more than 200,000 visitors per month, and has helped to organize campaigns involving numerous on- and off-campus organizations around issues such as global warming, student debt, and the war in Iraq.[11]

- **The Roosevelt Institute**, one of a handful of fledgling progressive think-tanks organized by Millennials as a direct response to such massive and powerful right-ring think tanks as the Hoover and Cato Institutes and the Heritage Foundation. Founded in 2004 by Kai Stinchombe, then a 22-year-old doctoral student in political science at Stanford University, the Roosevelt Institute now has over 7,000 members at 60 universities, who conduct research and hold conferences on topics ranging from health care reform to the living wage.[12]

The millions of progressives in Generation We have quite a way to go before they can equal the institutional, financial, and electoral clout the conservative movement has amassed over the past 40 years. But the demographics are on their side—and so is time. Today, the progressive resurgence spearheaded by Generation We is of similar proportion to the progressive swing in 1932, when Roosevelt was ushered into power for four terms and implemented the New Deal. We may be in a place that is roughly comparable to that occupied by the conservatives in the late 1960s and early 1970s—witnessing the massive failure and crack-up of the opposition and just beginning to mobilize the positive response that will ultimately sweep the nation.

AN EMERGING GENERATION OF LEADERS

If you're a Baby Boomer, you may have noticed that one kind of social activism your generation was famous for back in the day has gone practically unmentioned in this chapter about the emergence of the Millennials—political protest in the form of marches, demonstrations, sit-ins, rallies, and acts of civil disobedience. Maybe you're wondering—when can we expect to see Generation We taking over the streets of America's great cities as a way of promoting change?

It may or may not happen. We live in a new era where new forms of activism are likely to take center stage. The coming wave of change may have a shape that is quite unfamiliar to older veterans of the civil rights marches, antiwar rallies, teach-ins, and campus protests of the 1960s and 1970s.

We live in a new era where new forms of activism are likely to take center stage. The coming wave of change may have a shape that is quite unfamiliar to older veterans of the civil rights marches, antiwar rallies, teach-ins, and campus protests of the 1960s and 1970s.

It would be false to imply that today's youth has completely abandoned traditional street protests and similar kinds of demonstrations. Beginning in 1999, demonstrations against economic globalization have been widespread around the time of significant meetings of groups like the World Trade Organization and the Group of Eight. During the run-up to the Iraq war, protest marches were held in cities around the world, reaching a peak when millions of demonstrators marched against the war on 15 February 2003.[13] However, it's true that demonstrations such as these have drawn less media coverage than similar events in the convulsive years of 1968 and 1969, and partly as a result of the diminished press attention, political activists have looked toward other methods of organizing and mobilizing around their demands for change.

As we'll discuss later in this book, marches, demonstrations, and other forms of "visible activism" can have an impact unmatched by other political activities and therefore should play a role in the coming Millennial-led revolution. But as you're about to discover, taking to the streets isn't the only or even the dominant form of political action in which the Millennials engage.

MILLENNIAL CHANGEMAKERS

The fact is that Generation We is already pioneering new forms of social, economic, and political activism. In the next few pages, we'll briefly profile some of the young leaders who are at the forefront of this movement. Some might be called "liberal," others "conservative," but when we look more closely we see that, in different ways, they all represent the new vision America needs. And they all symbolize the rising activism, energy, creativity, and power of America's Millennials—a group that is coming of age and ready to begin sharing the reins of power. Most important, *they know it.*

Using Film to Spur International Activism

Filmmakers Jason Russell, Bobby Bailey, and Laren Poole hail from San Diego. All Millennials, they made a film called *Invisible Children* dealing with the plight of the people of northern Uganda caught in the midst of a civil war in which thousands of children have been kidnaped and forced to become soldiers. They followed up by creating an organization called Invisible Children, Inc., which holds showings of the film at various educational and cultural centers—mostly high schools and colleges—to raise public awareness in the United States in an attempt to spur youth into action and to change the current policies of both the American and Ugandan governments. On April 28, 2006, 80,000 young people—almost all Millennials—attended peaceful overnight protests to call attention to the Invisible Children cause and to raise money for schools and refugee camps in northern Uganda.[14]

A Social Entrepreneur Making Homes Affordable

Against all odds, the students fended off a proposed 100-million-dollar increase in student fees and obtained a 15-million-dollar bond for low-income student housing.

Bo Menkiti is a real estate mogul with a twist: He is a Millennial based in a rundown neighborhood of Washington, D.C., whose focus is on developing residential properties for low-income home buyers. A cum laude graduate of Harvard Business School, Menkiti founded the Menkiti Group in 2004 to renovate and convert abandoned or neglected buildings into homes and condos for teachers, firefighters, and other first-time real estate buyers. To change the incentives that normally push real estate agents to promote high-end properties rather than affordable homes, Menkiti pays members of his sales team a fixed salary and a commission based on number of homes sold rather than property value. "Housing is a fundamental social good," Menkiti explains, and he says that his agency strives to operate as a for-profit business driven by social objectives.[15]

Collaborating to Create the Automobile of Tomorrow

One of our world's most urgent technological needs is for the next generation of fuel-efficient, ecologically friendly automobiles—a new vision of the motor vehicle that will enable the emerging middle-class millions of China and India to get their own wheels without ravaging our already weakened environment. Rather than waiting for General Motors or Toyota to invent this technology, a group of engineering students at M.I.T. decided to tackle the challenge themselves.

Collaborating with their peers at 35 other universities, students Anna S. Jaffe, Robyn Allen, and the other members of the Vehicle Design Summit (VDS) are at work designing a high-performance four-passenger car that will get 200 miles to the gallon and minimize cradle-to-grave costs for materials, shipping, and waste disposal as

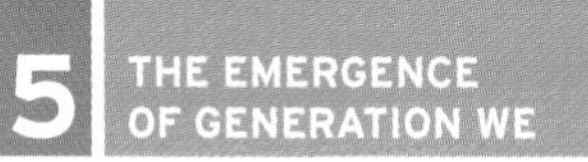

©COMSTOCK/FOTOSEARCH PR99581

well as energy. Perhaps most remarkably, the VDS team has taken a leaf from the Open Source software movement, not merely in its use of Internet-based long-distance collaborative tools but also in its approach to intellectual property rights: All the members of the VDS team are committed to making their inventions freely available to anyone who wants to use them.[16]

Mobilizing Generation We to Shake Up Politics

In 2002, David Smith was the 21-year-old chief of staff of the External Affairs Office of the student government at UC Berkeley. When word got around that the university budget was threatened by the state government's financial woes, Smith organized 150 of his fellow students to travel to the state capital in Sacramento to protect their interests. Against all odds, the students fended off a proposed 100-million-dollar increase in student fees and obtained a 15-million-dollar bond for low-income student housing.

"*What old people say you cannot do, you try and find that you can. Old deeds for old people, and new deeds for new.*"

HENRY DAVID THOREAU

The experience inspired Smith to devote his life to mobilizing Generation We to exercise their political clout. Today he helps run the Democracy 2.0 campaign, a grassroots effort to promote deliberative democracy—a process whereby ordinary citizens gather to study issues, voice their concerns, and develop solutions to our society's most pressing problems. He has also founded Mobilize.org, an "all-partisan" network dedicated to education and empowering young people through its 100 member organizations, 2 million youth advocates, and 75 Mobilizer teams working on college and high school campuses to organize young people around local community issues.[17]

Reaching Across Borders to End Sex Exploitation

Founded in 1995 by Canadian-born Millennial Craig Kielburger (then just 13 years old), Free The Children is the world's largest network of children helping children through education. The organization boasts more than 1 million youth in 45 countries involved in innovative education and development programs, ranging from rescuing Asian teenagers from the sex trade, setting up job cooperatives so parents of Latin American kids won't have to send their children to work, and creating rescue homes for child camel jockeys in the Middle East.

Free The Children has received the World's Children's Prize for the Rights of the Child (also known as the Children's Nobel Prize), the Human Rights Award from the World Association of Non-Governmental Organizations, and has formed successful partnerships with leading school boards and Oprah's Angel Network.[18]

Challenging Charities to Demonstrate Their Effectiveness

Holden Karnofsky and Elie Hassenfeld started their careers at Bridgewater Associates, a financial management firm where their job was to analyze the performance of companies as possible investment opportunities. In 2006, when both were 25, they decided to apply some of the same expertise to nonprofit organizations. Which were achieving real results? Which showed the greatest bang for the buck? Which used their resources most effectively to save or transform lives?

Today Karnofsky and Hassenfeld have abandoned their high-priced financial careers to run GiveWell, a research firm that studies charities and ranks their effectiveness. It's sponsored by the Clear Fund, a philanthropic organization the pair also founded, which makes grants to the charities that GiveWell deems most powerful. If Karnofsky and Hassenfeld get their way, charities in the future will routinely be challenged to *prove* their ability to use donations wisely to improve society—not just to assert it.[19]

Forcing a Social Networking Site to Change Its Policies

Many commentators have pointed to the popularity of social networking sites such as MySpace and Facebook as potential forums for organizing young people in support of political and social causes. As we've noted, progressive activists, including supporters of Barack Obama's presidential campaign, have used the sites to galvanize interest in their causes. Yet the sites themselves are controlled by corporations and run for profit, not for the benefit of their users.

Now some Millennials are trying to change this dynamic. In the fall of 2006, when Facebook unrolled a new feature called "News Feed," which allowed members to track activities of their friends online, Ben Parr, a student at Northwestern, launched a movement to protest the violation of privacy rights. Within days, 700,000 young people had signed on to Parr's protest, and the company was forced to back down.

A year later, when Facebook created "Beacon," a so-called social-advertising program that used member activities to promote products, MoveOn.org created a Facebook group to push back. The MoveOn protestors got Facebook to make Beacon an opt-in rather than an opt-out feature and even convinced some advertisers to steer clear of the program altogether.[20]

Saving AIDS Orphans from Lives of Hopelessness

When Andrew Klaber spent the summer after his sophomore year in college visiting Thailand, he was appalled to see children forced into prostitution after losing their parents to the AIDS epidemic. Determined to make a difference, Klaber—now a 26-year-old student at Harvard Business School—founded Orphans Against AIDS, which pays school expenses for hundreds of parentless kids in Asia and Africa. Klaber and his friends donate their time to running the organization and pay all administrative expenses out of their own pockets, so every dollar donated goes directly to help the children.[21]

These stories and numerous others we could cite all demonstrate the same point—many members of Generation We already beginning to change our world for the better. All they need now is the support of other generations and an overarching plan behind which we can unite.

6 GRAND ALLIANCE

A Turning Point for America

As we've mentioned, Generation We is already the largest generation in U.S. history. *By 2016, American Millennials—including young people who immigrate to this country from overseas—will be 100 million strong.* Age 16 to 38, they will also be in the prime of young adulthood—graduating from colleges, universities, and graduate schools; starting families; launching careers; founding businesses and not-for-profit organizations; and in some cases, beginning careers in politics and public service. By 2016, there may even be a handful of older Millennials serving as U.S. senators, members of Congress, and state governors, and beginning to be mentioned as possible future presidents.

Generation We, it's clear, will be poised to take control of the United States and thereby play a major role in determining the future of humankind on this planet. For the reasons we've explained throughout this book, we're excited about the prospect. We're looking forward to the Millennials helping to make America a better place and reversing many of the dire trends that have harmed our country and our world in recent years.

"Change does not roll in on the wheels of inevitability, but comes through continuous struggle. And so we must straighten our backs and work for our freedom. A man can't ride you unless your back is bent."

MARTIN LUTHER KING, JR.

But no single generation, no matter how numerous and gifted, can change a nation or the world on its own. Even at the height of their power and influence (which will probably arrive during the decade 2025–2035, when members of Generation We will be in their forties and fifties), the Millennials will never be an absolute majority of the population or of the electorate. To achieve their full potential, they will need help and support from others, including both those who are older and younger than they are.

This is the same pattern we can see in the life cycle of every notable generation in history. The so-called Greatest Generation, which was born between 1901 and 1924 and successfully tackled the twin challenges of the Great Depression and World War II, is a vivid example. They achieved an enormous amount as young workers for the Civilian Conservation Corps and the Works Progress Administration; as the GIs who liberated Europe from the Nazis and the female factory workers who supplied the Allied war machine; and as the entrepreneurs, corporate employees, and family men and women who helped jumpstart the economic boom of the 1950s. Eventually, a few of their number went on to guide the nation personally in the form of leaders such as John F. Kennedy (born in 1917), Lyndon Johnson (1908), and Ronald Reagan (1911).

But the Greatest Generation didn't do any of these things completely on their own. They were inspired by the leadership of people from earlier generations, including Franklin D. Roosevelt (born in 1882), George C. Marshall (1880), Winston Churchill (1874), and Dwight D. Eisenhower (1890). Of course, these great wartime figures could never have defeated the Axis powers without the sacrifices of millions of Greatest Generation soldiers; but neither could those armies have prevailed without the wisdom of Roosevelt, Marshall, Churchill, Eisenhower, and others.

When a nation faces its greatest challenges, generations must work together for the common and greater good.

When a nation faces its greatest challenges, generations must work together for the common and greater good.

And so it will be with Generation We. The 2008 election cycle marks their coming of age, as the oldest members of their age group turn 30. It's a moment in time that is almost exactly the equivalent of 1932, the election year when the oldest members of the Greatest Generation turned 31. That election, occurring in the depths of the Great Depression, proved to be a major watershed in American history.

Repulsed by the clear failure of laissez-faire Republican conservatism, Americans by the millions turned to Franklin D. Roosevelt and the Democrats—led by the young voters of what would become the Greatest Generation. FDR's victory ushered in 40 years of political dominance for Democratic liberalism and the greatest period of benevolent American influence in history, including the defeat of fascism;

the founding, under U.S. guidance, of a series of great international institutions (the UN, NATO, SEATO) that successfully averted any further global war; the rebuilding of the defeated Axis powers as peace-loving democracies; and the biggest economic boom in world history.

There is another striking coincidence: Generation We today is trending approximately 60 percent Democratic to 38 percent Republican, which is the highest generational difference in voting tendency *since* 1932.

It's impossible to predict with certainty how history will judge the events of today. But someday the election of 2008 may be viewed as a turning point comparable to 1932 in the American saga. If so, it may well be seen as a moment when Generation We took the stage, and with help from millions of older Americans, gave the wheel of history a decisive turn.

If this happens, it will be because of a grand alliance between Generation We and like-minded Americans from other generations. In that alliance, several specific groups are likely to play important roles.

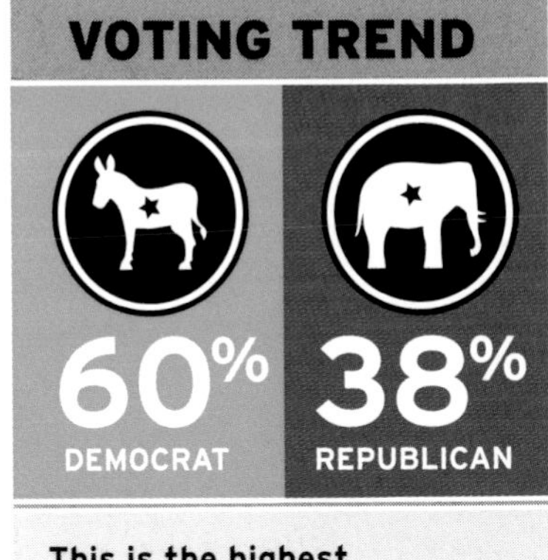

This is the highest generational difference in voting trends since 1932.

"YOUNG VOTERS IN THE 2006 ELECTION," CIRCLE

THE LEGACY BEARERS

Legacy-bearing Baby Boomers and prior generations are seeking to redeem the failed hopes and dreams of their youth by helping younger generations to reshape America along the lines of their most idealistic imaginings.

"Grandparent" is a role you grow into, and it's the stage in life millions of Baby Boomers have already entered or are now entering. Ideally, it should be the culmination of a life well lived—a time of serenity in which to enjoy the fruits of your hard work, to enjoy the spectacle of younger generations taking over their inheritance, and to pass along the wisdom you've developed through a lifetime of challenging and rewarding adventures. It's also a time when the deeper meaning of life begins to emerge, and maturity and perspective start to blunt the dogmatism of youth.

Unfortunately, for many of the women and men now moving into this stage of life, the serenity and the sense of fulfillment they rightfully seek are proving elusive.

Part of the reason is selfish—the fear many of these elders feel when they contemplate their own futures. Will their personal safety nets hold? Will Social Security and Medicare remain intact? Will the corporate pensions and IRAs and 401(k)s they built up over time retain their value? Will they be able to enjoy the retirements they planned—or will they have to go back to work, or live a hand-to-mouth existence, unable even to pay for healthcare and medicines, let alone the amenities of a rich, rewarding life?

And part of the reason is selfless—the concern many elders have about the kind of world they are passing along to the younger

©GIDEON MENDEL/CORBIS

generations. Will today's elders be the first American generation to give their children and grandchildren a less secure, less hopeful world than the one they received from their parents? Will their offspring be doomed to a lower quality of life than their parents enjoyed—a life of cramped horizons, diminishing prospects, increasing helplessness, and expanding anxiety? Has the Baby Boom generation failed not only to match the achievement of its own ancestral elders, the legendary Greatest Generation, but failed even to live up to the minimal mandate of every cohort—to leave the young a world they can call their own?

Will they be able to enjoy the retirements they planned—or will they have to go back to work, or live a hand-to-mouth existence, unable even to pay for healthcare and medicines, let alone the amenities of a rich, rewarding life?

Today's legacy-bearers grew up with enormous expectations. Raised in the post-war world by often-indulgent parents, given unprecedented access to education, technology, and the riches of the world, the children of the 1950s and 1960s were considered golden, a generation of superstars with the potential to reshape society for the better.

Much of what they did with their opportunity was admirable. The Boomers have made America a more affluent place. They have created an amazing array of new technologies and helped introduce the world to the marvelous freedoms of contemporary life. They also have made America a more open, tolerant society, having taken long strides toward creating real equality for both sexes and for people of all religions, races, ethnic backgrounds, and sexual orientations.

But the vision on which they were raised—of a world without poverty, disease, inequality, war, bigotry, crime, or hatred—has long since faded from sight. It's hard not to feel a sense of disappointment, even bitterness, when we compare the brilliant promise of the Baby Boom generation with the troubled legacy they would leave behind if their story ended today.

Fortunately, their story doesn't end today. There is at least one more chapter yet to be written. And it is one they will write in collaboration with the generations they spawned—the generations of their children and grandchildren, including the members of Generation We who are now poised to take center stage.

But the vision on which they were raised—of a world without poverty, disease, inequality, war, bigotry, crime, or hatred—has long since faded from sight. It's hard not to feel a sense of disappointment, even bitterness, when we compare the brilliant promise of the Baby Boom generation with the troubled legacy they would leave behind if their story ended today.

THE CARING MOTHERS AND FATHERS

Caring mothers and fathers are determined not to become the first generation of Americans to bequeath their children a poorer, sicker, weaker, and more dangerous world, and who will work with youth to prevent that.

Unfortunately, at this moment, the relationship between Generation We and the older generations in American society is a dysfunctional one. On an individual basis, there are many healthy, nurturing parent-child relationships (and it's noteworthy that Millennials report more positive, loving connections with their own elders than other recent American generations). But on a societal basis, the relationship is more like that between an abusive parent and a victimized child.

Does this seem extreme? Think about it. Right now, the parental generation that is running the United States has created—or tolerated—the following:

- A nation in which massive debt has been created for the benefit of a relative handful of older people (mainly business oligarchs) and which young people of every class will have to pay off for decades to come

- A nation in which opportunities for decent work, housing, education, healthcare, and good nutrition are becoming more and more scarce and expensive

- A nation in which the news and entertainment media are dominated by fear-mongering, mind-numbing trivia, and soul-sapping consumerism

- A nation in which natural environment and resources are being squandered for short-term gain, leaving behind a world in which the young will have to scramble even to survive

Isn't this relationship fairly described as an abusive one?

Today, many mothers and fathers are welcoming home caskets, and children without limbs. Most were too young to participate in Vietnam, so they are now experiencing for the first time the indignation of paying personally for oil wars and imperialistic foreign policy. When politicians call this a war for a lifetime or 100 years in Iraq, they shudder—especially given that their precious grandkids could be sent off and brought home in the same way. They do not want their children to be fodder for military conquest. They want to keep their families intact.

©LUSHPIX/UNLISTED IMAGES

We don't believe most mothers and fathers want to bequeath a world of insecurity and violence to their children, nor was it ever their intention to create such a world in the first place. The parents themselves are victims alongside their children, trapped in patterns of behavior that have been imposed upon them by deceptive and (in some cases) near-psychotic leaders. Now is the time to reverse these deadly trends and to break out of the mutually destructive habits that have created the patterns of abuse.

We don't believe most mothers and fathers want to bequeath a world of insecurity and violence to their children, nor was it ever their intention to create such a world in the first place.

THE CULTURAL CREATIVES

Cultural creatives are Americans who have already moved beyond old divisions of "traditionalist" versus "modernist" to embrace new forms of spirituality, social experimentation, and personal growth. These are the people who are ready to respond to the new vision of the Millennials. It's a term originally coined by sociologist Paul H. Ray and psychologist Sherry Ruth Anderson to describe a large segment in Western society that has recently developed beyond the standard paradigm of "modernists" versus "traditionalists" or "conservatives." The concept was first presented in 2000 in their book *The Cultural Creatives: How 50 Million People Are Changing the World.*[1] Since then it has been elaborated in other writings by Ray, Anderson, and other analysts. Ray also sometimes refers to this segment of the population as the New Progressives.

This growing section of the population—estimated by Ray at 26 to 28 percent of the population, or around 50 million Americans—is spiritual in orientation and embraces the practice of spiritual values in daily life, even without practicing any formal religion. Many cultural creatives are familiar with a variety of religions and seek to identify with principles that are universal among religions. The intention is to search for universal, practical spiritual principles that have intrinsic value and do not depend on ecclesiastical authority.

The cultural creatives generally avoid identification with the traditional "left" and "right" of the political spectrum, although they are "progressive" or "liberal" in their disdain for corporate power. Instead, they are known for their support for diversity along ethnic, gender, religious, and sexual lines; their commitment to civil rights and civil liberties; their concern for the environment; and their opposition to militarism.

The cultural creatives are natural allies for the emerging Generation We. Paul Ray has long been pointing to the growing anxiety that this group of Americans has about the future of our planet. In his essay "The New Political Compass," in which he describes the cultural creatives as occupying the northern point on a four-point political map, Ray writes:

What most upsets the people of the North part of the Compass is that politicians are not dealing with the issues that affect their children's future. Historically, these have been seen as women's concerns. No longer. My 1999 survey showed that a full 60 percent of all Americans, and it now appears, 80 percent of Political North, are very worried that their own children and grandchildren will inherit a worse world than they themselves grew up in.

The fears of cultural creatives concerning the future of their children are becoming all too real.

This is a complete flip from Americans' historical optimism. It is a deep anxiety, but it has no present focus. Though it is important, it is easily pre-empted by whatever is more urgent. In that respect, it's rather like buying life insurance, indefinitely postponable until some crisis comes along to remind us how risky life really is, and how transitory. It is easily arguable that our inept and corrupt politics is about to harm us. The West is about to face a cascade of crisis that political business as usual cannot handle, whether it is led from the right or the left. Our most recent big crisis, 9/11/2001, has already brought that latent pessimism about the future to the surface.[2]

We think Ray was prescient. From today's perspective, the crises of the West have become all too clear—not just the terror attacks of 9/11 and the inept response to them by the U.S. government, but also the war in Iraq, the onrushing climate crisis, the increasing gulf between rich and poor (both nationally and globally), the continued erosion of civil liberties, the looming risk of economic meltdown, and the danger of worldwide pandemics.

The fears of cultural creatives concerning the future of their children are becoming all too real. Now that a vast cohort of those "children"—Generation We—is reaching the age at which they can begin to mobilize themselves in response to these crises, there's every reason to believe that Ray's "new progressives" will be eager to line up behind them in support of the causes and leaders they embrace.

THE JUSTICE SEEKERS

There's a final large group of Americans who we think will play an important role in the grand alliance that will support the Millennials in their quest to redeem our national promise. These are the justice seekers—fair-minded citizens who are troubled by the large and growing gap between our stated ideals of democracy, freedom, and opportunity and the harsh reality of life in twenty-first century America.

Earlier in these pages, we've discussed how growing income inequality, dwindling educational opportunity, lack of access to healthcare, and the increasing concentration of power in the hands of elites are all helping to undermine the traditional American values of fairness and equality. Millions of Americans are disturbed by these trends, and many are prepared to demand redress for these injustices.

Here are examples of some of the events and trends that have aroused the feelings of the justice seekers and that will mobilize them to support a movement for social and political change:

- The horrific aftermath of Hurricane Katrina, in which government indifference and incompetence combined with poverty and racism created a nightmare in which a great American city was nearly destroyed by a natural disaster whose worst effects could have been and should have been foreseen and forestalled.

- Corporate scandals, such as those involving Enron, WorldCom/MCI, Tyco, and Global Crossing, in which white-collar criminals lavishly and fraudulently enriched themselves and their cronies at the expense of customers, investors, and lower-level employees.

- The failure of our military to adequately equip, train, protect, and reward our men and women in uniform, even as we sent them into the line of fire in Iraq and Afghanistan for repeated tours of duty, and squandered billions in unaccounted funds paid to private contractors and Iraqi politicians.

- The transformation of our prisons into a vast system for social control, in which more than 2.3 million Americans—more than one in every hundred adults—are incarcerated, many of them charged with nonviolent offenses, such as drug abuse, for which therapeutic and remedial care would be far more effective and humane. Racial disparities are enormous: If you're a Hispanic male, your chance of being in prison is 2.2 times greater than of a white male, and if you're a Black male, your chance is almost 6 times as great.[3]

- The increasing difficulties faced by young people who try to better their lot through higher education, caught between ever-growing tuition costs, ever-shrinking access to government grants and low-cost student loans, ever-increasing mountains of debt, and ever-worsening job prospects.

©NATIONAL GEOGRAPHIC/GETTY IMAGES

Notice that none of these is a partisan issue. You don't have to be a Democrat or a Republican to be outraged over the destruction of the Ninth Ward of New Orleans, the obscene money-grubbing by the energy-market manipulators at Enron or those who drove the price of oil to 140 dollars per barrel, or the disgraceful conditions in which wounded veterans are treated at Walter Reed Army Medical Center. All you need is a sense of fair play and a commitment to the idea that America should be better than this.

Millions of Americans who have that sense and that commitment are ready to become part of the grand alliance that will usher in a new progressive era in our national politics.

...today's young people respect and are eager to learn from well-intentioned people of their parents' and grandparents' generations.

IT'S NOT "US AGAINST THEM"

The revolution led by Generation We will *not* be about intergenerational conflict. Some have suggested that conflicts over the national debt, troubled entitlement programs for the elderly, and weakened support for programs in education and health must inevitably pit aging Baby Boomers against burdened Millennials (with Gen Xers caught somewhere in the middle). But the solutions to these and other major social, political, and economic problems can't be achieved by any one group, and that means warfare among groups will only make matters worse.

Thankfully, there is every sign that the real-world members of Generation We have no interest in fomenting resentment, scapegoating, or intergenerational battles. Every survey and attitudinal study—including our own—confirms that today's young people respect and are eager to learn from well-intentioned people of their parents' and grandparents' generations. This is a dramatic change from the experience of many people from past generations, who grew up believing that intense intergenerational conflict is natural and unavoidable. In their massive study *Millennials Rising*, generational scholars Neil Howe and William Strauss report, "Most teens say they identify with their parents' values, and over nine in ten say they 'trust' and 'feel close to' their parents. The proportion who report conflict with their parents is declining."

Although Baby Boomers may have invented the motto, "Don't trust anyone over 30"—and even lived by it, at least until they themselves turned 30—their children, Generation We, are ready to trust and work with them.[4]

The Millennial revolution will also not be about moral judgments, a religious revival, or a return to "traditional lifestyles." We've already noted the fact that Generation We is more tolerant, open-minded, and accepting than any previous generation in American history. They see those far-right dogmatists espousing "traditional" rhetoric today as a cog in the machine that created the mess they are in. When it comes to lifestyle choices—whether we're talking about sexual orientation, abortion, divorce, or gay marriage, or about gambling, drinking, drug use, and church attendance—their all-but-explicit motto is "Live and let live."

It's not that Millennials don't have preferences or beliefs about the right and wrong ways to live. Survey results, statistics about behavior choices, and mounds of anecdotal evidence all show that Millennials believe in responsible lifestyles, strong relationships, and the values of family and community. But they *don't* believe that anyone has the right to force their opinions on anyone else, and they generally look askance on people who judge or condemn others for the lifestyle choices they make. As long as you aren't harming others (neglecting your children, for example), you have the right to decide for yourself how you want to live. And the members of Generation We respect that right.

This tolerant attitude is one reason for the growing rift between most Millennials and organized religion. Having grown up in a world where religious dialogue is dominated by headlines about evangelical preachers threatening nonbelievers with fire and brimstone, about blaming 9/11 on homosexuality, and about Islamic fundamentalists employing terrorism against *"infidels"* who don't share their exact beliefs, Millennials have come to associate piety with hateful, us-against-them attitudes.

Many studies of Generation We bear out these findings. For example, according to surveys by the Barna Group, which examines the religious attitudes of young people, 87 percent of Americans between the ages of 16 and 29 describe mainstream Christianity as "judgmental," 85 percent call it "hypocritical," 78 percent say it's "old-fashioned," and 70 percent call it "insensitive to others."

"For in the end, freedom is a personal and lonely battle; and one faces down fears of today so that those of tomorrow might be engaged."

ALICE WALKER

Obviously these findings pose a challenge for religious leaders—including progressives—who hope to reach out to Generation We. But our point here is a simple one: *Generation We is fed up with leaders who seek to divide Americans against one another, whether on moral, ethnic, religious, geographic, racial, or economic grounds.* They are looking for leaders who will unite the country around common goals for the greater good that will benefit everyone.

Together, we can create the greatest change in human history—one that combines and builds upon the impact of some previous epochs of change as the Enlightenment, the Industrial Revolution, the Democratic Revolution, and the Digital Revolution. We can usher in an era of plenty for all people on a shared planet that is environmentally sustainable, culturally diverse, and permanently at peace. The Millennials can lead the way—and all of us can help.

7 THE MILLENNIAL AGENDA

The Mission of a Generation:

Restoring the American Dream

History shows that every generation has a mission. Some rise to the challenge nobly, as the Greatest Generation rose to the challenge posed by the Great Depression and the rise of fascism. Others muddle through, as did the Silent Generation of the 1950s, who largely maintained the comfortable status quo they inherited from their parents.

For the Baby Boomers, the verdict seems to be mixed. They played a key role in expanding human rights to previously oppressed groups (Blacks, women, gays), ushered in the information technology and Internet revolution, and opened the national consciousness to new forms of intellectual and social experience. But they have failed (so far) to find the right balance between economic and social values, as evidenced by a wealthy nation plagued by a sense of moral and spiritual emptiness.

It is always easier to define a generation's mission after the fact. But it's already possible to identify many of the crucial challenges Generation We faces in the early decades of the twenty-first century.

Generation We is inheriting a damaged future and a series of problems that are of crisis proportions. Things are not going to get better on their own; without decisive action, we face societal decline and potential collapse. Generation We has no choice other than to innovate their way out of the mess they (and we) are in.

We have spent a lot of time talking about the issues of the day. This book is a call to action. It has been written to suggest an agenda, a slate of actions that the entire Millennial generation must rally around, no matter what their party or their religious, geographic, gender, or racial characteristics. The agenda becomes a plan when the voters insist that elected officials and private industry must address it and when measures for implementation, including accountability and deadlines, are instituted. The plan must be inclusive and multipartisan, and it

©IMAGESTATE RM/FOTOSEARCH

must be supported by the political will to implement it.

Like any large group of people, the members of Generation We don't agree on everything. But they all share the need for a future worth living, where they can enjoy—in the immortal words of the Declaration of Independence—"certain unalienable rights, that among these are Life, Liberty, and the Pursuit of Happiness." Remember that the majority of our nation's founders were only in their twenties and thirties during the crucial years from the Revolution in 1776 to the implementation of the Constitution in 1789. Like Generation We, they shared an agenda, worked out solutions together, and in the end created the greatest form of government the world has ever seen.

Today's youth don't yet realize how powerful they are or how deeply they agree on basic values, despite differences in race, religion, party affiliation, geography, and gender. They don't yet share an agenda, largely because the power elites and the industries and media they control have prevented the unification of youth around a common purpose. We hope this book will help change this dynamic.

PROJECT FREE–INNOVATING THE NEXT GENERATION OF ENERGY

Many times in the past the world has changed when ordinary people—the offended masses being oppressed by those in power—got fed up with their condition and did something about it. The thing that will change our world today is the vote of the youth. We need the political will to blunt the power of the special interests, to elect those who are fit to serve and will focus on the best long-term interests of our country, and to vote out those who are obstructionist, short-sighted, and self-interested.

We believe Generation We, together with their supporters from other generations, can and will band together to create the greatest political force in the history of our nation. The first step in the restoration of their birthright and the revival of the American dream: Project FREE, to technologically innovate the next generation of energy.

Inventing the next source of energy is the single greatest thing we can do to change the world for the better. There is nothing more important to our society. It is the call and legacy of Generation We and will be the greatest achievement in the history of mankind.

In 1962, John F. Kennedy set the seemingly impossible goal of sending a man to the moon and returning him safely to Earth within a decade. Kennedy said:

> We choose to go to the moon in this decade and do the other things, not because they are easy, but because they are hard, because that goal will serve to organize and measure the best of our energies and skills, because that challenge is one that we are willing to accept, one we are unwilling to postpone, and one which we intend to win, and the others, too.

Kennedy was taking a page from the playbook of World War II. Like the Apollo moon-landing project, the Manhattan Project was a seemingly audacious technological challenge that an earlier generation of Americans had met, keeping us free by developing atomic weapons just months ahead of our Nazi enemies.

Today, an equally bold vision is required. We must immediately implement an Apollo- or Manhattan-like project to invent new sources of nonfossil fuel energy free from carbon emissions, based on hydrogen, fusion, or other means.

The ultimate goal of this effort will be to take Americans "off the grid"—to free us from dependence on one or a few centralized sources of energy and instead to generate most energy at the point of need, without having to be wired. The goal is to create a power source generated within the place of consumption—the car, home, business, or factory. This will liberate us from the limiting factors introduced by long-distance transmission, which is an impediment to large-scale implementation of clean energy, such as wind and solar, and getting it into large markets quickly.

We call it Project FREE, because the four letters that spell the word serve as a handy reminder of the benefits the project will provide if successfully completed:

F stands for FREEDOM FROM ENERGY WARS

Freedom from dependence on foreign sources of energy that threaten to embroil us in wars and conflicts that could put our security and our future in peril.

R stands for RIGHT TO AFFORDABLE, CLEAN ENERGY

The right of every American, and ultimately, every person on the planet to affordable and clean energy.

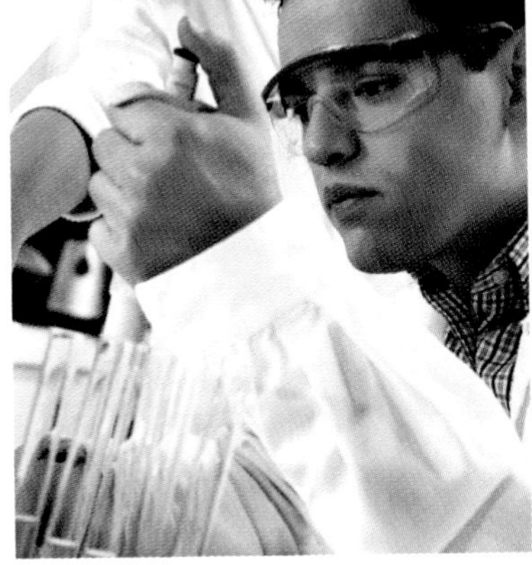

©LAJOS RÉPÁSI/ISTOCK INTERNATIONAL

Inventing the next source of energy is the single greatest thing we can do to change the world for the better.

E stands for **ECONOMIC GROWTH**

The incredible boon to global productivity, financial savings, and wealth creation that will be sparked by the discovery of a permanent form of cheap, renewable energy and the infrastructure to support it, not to mention the industries it will create and re-create.

E stands for **ENVIRONMENTAL RENEWAL**

Renewal and preservation of our natural environment and a sustainable future for our planet, which will result from an end to the burning of fossil fuels and carbon emissions.

Project FREE is not incremental technology, formed to improve the 100-plus-year-old coal, gas, and oil platforms we use today. Instead, we will seek radical innovations that can completely free us from foreign oil dependence and the conflict, environmental damage, and economic weakness it fosters. Conservation and improved use of current technologies are necessary but insufficient to create a future that takes mankind into its next epoch.

Project FREE must be a national program driven by the president, headed by an official with cabinet-level authority, endowed with 30 to 40 billion dollars in spending authority per year, and like the Federal Reserve, independent of partisan machinations. The mandate: to invent our way out of our energy dilemma within the next 10 to 15 years.

Forty billion dollars may sound like a lot of money, but it barely equals one year's worth of profit earned by a single multinational oil company. (In 2007, ExxonMobil posted record annual profits of 40.61 billion dollars after taxes. They made 80 billion dollars in profit before taxes, an amount equal to almost 1,300 dollars *per second.*[1])

The budget of Project FREE is also dwarfed by the obscene sums already committed to the war in Iraq (a war driven largely by the desire to ensure the continued flow of oil from Iraq's vast reserves) and the huge amounts we are currently sending overseas in exchange for foreign oil. In 2006, for example, the United States sent about 280 billion dollars to foreign oil producers—around a thousand dollars for each man, woman, and child in the country.[2] At that time, the average cost of oil was less than 70 dollars a barrel. As of this writing—just two years later—oil costs over 140 dollars a barrel, more than twice as much. With this gigantic and steadily growing drain on our national resources, no wonder our economy is floundering—and no wonder more and more Americans are recognizing the urgency of the need for energy independence.

There are two important points to note. First, Project FREE should be established with powers akin to those granted high-priority wartime programs, so as to remove all clearance and cooperation impediments that might otherwise slow or stop its progress.

Second, it should be temporary, as permanent bureaucracies tend to become special interests, intent on prolonging their own existence rather than on getting the job completed. The legislation creating the project must mandate its dismantling either upon fulfillment of its commission or after 15 years have passed, whichever comes first. Just as built-in deadlines existed for both the Manhattan Project (finish the bomb before the Nazis do) and the Apollo Project (to land a man on the moon "before this decade [the 60s] is out"), there should be a deadline for Project FREE.

It has been a long time since America has heard a rallying cry to launch an extraordinary effort to achieve the seemingly impossible. Today, with our nation's greatness apparently in decline and with our people divided by partisan rancor and social discord, it would benefit the nation enormously if we could join forces to pursue an important and truly valuable goal.

We have so many neglected priorities that several such projects can easily be identified. But there is no other project so important to our economic and military security.

It's vitally important for Project FREE to be done right. It will need to be headed by a visionary public official with a broad understanding of technology, government experience, and a creative mindset. He or she must be given the visibility and clout needed to overcome the efforts of special interests to impede the solution of our energy crisis. Imagine where the world would be if microprocessor technology had remained unchanged for more than a hundred years. That is precisely what has happened with oil, gas, and coal. We cannot afford to let these special interests control our energy policies any longer.

Today, with our nation's greatness apparently in decline and with our people divided by partisan rancor and social discord, it would benefit the nation enormouslyif we could join forces to pursue an important and truly valuable goal.

Of course, there are downsides to any government program, of which we, as advocates of free markets, are well aware. But Project FREE is the kind of challenge that private enterprise alone can't meet. The new technologies to be pursued under its auspices can't guarantee any commercial return in the short run, which means that businesses cannot invest in them because of their inherent risk and unknown commercial prospects. Only government is positioned to address this issue.

The challenges facing Project FREE will be great. Unlike the Manhattan or Apollo projects, the scientists and engineers involved will not be pursuing a single solution to a single challenge but rather exploring an array of innovations with one shared objective—to reduce America's dependence on fossil fuels.

In 2006, the US sent 280 BILLION dollars to foreign oil producers which equals a thousand dollars for each person in the country.

The cost of oil has doubled in 2 years from 70 dollars a barrel to 140.

In 2007, ExxonMobil made annual profits of 40.61 BILLION dollars after taxes.

SOURCE: SANDALOW, *FREEDOM FROM OIL*, CNNMONEY.COM

Some of these innovations will focus on the demand side, where there are huge opportunities for conservation and improved efficiency *without* any dramatic reduction in Americans' lifestyle. For example, plug-in electric cars—a technology that is available today—could meet the total transportation needs of 60 percent of American drivers using the unutilized nighttime generating capacity of existing power plants.[3] However, the advances that will be more significant in the long run will focus on the supply side, where one or more breakthroughs are needed to make nonfossil energy technologies more cost-effective.

Perhaps the most exciting possibilities include a commercially viable hydrogen-based energy program and energy from low-energy nuclear reactions, or fusion, the method of producing energy that takes place on the sun itself. The latter concept is one of 14 "Grand Challenges for Engineering" selected by the members of the National Academy of Engineering in February 2008, as top priorities for the twenty-first century. (Solar power and carbon sequestration also made the list.[4]) If we can achieve the breakthroughs needed to turn fusion power from dream into reality, we can transform the world economy for decades, perhaps centuries to come.

Once the scientific breakthroughs have been achieved, the work of Project FREE will not be done. A series of daunting engineering and economy challenges will still have to be met. Here is how physicist David J. Eaglesham, managing director for advanced technologies at Applied Materials and president of the Materials Research Society, explained these challenges in an article endorsing the idea of a large-scale Manhattan-style project to meet the energy crisis:

> The [original] Manhattan Project required one device (or a few) that could be built as expense-is-no-object. Don't know of an efficient way to separate isotopes of uranium? Just go ahead and build enough accelerators to send a few kg of material round a mass spectrometer. Energy is different. We don't need *one* of anything. We need 100 billion m^2 of photovoltaic systems, 10 billion solid-state lights, and a billion high-efficiency cars. And, most importantly, we'll need it all cheap.... So the Energy Manhattan will require not only an unprecedented international collaboration; it will require unprecedented coupling of the public and private sectors. It will call for simple and pragmatic approaches as well as visionary leaps. Getting industry involved could be simple (carbon credits, incentive schemes) or very complicated (joint government/industry projects), but the scale of the challenge makes it essential that we learn how to do it.[5]

Eaglesham is right; Project FREE will be the greatest technological challenge America has ever tackled. But it is also essential to our future. As Eaglesham goes on to say, "The solutions will be complex and multifaceted,

Imagine where the world would be if microprocessor technology had remained unchanged for more than a hundred years. That is precisely what has happened with oil, gas, and coal. We cannot afford to let these special interests control our energy policies any longer.

Manhattan Project

Apollo Project

Project FREE

and the programs unwieldy. But I think we have to take this challenge on because the alternative is too terrible to contemplate."

Think back to the two historic projects to which we've compared Project FREE—the Manhattan and Apollo projects. Both were crash projects driven by national anxiety over looming threats: in the case of the Manhattan Project, the danger that the Nazis might beat us to the secret of atomic weaponry and use it to complete their mission of world conquest; in the case of the Apollo program, the fear that the Soviet Union would colonize space and use it as a new form of military "high ground" from which to launch missile attacks on the West.

Maybe it takes a life-or-death threat like these to mobilize a great national effort. We are at that point today. The combined dangers we now face from global warming, dependence on totalitarian regimes for fossil fuels, and the risks of war for control of the world's energy supplies are at least as great as the dangers that prompted those earlier national triumphs.

As you can imagine, getting us off the grid will be a revolutionary step that will drastically reduce the influence of powerful special interests that currently wield enormous clout in Washington and around the world—not just the oil barons and the overseas potentates who control the great fossil fuel reserves but also the utility companies, the oil refiners, and the agribusiness conglomerates currently pushing ethanol (which is, at best, an inadequate half-measure).

This is another reason why Project FREE *must* be a government-sponsored program. Only a project that is independent of today's most powerful energy companies can be free to think outside the box of current technology. Optimizing today's century-old technologies will take us only so far. It's time to look for brand-new solutions. That will be the ultimate mandate of Project FREE.

If Project FREE is successful, the potential benefits are so great they are almost incalculable. Having one or more new, clean energy sources to power growth in our nation and the world over the next century will:

- Produce millions of new jobs—some directly, in the new energy industry itself; others indirectly, in the new businesses made possible by the availability of an abundant, reliable source of clean new energy.

- Dramatically reduce the environmental damage caused by carbon emissions and make it possible for us to slow or even reverse the danger of global warming.

- Free the United States from its current dependence for energy on unreliable, often hostile foreign regimes.

- Stimulate history's greatest-ever economic boom, fueling innovation, entrepreneurship, and business expansion.

- Produce a "positive domino effect" by unleashing the power of cheap energy to solve many other problems—for example, by making the current costly technology of desalination affordable and thereby making safe water available to all. This is perhaps the most outstanding humanitarian achievement of the project. It can effectively end starvation, turn deserts into oases, and make large-scale sustainable agriculture a global reality.

- Dramatically reduce the likelihood of wars over resources, defusing the economic tensions that profoundly complicate the already challenging task of forging peace in regions of the world such as the Middle East, the Horn of Africa, and Chechnya. People will be so busy industrializing, making money, and rebuilding infrastructure, they will have no desire to fight over resources.

You can get a sense of the seriousness of today's interwoven energy/climate crises by noting the fact that many politicians from both parties—people not normally known as profiles in courage—have been willing to express support for the idea of a vast, costly, and difficult Apollo-style project for energy. Notable political figures who have endorsed the concept include Barack Obama, Hillary Clinton, Newt Gingrich, Mitt Romney, Rudy Giuliani, and Lamar Alexander. Leaders from industry, academia, and the sciences have also signed on.

Does this mean Project FREE is a done deal—that it will surely be part of the agenda of the next president? Unfortunately, no. We've all seen how other worthwhile initiatives—projects that "everyone" agrees are important and necessary—have gotten sidetracked, delayed, distorted, and ultimately killed by political timidity, interference by special-interest lobbyists, budgetary constraints, and public indifference. Think about all the efforts over the years to fix our healthcare system, put Social Security and Medicare on a firm financial footings, or reform our immigration and border security programs. In every case, smart, well-meaning people have put forward plans that made sense, only to see them scuttled and abandoned. Under "politics as usual," it's all too likely the exact same thing will happen to Project FREE.

That's why it's essential that today's most important rising political force, Generation We, must choose *not* to let "politics as usual" carry the day.

During the turmoil of the late 1960s, in the midst of nationwide struggles over civil rights and the war in Vietnam, legendary independent journalist I. F. Stone taught an important lesson about how politics works:

> There is a wonderful story of a delegation which came here [to Washington, D.C.] to see Franklin D. Roosevelt on some reform or other. When they were finished the President said, "Okay, you've convinced me. Now go on out and bring pressure on me." Every thoughtful official knows how hard it is to get anything done if someone isn't making it uncomfortable *not* to. Just imagine how helpless the better people in government would be if the rebels, black and white, suddenly fell silent.[6]

Like the late 1960s, these early years of the twenty-first century are no time for us to fall silent. We need to mobilize to keep up the pressure on our public officials to do the right thing.

Project FREE must be the great cause around which the Millennial generation can rally. Like Generation We itself, it is "post-ideological"—"liberal" because it will help save our environment, "conservative" because it strengthens our national security, a potential source of pride and (not incidentally) tremendous economic riches for the entire nation. It calls for cooperation between all of the most powerful and effective institutions of our society—government, business, academia—and its benefits will flow to everyone, not just in the United States but around the planet. It is not directed *against* anyone but rather *for* everyone—young and old, rich and poor, black and white, urban and rural, women and men. Thus it has the power to inspire and unite our people, and to return the United States to its place as the most admired nation in the world.

©RUSSELL DU PARCQ/DREAMESTIME.COM

Generation We is ready to rally around Project FREE, as shown by multiple findings from our surveys. Ninety-four percent of those in the GMS agreed with the statement, *Our country must take extreme measures now, before it is too late, to protect the environment and begin to reverse the damage we have done.* Seventy-four percent agreed that *We must make major investments now to innovate the next generation of nonfossil fuel based energy solutions.* And as we've already noted, seventy percent rated "very effective" the idea that America should *Launch a concerted national effort, similar to the Apollo Program that put a man on the moon, with the goal of moving America beyond fossil fuels and inventing the next generation of energy, based on new technologies such as hydrogen or fusion.*

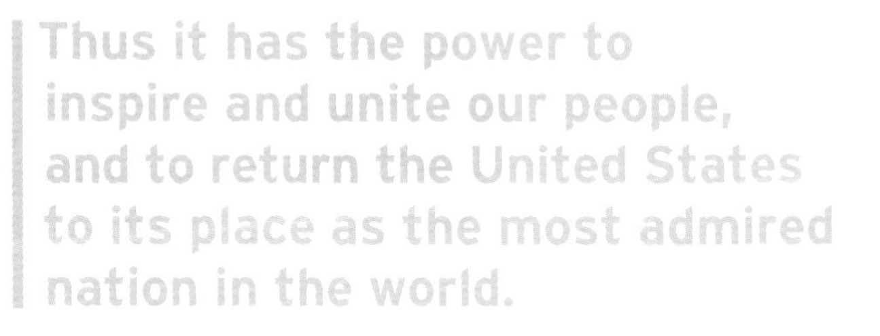

Project FREE is an ambitious, challenging concept. But except for the opposition it will attract from entrenched interests, it is *not* controversial. It will be eagerly supported by tens of millions of Millennials, the greatest power bloc of the next several decades.

Whichever political party espouses, leads, and successfully implements Project FREE will be an enormous benefactor to America and the world. It will also seize the moral and political high ground from which to command the allegiance of Generation We for decades to come. The fact that it is based on clear, nonpolitical objectives and a deadline makes the future of Generation We, and their children, something to look forward to rather than something to fear.

THE REST OF THE AGENDA

There are other major projects for creating America's future that also need and deserve investment during the next generational cycle. Some require literal investment—financial commitments by both the government and the private sector. Others require investment of social and political capital. Here is our list of important items for the Millennial generation to consider when shaping its agenda:

- Restoring and protecting the environment and the planet—not only through the innovations that Project FREE will provide, but also through fair, firm, market-based rules and systems that will reduce air and water pollution, incentivize and reward clean technologies, and protect the natural diversity of species and ecosystems that represents one of our most precious legacies to future generations.

- Providing quality nutrition and healthcare for all—replacing America's jerry-rigged healthcare system (which channels profits and benefits mainly to the owners of for-profit insurance companies and healthcare providers) and its industrial food supply system (which encourages obesity and chronic illness) with a medical system that covers the basic healthcare needs of every American and encourages preventive care, along with a reformed, sustainable agricultural system that provides affordable access to natural, healthful foods.

What we want and how we get to it depends on our mindsets. It is extremely difficult to change mindsets once they are formed. We create the world in accordance with our mindset. We need to invent ways to change our perspective continually and reconfigure our mindset quickly as new knowledge emerges. We can reconfigure our world if we can reconfigure our mindset.[7]

We are proposing an agenda—a list of items for discussion—not a plan. It is up to you, and every concerned citizen, to take part in shaping the strategy.

Yunus is right. As a society, we get what we want—or at least, what we set our hearts on achieving. Right now, we have a world run by plunderers, focused solely on individual material gain, and headed toward destruction through war, disease, or environmental catastrophe. But all these problems are the results of human action or inaction—and all can be solved if we put our minds to it.

DEFENDING THE MILLENNIAL AGENDA

Right-wing, special-interest, and corporate opponents of the Millennial agenda will employ their usual tactics to attack those who support it. They will say, "We live in a dangerous world"; they will label those who oppose needless wars as "wimps," "cowards," "traitors," and "surrender advocates"; and they will insist that only a totalitarian government focused on war-making can protect Americans from external threats.

These are lies that must be labeled as such. History shows that, when American values of democracy and freedom have been truly threatened, the successful battles to defend those values have been led and won not by tough-talking right-wing reactionaries, but by progressives. It is the freedom-lovers who win our wars—not the freedom-haters.

America's victorious involvement in World War I was led by the progressive president Woodrow Wilson. (If Wilson's brainchild, the League of Nations, had been supported vigorously after the war, it's possible that World War II might have been prevented.) America's triumph in World War II was led by the progressive president Franklin D. Roosevelt. (It was Roosevelt and his progressive successor Harry S. Truman who guided the creation of the international institutions, from NATO to the United Nations, that helped prevent the outbreak of a third world war.) Even the Cold War, which was waged by politicians of both parties, was managed with the greatest wisdom by progressive presidents like John F. Kennedy, whose strength and forebearance during the Cuban Missile Crisis of 1962 arguably helped prevent the thermonuclear destruction of the world.

By contrast, the "tough guys" of the extreme right are experts at bluster, unilateral saber-rattling, and ill-considered military actions that kill thousands and ultimately end up weakening America's position in the world, as exemplified by the current war in Iraq. The progressives of Generation We will need to lead a clean break from this kind of mindless "toughness" in favor of a deeper understanding of what it *really* takes to maintain the freedom and safety of our nation and our planet.

True bravery comes when the spirit of a nation resists evil and faces its greatest challenges with resolve and optimism. The accusations of cowardice often come from pundits, politicians, and special-interest advocates who are devoid of any personal bravery. They are so wedded to their own dogma or self-serving interests they do not have the courage to open their minds and admit there may be a better way.

True toughness is the spirit showed by Martin Luther King, Jr., in facing down the hate-mongers to create a civil rights movement that ultimately claimed his life. It was the bedrock of a handicapped FDR who, in one of our nation's darkest hours, famously declared, "The only thing we have to fear is fear itself." It was the Spirit of 1776—the readiness to face a terrible threat without fear and keeping the resolve to fight until victory is won.

The most important battles to be fought and won in the years to come are not just military battles against foreign aggressors—although, as history shows, progressive leaders will wage such wars with courage and determination if and when they are necessary. The *real* battles the future is calling on us to wage are against oppression, tyranny, manipulation, exploitation, and cruelty. The biggest enemies are not tin-pot dictators in faraway lands or terrorists crafting squalid schemes for murdering innocents—although progressive leaders understand and will deal with the threats both of these groups can pose. The *real* enemies are the plunderers who exploit jingoism, machismo, fear, and anger to seize and maintain power for their own selfish ends.

The greatest battles Generation We will be called upon to wage will be mental battles—disputes to free their own minds and spirits of the shackles of false consciousness imposed by our manipulators. The kind of toughness they need will be the Spirit of 1776—the chutzpah that was in our ancestors when they shook off tyranny, saying to their British overlords, "Enough!"

Surely military strength and battles will be necessary. But the toughest battles will call for heroic resolve to create a new style and method of achieving solutions, and to stay the course no matter how difficult the road. This battle calls for the same bravery and resolve our founders expressed. Today's youth are called to say "Enough!" to the older generation and the oligopolistic business/government power structure, peacefully asserting their own interests and those of the nation and forcing change through the existing political process.

They can follow no better spiritual guide than George Washington himself, a hero for the ages—steadfast in purpose, a courageous freedom fighter, and the man who turned down the offer to become the American monarch and instead insisted on democracy.

FINDING OUR VOICES

Part of the challenge Generation We will face is finding their own voices and the boldness to defend their own interests loudly and clearly. There's no doubt that tackling all of the items on the proposed Millennial agenda successfully will be a tall order. Generation We faces a list of challenges perhaps as great as that faced by any generation of Americans.

We've written elsewhere in this book about the change in the past generation whereby ownership and control of the media has passed into the hands of giant corporations whose interests run directly counter to those of Generation We—and in fact, to those of the vast majority of citizens. Part of the solution must involve returning to the media regulatory structure that existed in the United States prior to the Reagan administration, under which the ownership of mass media distribution systems had to be separate from content creation. This system, while far from perfect, as least created a modicum of independence among those who reported and wrote the news, as well as those who created entertainment and information content for most Americans.

Part of the solution must involve returning to the media regulatory structure... under which the ownership of mass media distribution systems had to be separate from content creation.

An important intermediate step may be the creation of a media organization run by and for Millennial youth. This could include a wire service to create and distribute news content; a television news network analogous to and competing with CNN, MSNBC, and Fox News; and a network of Internet sites to encourage young people to create and share their own information.

Most daunting is the fact that if Generation We is to tackle massive social problems effectively, they will need to envision and then implement a major restructuring of our economic and political systems, so the inherent creativity of all people can be unleashed. Just as the reforms of the Jacksonian and Progressive eras produced new opportunities for working- and middle-class people to participate in the political and economic system, and as the twentieth-century human rights movement brought similar opportunities to women, religious and ethnic minorities, and people of color, so Generation We must find ways to free twenty-first century America from the control of plundering economic and political elites, liberating the innovative powers of our whole nation. Only in this way can the huge problems we face be solved.

Fortunately for our nation and the world, Generation We has what it will take to meet the enormous challenges of tomorrow. Resilient, optimistic, well-educated, thoughtful, generous, open-minded, and practical, they have the potential to be the next "greatest generation" in American history. They are all about the greater good. When they are finished making their mark (40 to 60 years from now), there is every reason to believe they will leave the planet a very different place—and a much better one.

AN EMPOWERING VISION OF THE FUTURE

The urgent need to invest in our future is more than just another way of defining the Millennial agenda. It's also a vitally important antidote to the onslaught of negativity, pessimism, and apocalyptic thinking that dominates the conservative, corporate media—especially on those rare occasions when they attempt to glimpse the future.

There's no doubt we live in an era of accelerating crises—political, economic, environmental, biological, social, and spiritual. But there is a positive vision for the future we can offer the world, showing what our planet can be like once we confront and seize control of these crises and use them to reverse the destructive course we've been on. It's a vision that incorporates the best traditions of Western civilization even as it embraces the need for dramatic change and revitalization in the face of unprecedented challenges.

Sociologist Paul Ray, whose work we cited earlier in our discussion of the "cultural creatives," has written insightfully about the kind of new vision that is essential to inspire the change we seek. In one essay, Ray describes "the Wisdom needed for our time" in terms of opposed dualities. According to Ray, the Wisdom our world needs includes:

> The *wise elder's* long-term perspectives and reasoning: what is good for *all* the children? *Not* short-term, immature, selfish, greedy, power-mad perspectives and reasoning.
>
> Linking future-oriented perspectives and concerns to our deep collective past, and drawing from its themes for legitimacy. *Not* just focused on our shallow past and present to the exclusion of our evolution into the future.
>
> Showing maximally inclusive concerns across all kinds of people and all species, for humans and nature alike. *Not* narrowly focused on particular tribes, traditions, or humanity only, and not exclusion, or ignorance, of nature.
>
> Linking spiritual realization and concerns to practical action to the needs of "the planet and the people and species on it." Not otherworldly, abstruse, or lacking relationship to people's real concerns in their "life worlds," and in their ecologies.
>
> Placing crucial emphasis on the growth and transformation of both persons and the culture, both organizations and life worlds, both spirit and civilization, both local and planetary. *Not* static ideals, not moral absolutes lacking reference to human growth/transformation; and not focused just on individual change, lacking reference to cultural change issues.
>
> Concerns of the elders of humanity for the well-being of *all* the children of the world, now and in the longer term fu-

"What's the use of a fine house if you haven't got a tolerable planet to put it on?"

HENRY DAVID THOREAU

resilient
open-minded
generous
well-educated
practical

ture. Not excluding anyone, not immature in the manner of the adolescent consciousness typical of humanity today.[8]

Ray's vision of a planetary "wisdom civilization" is one we think today's Millennials are ready to respond to and work toward. It's just one version of the kind of overarching vision we need to inspire and empower young people and those who would support them—a vision that embraces and transcends individual agenda items and embodies long-term goals far greater than any checklist of particular political or economic projects, no matter how ambitious.

It's also a vision that embraces the need for personal sacrifice—not in a mood of joyless self-denial or rejection of pleasure, but out of a desire to transcend the petty and the purely personal in favor of bigger, broader social goals.

Many commentators have decried the narrow and selfish perspective of the Bush administration, and more broadly, the conservative power structure currently ruling the United States. Noted particularly is its failure to call for any personal contribution to the supposedly epochal "war on terror" other than urging Americans to "borrow money and go shopping"; its insistence on massive tax cuts even as overseas wars are draining the treasury and incurring enormous future debts; and its willful blindness to the need for long-term thinking about the energy and environmental crises in favor of short-term fixes such as drilling for oil in the Alaskan wilderness.

Generation We rejects this kind of petty, self-centered thinking and are ready to embrace the need for dramatic personal and social efforts in support of worthwhile goals. In the GMS, 78 percent of the Millennials we surveyed agreed with the statement, *I am willing to personally make significant sacrifices in my own life to address the major environmental, economic, and security challenges facing our country,* and fully 91 percent agreed that *In our country, each generation has a responsibility to wisely use the country's resources and power so that they can provide the next generation a secure, sustainable country that is stronger than the one they inherited.*

Clearly the sense of responsibility and personal mission is already in place. All that's lacking is the vision, the will, and the leadership.

"Dependence begets subservience and venality, suffocates the germ of virtue, and prepares fit tools for the designs of ambition."

THOMAS JEFFERSON

Q70

Now let's look at some potential solutions for some of the major challenges facing our country today. For each, please tell us how effective you feel each of the following would be in addressing that issue, on a scale of 0-10, where 10 means it would be extremely effective in addressing that challenge and 0 means would not be at all effective.

You can choose any number between 0 and 10 – the higher the number, the more effective you feel the solution would be in addressing that issue.

	Mean	10	8–10	6–10	0–5	DK/ Ref
Launch a concerted national effort, similar to the Apollo Program that put a man on the moon, with the goal of moving America beyond fossil fuels and inventing the next generation of energy, based on new technologies such as hydrogen or fusion. This aggressive plan would require a huge national investment but would produce millions of new jobs, could dramatically reduce environmental damage, and free us from our dependence on fossil fuels and foreign oil.	7.0	21	49	71	29	0
Commit ourselves to a comprehensive effort to not only reduce the pollution we are putting into the environment but reverse the damage we have done. That damage is not only polluting the earth, it is causing unprecedented disease and suffering in communities throughout our country and across the globe.	6.9	20	46	69	30	0
Provide quality healthcare and nutrition for all children in our country, regardless of their financial condition. Poor nutrition is creating an epidemic of preventable chronic diseases, including diabetes and obesity, that will cost our country billions of dollars and ruin the lives of millions of children.	7.3	29	53	75	25	.
Provide equal funding for public education and learning resources for all children and all communities, regardless of economic class. This is a critical investment in the human potential of our country and its ability to compete in a global economy.	7.2	27	53	73	27	0
Balance the federal budget, but also eliminate the 8 trillion dollars of national debt that have been built up over decades of irresponsible spending. This debt makes it impossible for our country to keep pace and leaves us indebted to other countries who are potential competitors.	6.8	16	43	69	31	0
Fully fund Social Security, Medicare, and other social insurance commitments being passed on to future generations, which have doubled to over 40 trillion dollars just since 2000 and are increasing by several trillion every year. These commitments must be met by current generations because it would be morally wrong to pass on unfunded liabilities of this size to our own children.	6.7	17	43	66	33	0
End trade imbalances that see us importing nearly 1 trillion dollars per year more than we export to other countries by restoring our industrial base. Restoring our industrial base and eliminating our trade deficit will provide secure jobs with good wages and benefits and rebuild our shrinking middle class.	6.6	16	39	66	33	0
Begin to rebuild America's economic self-sufficiency by restoring our industrial base to provide the essential components needed to provide for our defense and basic economic needs. As we have seen with oil, we can no longer afford to rely on other countries for our most vital economic and security needs.	6.8	16	41	70	30	0
Protect our civil rights by reversing recent actions to restrict our right to privacy and to limit access to government information, ensuring survival of a free and unrestricted Internet, and restoring an objective, unbiased media. Protecting our civil rights also requires eliminating the influence of special interests over our government and creating more transparency in government and business.	6.6	17	40	65	35	0

8 MAKING CHANGE HAPPEN

It Has Happened Before

When we look back at great turning points in history, we see that each was driven by a unique confluence of events: a society ripe for change; a new generation ready to drive that change; the emergence of one or a few leaders to articulate the need and set the agenda; and in many cases, technological or economic shifts that made innovative action possible. In various ways, these great changes provide models for the coming Millennial revolution.

The European Enlightenment: *The Power of Technology*

After centuries in which church authorities dominated government and daily life, Europe was ravaged by religious wars in the late sixteenth and seventeenth centuries. Finally, Europeans said, "Enough!" Turning away from superstition and authoritarianism, they launched new modes of thinking that included the birth of modern science, the political ferment that led to the French and American revolutions and eventually the freedom of the world's colonial peoples, and the rise of democracy.

Although many factors played a role in stimulating the birth of the Enlightenment, scholars agree that it was made possible largely by the invention and spread of the printing press, which made scholarship and information accessible to millions of people for the first time. In the same way, the coming Millennial revolution will be shaped in large part by today's new technologies—the Internet, instant messaging, text messaging, streaming video, the cell phone, and Wi-Fi—which are bringing new knowledge and power to millions of people who were once voiceless and able to access only the information and ideas provided by corporate media masters.

The Industrial Revolution: *Economic Creativity*

In the late eighteenth and early nineteenth centuries, the Industrial Revolution created a surge of economic productivity, freed millions from back-breaking labor, and ultimately fueled an incredible increase in individual and societal wealth that is still driving unprecedented improvements in living standards around the world. This change in the basic conditions of human life was driven not only by scientific and technological advances (such as the steam engine and iron founding) but also by new economic structures (including mass production, the assembly line, and the emergence of the corporation).

In the same way, new forms of creative capitalism are already being unleashed by Generation We, including the application of modern management techniques to nonprofit socially oriented businesses (social entrepreneurship); the use of social networks to spread, consolidate, and mobilize ideas and information; the organization of work through electronic networks that connect people from many geographic locations; and the growth in self-employment, entrepreneurship, and independent initiative among young workers.

The American Revolution: *The Spark of a Powerful Issue*

The American colonies had existed for almost two centuries before the movement toward political and economic independence came to fruition. The revolution occurred when the growing American colonies were psychologically and socially ready to embrace an independence movement, and when a particular issue—"taxation without representation"—provided the spark that ignited national outrage and patriotism, and convinced a majority of Americans that political freedom was both necessary and achievable.

In a similar way, the rising discontent felt by millions of Americans today will eventually spark a reaction, in which the vast numbers of Generation We will surely play an important role. The specific cause the Millennials will rally around may be global warming, poverty in the developing world, economic fairness in the United States, peace in the Middle East, censorship and authoritarianism—or some emerging issue we can't even imagine today. But when the revolution begins, it is likely to have far-ranging consequences that extend well beyond the initial stimulus.

The Abolition of Slavery: *A Spiritual Awakening*

The movement to eliminate the national shame of slavery was, of course, driven by a growing social, moral, and spiritual awareness on the part of millions of Americans. However, that sense of awareness did not turn into action until a series of political events brought the conflict between North and South to a head, culminating in the election of Abraham Lincoln and the decision by the southern states to attempt secession.

Today's Millennials are ripe for a similar awakening of conscience that will help produce massive social changes. In fact, there are some startling similarities between the pre-Civil War era in the United States and the situation we face today. In a recent *Time* magazine article, historical novelist Kurt Andersen penned this description of the United States in 1848, when the Civil War generation was just coming of age:

> Miraculous new communications technologies have suddenly appeared, transforming everyday life. Everything is moving discombobulatingly fast. Globalization accelerates. Wall Street booms. Outside San Francisco, astounding

"An army of principles can penetrate where an army of soldiers cannot."

THOMAS PAINE

> fortunes are made overnight, out of nothing, by plucky nobodies. The new media are scurrilous and partisan. Marketing spin and advertising extend their influence as never before. A fresh urban-youth subculture has emerged, rude and vibrant, entertainment-fixated and violence-glorifying. Christian conservatives are furiously battling cultural decadence, and one popular sect insists that the end days are nigh. Ferocious anti-immigration sentiment is on the rise. Both major American political parties seem pathetically unable to deal with the looming, urgent issue of the day. Insurgents practicing asymmetrical warfare have, practically overnight, threatened to bring down the political order of Western civilization. And the President has tapped into patriotic rage to invade a poor desert country, having dubiously claimed that the enemy nation represents a clear and present military danger to America.[1]

The pre-Civil War period was a time of unprecedented national peril in a country deeply divided along social, racial, economic, geographic, and political lines. It's entirely possible that the resulting upheaval might have destroyed the country permanently. But thanks to the emergence of a number of inspiring, farsighted leaders (including Robert E. Lee, Ulysses S. Grant, and above all, Abraham Lincoln), as well as the remarkable dedication and selflessness of an entire generation of Americans from every background, the nation emerged stronger than ever—purged of the curse of slavery, politically reunited (though still split by bitter disputes and resentments), and poised for two generations of amazing geographic expansion and industrial growth. It is hoped Generation We will rise to the challenge with the same courage and wisdom their ancestors showed a century and a half ago.

The Progressive Movement: *Social Reform Reshapes Politics*

Yet another model of revolutionary change for America can be found in the Progressive Movement of the first two decades of the twentieth century. Driven by discontent over how our economic and political systems had adapted—or failed to adapt—to the impact of such changes as industrialization, westward expansion, massive immigration, and growing demands for equality among citizens, the Progressive Movement mobilized hundreds of thousands of Americans across the country behind a broad array of causes.

Some of the reforms championed by the Progressives are now taken for granted—antitrust laws, conservation of natural resources, banning of child labor, limitations on hours of work, workplace health and safety regulations, and rules concerning food and drug safety. Others have been forgotten or superseded—"bimetallism" rather than the gold standard, prohibition of alcohol, nationalization of industry.

But on balance, the legacy of the Progressive Era was a giant step toward making the United States a more democratic nation—one in which the rights of all people, from manual laborers to captains of industry, were recognized and respected, and in which economic freedoms are sensibly and fairly balanced against the needs of working people who might otherwise be exploited. And on the constitutional level, three amendments that helped bring the United States into the twentieth century—the 16th (the income tax, passed in 1913), the 17th (direct election of U.S. senators, 1913), and the 19th (women's suffrage, 1920)—were all products of the Progressive Movement.

Many leaders were responsible for the accomplishments of the Progressives, including social reformers (Jane Addams, Jacob Riis, Lewis Hine, Margaret Sanger), writers (Jack London, Upton Sinclair, Lincoln Steffens, Ida Tarbell), and organizers and educators (W.E.B. DuBois, John R. Mott, Booker T. Washington, Gifford Pinchot). Ultimately, the support of elected political leaders was needed to give the Progressive reforms the force of government and a permanent place in national life. Politicians such as William Jennings Bryan, Robert La Follette, and Theodore Roosevelt each adapted or developed portions of the Progressive agenda and used them to spearhead national movements for reform.

In a recent speech he gave when accepting an award from the Woodrow Wilson National Fellowship Foundation, journalist and television commentator Bill Moyers aptly summarized the role played by yet another visionary politician in bringing many of the causes of the Progressives into the political mainstream. Moyers also noted how the Progressive Era foreshadowed our own time, in which America again stands poised to pursue dramatic and long-overdue systemic reforms:

> In his forgotten political testament *The New Freedom* (1913), [Woodrow] Wilson took up something of the ancient, critical task of the public intellectual, a fact all the more remarkable in that he was president at the time. Louis Brandeis, the people's lawyer, was his inspiration and the source of this vision, but Wilson stood for it, right there at the center of power. "Don't deceive yourselves for a moment as to the power of the great interests which now dominate our development." "No matter that there are men in this country big enough to own the government of the United States. They are going to own it if they can." But "there is no salvation," he said, "in the pitiful condescensions of industrial masters. Guardians have no place in a land of freemen. Prosperity guaranteed by trustees has no

prospect of endurance." From his stand came progressive income taxation, the federal estate tax, tariff reform, and a resolute spirit "to deal with the new and subtle tyrannies according to their deserts."

Wilson described his reformism in plain English no one could fail to understand: "The laws of this country do not prevent the strong from crushing the weak." That was true in 1800, it was true in 1860, in 1892, in 1912, and 1932; it was true in 1964, and it is true today. We have often been pressed to the limit, the promise of the Declaration and the ideals of the Gettysburg Address ignored or trampled upon and our common interests brought low. But every time there came a great wave of reform, and I believe one is coming again, helped along by the bright young people this foundation is nurturing.[2]

Freedom Movements of the Twentieth Century: *The People Rise Up*

The twentieth century saw more than its share of revolutionary movements. Some were destructive, such as the Communist upheavals in Russia and China, and the fascist movements in Germany and Italy. But others were largely peaceful and almost entirely beneficent, including a variety of third-world independence movements spearheaded by India's Mahatma Gandhi and symbolized, a generation later, by Nelson Mandela's battle against apartheid in South Africa. For Americans, the greatest example is our own civil rights move-

©XAVI ARNAU/ISTOCK INTERNATIONAL

ment, led by the martyred Martin Luther King, Jr., and supported by hundreds of thousands of brave activists—black and white, women and men, young and old—who put their bodies and their honor on the line in support of the cause of justice.

In these movements, the pent-up longing for freedom shared by millions of people was channeled by great leaders into demands for peaceful change and the overthrow of once-powerful repressive elites—changes much like those we believe Generation We will soon demand.

WHAT CAN I DO?

For historians, social scientists, and journalists, it's fascinating to speculate about where and how the next great change in American society will emerge. More important for the rest of us is our role as citizens—to *make it happen* and to ensure that the change, when it comes, will be a positive one.

We hope every reader of this book, whether a member of Generation We or some other age cohort, feels excited by the vision of generational change we've painted. And we hope it will leave you wondering, "What can *I* do to help turn this vision of a better America into reality?"

Here are some answers.

Vote!—And Insist That Everyone Gets the Same Right to Vote

Voting is the most important action we're calling for in this book. It provides the political impetus and will that allow great things to be achieved. You *must* vote! If you don't, you waive your right to complain.

Generation We believes that everyone makes a difference, as evidenced by the GMS findings and several other sources on the sentiments of the generation. This means that every citizen has an obligation to participate in the democratic process, and voting is the most basic and essential way to start.

In today's political system, organized groups such as the American Association of Retired Persons (AARP) and the National Rifle Association (NRA) have power largely because politicians know their members express their values at the ballot box—and they use that power, sometimes wisely and sometimes not, to benefit the causes in which their members believe.

As a Millennial, you need to start building your own power base so the causes you believe in will be supported. That effort begins with the vote. If you care about the environment, economic justice, human rights, world peace, or any of the other causes we've mentioned in this book, you need to express those values on Election Day.

During the 2008 primary elections, voting by young people surged. It was a hopeful explosion of interest and activity by Millennials that suggested this generation may exercise its civic clout to a degree other recent generations have failed to do. But those who have studied the 2008 youth surge note that it was largely concentrated among college students. One estimate says that 80 percent of young voters during the 2008 cycle were college youth—despite the fact that noncollege youth make up a larger portion of the Millennial-age electorate. Obviously more must be done to get noncollege Millennials to get involved in the political process.

One way we can do more to encourage participation in the electoral process is by simplifying the process and eliminating barriers that discourage voting. Look at the state of Minnesota, for example. With its long tradition of progressive activism, Minnesota has some of the least-restrictive voting rules in the country, including same-day registration based on any state-issued ID or a wide range of acceptable substitutes, such as a student ID and a recent utility bill. Small wonder the state enjoys enormous turnout among youthful voters—69 percent in 2004, which is not only 50 percent higher than the national turnout among young voters (47 percent) but higher than the national average among all voters (60 percent)[3].

Some politicians—especially conservatives and Republicans—claim that making it easy for people to vote opens the door to electoral fraud. They use this as a justification for tough voter ID laws, such as the Indiana statute upheld by the U.S. Supreme Court in April 2008. But as even advocates for the law admitted, there is scanty evidence that such fraud exists. ("Indiana Secretary of State Todd Rokita has conceded the state has never presented a case of 'voter impersonation,' which the law was designed to safeguard against." [4])

It's hard not to attribute the demands for restrictive voting laws to a desire to keep young people and other progressive blocs away from the polls. (Because young people are more geographically mobile and less economically settled, they are less likely than other age groups to own government-issued photo ID cards, a trait they share with racial and ethnic minorities, the elderly, the poor, and other groups that tend to vote for progressive causes and candidates.) We need to push back against this trend toward rules that disenfranchise voters, which is so clearly un-American and antidemocratic.

At the same time, there are demonstrable, documented cases of fraud that represent a real threat to free elections in this country. We need to fight against electoral dirty tricks designed to deprive people

Q90

Are you registered to vote?

A	%
YES	75
NO	24

Q91

What are your chances of your voting in the election for president ?

A	%
WILL VOTE	63
PROBABLY	16
WILL NOT VOTE	9
DON'T KNOW	1

SOURCE THIS PAGE: GREENBERG MILLENNIAL SURVEY 2007

You must vote! If you don't, you waive your right to complain.

of their right to vote. Bizarre problems with voting machines (including thousands of votes that simply "disappear"), automated robocalls spreading false information about candidates and voting procedures, intimidating threats to prosecute voters for nonexistent or minimal rule violations, and other similar abuses have become a perennial problem. In closely contested elections, they can make a decisive difference. Progressives—including Millennials—should work together on efforts to eliminate these practices and prosecute political operatives who organize them.[5]

Hold Our Leaders Accountable

It's not enough merely to vote. Democracy requires our participation more frequently than once every year or two. As citizens, we need to stay involved in the workings of government on a year-round basis, making both elected officials and administrative appointees aware of our needs and wishes, and holding them accountable for delivering.

Keeping up the pressure on those who represent and serve us in government involves several specific strategies. It means staying informed—periodically checking up on what your governor, state legislator, U.S. senator, representative, and other key officials have been doing. It means questioning their actions and motives—looking behind the speeches and the press releases to ask, "Who benefits from this piece of legislation or that policy initiative—the citizens or the special interest groups?"

It means attending public meetings and forums where you'll have a chance to question officials face-to-face, and coming prepared with a couple of tough but fair and specific challenges you expect them to answer. It means sharing your ideas and concerns with your fellow citizens via letters to the editor and simple word-of-mouth. It means writing letters, sending emails, placing phone calls, and even organizing petition drives when you have a program or policy you want to see enacted.

Of course, in the end, you always have the ultimate recourse: to vote out of office those who refuse or fail to carry out the people's mandate.

It's sad to say, but when the Millennial agenda rises to the forefront of the national debate, there will be plenty of people who oppose it—for reasons of ideology, self-interest, or just plain stubbornness. Some will be those in office. They have a right to their opinions. But they don't have the right to claim to represent you. You'll need to fight—peacefully—the enemies of progress with everything you have.

Get Educated

We don't have to be passive victims of the mass media and their celebrity culture. In today's wired world, there are millions of sources of information about what's *really* going on in the world and how it affects us. Invest some time and energy in learning about how the world works—and begin thinking about how to change it for everybody's benefit.

Even as Millennials revel in the power of the Internet to connect with sources of knowledge anywhere in the world, many worry about the long-term impact that being flooded with data may have on their minds. In our focus groups, some spoke about the "numbing" effect of *too much* information—about how seeing floods, famine, and violence in far-off lands on the evening news night after night eventually causes the sympathetic spirit to shut down, leading people to retreat into their own interests. Others talked about feeling emotionally disconnected from human beings as electronic communication supersedes face-to-face or voice-to-voice dialogue.

These are real dangers and the inevitable downside of today's miraculously powerful communications technologies. It's up to Generation We to find ways to master these tools and make them serve human ends. Start exercising personal choice and self-discipline when it comes to your media diet. Turn off the umpteenth celebrity gossip show, the latest goofy video on YouTube, the newest fear-mongering email from some shadowy online source. Much of this is distraction media that is intentionally sensationalized to keep people from focusing on the real issues of the day and being able to seek out solutions. Look for sources of information and ideas that enrich, ennoble, and empower you—or create your own.

Just as a daily menu filled with junk food eventually causes physical illness, a media menu made up of mental rubbish will eventually leave you brain-dead and spiritually empty. Don't let this happen to you. Think about what you take in.

Connect the dots in your own life. Recognize the links between the personal and the political. Look at how the food you eat, the work you do, the state of your health, the air you breathe, and the prices you pay are all connected to the political system we tolerate.

Connect the Dots!

After watching one of our Millennial focus groups, one of our expert observers made an astute comment:

> Some young people today have difficulty figuring out how to connect themselves to the political system. They have no real sense of the entry points—no idea of how to draw lines between their lives and the kinds of changes that are needed in government to improve those lives. A big part of the reason for this problem is the way we teach civics in our schools. There's little emphasis on the role that citizens need to play in driving change, influencing legislators, and organizing behind a cause. Instead, the focus is on the internal mechanisms of government: how a bill becomes a law, what the Supreme Court does, and so on. The implied message is very simple: the Founders were great, they created a perfect system, now all we have to do is go shopping and let the government handle everything for us.

Of course, this is the worst possible message for young people to absorb—and a big part of the reason for the troubles we face today.

Fixing this is a major challenge that Generation We must tackle. It starts with you, the individual citizen. Connect the dots in your own life. Recognize the links between the personal and the political. Look at how the food you eat, the work you do, the state of your health, the air you breathe, and the prices you pay are all connected to the political system we tolerate.

Exercise Your Clout

As you learn more about the issues, share your knowledge with those around you. Reach out to family, friends, and neighbors. Start connecting with the people in your communities, including your geographic community (i.e., your neighborhood), your electronic community (your friends and acquaintances on the Internet), and your social and professional communities (fellow members of your industry, religion, or avocation). Remember that politics is *not* just for elected officials or party operatives—it's for every citizen.

Speak your mind about the issues you care about. Write letters, voice your mind at community meetings, join local action committees and citizens' groups. In a world where many people are apathetic, the energized few can have surprising power. Take it and use it!

We've talked about how the power of technology is giving a voice to many people who previously went unheard, unable to gain a foot-hold in the centralized mainstream media controlled by the power elite. The Internet can be an effective tool for communicating with people around the neighborhood and around the world, and some of today's most provocative and insightful writing on social, economic, and political topics can be found on websites and blogs. We encourage you to participant in this movement.

At the same time, it's important *not* to get too comfortable sitting in front of your computer monitor all day, typing messages that float out into cyberspace and end up affecting and changing nothing. "Virtual activism" is fine—so long as it's a launching pad toward the real thing!

Make Your Message Visible, Audible, and Impossible to Ignore

The last big generation of political activists, the Baby Boomers of the 1960s, got some things right and some things wrong. One of the things they got right was when they took to the streets in support of their most important goals—claiming civil rights for all Americans (especially African Americans) and ending the war in Vietnam.

Some of the giant demonstrations the Boomers mounted—with support, of course, from people of every generation—were crucial turning points in the evolution of popular opinion. Images of peaceful marchers in the South having fire hoses turned on them and police dogs sicced on them revealed to millions of Americans the brutality of the segregation regime and the need to support the aspirations of Black citizens for freedom. The unforgettable words of Martin Luther King, Jr., when he addressed 300,000 demonstrators during the 1963 March on Washington in his "I Have a Dream" speech have inspired generations of people around the world. The antiwar marches of the 1960s and 1970s, in which moms and dads, college students and home-makers, ministers and nuns, veterans and pacifists, and working men and women of every age participated, gradually convinced the people of America that the cause of peace was a universal one, not just the province of a few "pinkos" or "hippies."

Of course, marching in the streets isn't important for its own sake, although there is a value in simply getting people together to recognize and appreciate how large their numbers are and how great their potential power can be. Demonstrations must be smartly planned and creatively executed so as to maximize their publicity value, media appeal, and impact on public opinion. Millions of people around the world participated in protest marches against the impending Iraq War in February 2003, but those marches failed to even slow the rush to war, perhaps in part because the news media dismissed them as "Just business as usual"—the same kinds of marches they'd seen hundreds of times before.

Our point is that one of the important challenges for the enormous creativity of Generation We will be to develop new forms of peaceful protest designed to be effective in today's world of 24-hour saturated news coverage via cable TV and Internet. It won't take a lot—just two or three people with a bit of media genius who can design events (even "publicity stunts") that will attract as much interest and attention as, say, the latest escapades of Lindsay Lohan or Paris Hilton, and then the mobilization of caring Millennials in support of those events.

Children of the electronic media age, Generation We should use their media wisdom to spread the word about the causes they believe in. And—importantly—they need to remember the lesson taught by Gandhi and King: that an absolute commitment to nonviolence is a prerequisite for any movement that hopes to generate public support for a cause.

We do not condone violence of any nature in this movement. Peace begets peace, and violence creates hatred. We must move past that world of divisiveness to a new world of kindness and togetherness. But never forget—that doesn't mean passivity in the face of evil. The willingness to take a public stand for what is right is the other essential legacy of Gandhi and King.

Practice Consumer Power

Big companies have enormous influence on our world. But ultimately they are at the mercy of the customers who support them by buying their products. Exercise your power by becoming an educated consumer. Spend your money with those that have your best long-term interests in mind and demonstrate it through their actions, not just empty rhetoric. Learn about the environmental, social, and economic practices of the companies you patronize; choose products and services that benefit society, not just a few shareholders or executives; and let companies know that you shop in accordance with your social and political values.

Of course, individual consumers can only do so much. Far greater power can be wielded when consumers band together to combine their influence. An economic union created by and for Millennials that will represent their interests and values, demand concessions and changes from big businesses, and promote inter-generational equity could be a crucial step toward many of the goals outlined in this book.

Push for Change in Your Own Sphere of Influence

Are you a student or teacher? Look for ways to bring greater democracy and participation to the classroom and the campus. Are you a business person? Examine how your company influences the broader society, and try to shift that influence for the better. Do you support a church, synagogue, mosque, charity, or foundation? Use your influence to promote reform throughout our society. In combination, a million small efforts can produce a huge impact.

Get Organized

A hundred and eighty years ago, Alexis de Tocqueville noted that the great strength of American democracy lay not in government institutions or even in the genius of our Constitution, but in the myriad of private organizations through which people expressed their opinions and shaped the world around them.

These organizations go to make up what scholars often call "civil society," and their absence goes a long way toward explaining why otherwise great nations like Russia and China have been unable to make a transition to democracy, even after their old autocratic regimes have been found wanting. Civil society includes charitable organizations, foundations, religious groups, fraternal societies, service clubs, political groups, professional and business associations, and dozens of other kinds of organizations representing every conceivable socioeconomic grouping and point of view.

Millennials interested in promoting a change agenda need to create organizations of their own. There are plenty of powerful models to learn from. Look at how AARP has fought effectively for the economic and social rights of its 50-year-old-plus members; at how Jewish organizations have made certain the United States stands staunchly in support of Israel; at how the NRA has defended the prerogatives of gun owners; at how the teachers' unions have battled on behalf of the professional privileges of their members. You probably agree with the positions of some of these organizations and disagree with others. So do we. But all illustrate the political clout that an organized group of people can wield.

We want to see the day when spokespeople for Generation We can visit representatives and senators on Capitol Hill and say, "We're here to talk with you about our country's most pressing issues—and we represent the perspective of a hundred million voters." Don't you think a statement like that will get a politician's attention—fast?

The problems faced by America and the world are serious. But everyone has a solution—if we act together for the common good.

The time of Generation We is here. Let's seize it—now.

15 MINUTES FOR CHANGE

Everyone is busy. We have jobs to do, families to care for, homes to maintain, bills to pay. But that's no excuse not to get involved in the crucial task of creating our country's future.

> *Here's a list of actions you can take in 15 minutes or less that will contribute in a meaningful way to the Millennial movement we advocate. Why not copy the list and put it somewhere you can refer to it daily—on the fridge at home, on the wall in your office, or in your calendar or diary? Then, whenever you have just 15 minutes to spare, carry out one of the tasks on the list. You'll be well on your way to becoming the kind of engaged, empowered citizen that the power elites fear—and that makes our country great.*

> *Each of these steps is fast, simple, easy, and even fun. But cumulatively—through your own daily efforts, as well as those of thousands or millions of other people—they can have a huge impact on our world.*

- ✓ **Write a letter or an email to an elected official.** Names and addresses are readily available on government websites.
- ✓ **Phone a friend and talk about an issue that's important to you.**
- ✓ **Pick a nonprofit or advocacy organization** whose programs you admire and offer your support—in the form of a check or by volunteering to help when you have more time to spare.
- ✓ **Distribute information about an important issue**—hand out a few flyers to friends, post one at the local supermarket or town hall, or send an email with a link to an informative article to people you know.
- ✓ **Write a blog** post (on your own blog, or a friend's), presenting your opinion about some issue and backing it up with a fact or two.
- ✓ **Join a social-networking group,** and link to one or more subgroups that focus on social, political, or economic concerns.
- ✓ **Help someone register to vote,** and make sure he/she has a ride to the polls on election day.
- ✓ **Rewrite your shopping list**—read an article or website explaining which companies do business in environmentally, economically, and humanly sound fashion, and make them your suppliers of choice.
- ✓ **Write a letter to the editor of your local newspaper.**
- ✓ **Help to raise funds for a group or cause you support**—it can be as simple as calling three friends and saying, "I'm donating X amount—how about joining me?"
- ✓ **Educate yourself**—learn more about a problem or cause you're concerned about through online research or offline reading.
- ✓ **Nurture yourself**—do something to make yourself more physically, psychologically, or spiritually fit (through exercise, diet, or meditation, for example). The healthier you are, the smarter, stronger, and more effective you'll be as an agent of change.
- ✓ **Nurture your children**—if you have kids, take a few minutes to impart your values through example, shared activity, or simple conversation.
- ✓ **Give a copy of this book to someone** who may find it interesting, enlightening, or inspiring.

THANK YOU !

"There are no constraints on the human mind, no walls around the human spirit, no barriers to our progress except those we ourselves erect."

RONALD REAGAN

epilogue:

THE WE DECLARATION

We, the Youth of the United States,

are badly served by the governance and direction of our nation and the world. Our future is in peril. If the misconduct against our generation, humanity, and the planet continues, the American Dream our parents and grandparents experienced will become our American Nightmare.

We believe that all people—and all generations—are created equal, and like the Founders, we hold that all are endowed with equal rights and responsibilities. Further, all people and generations are to be treated equally.

We believe that in a nation founded on equality, all people have a guaranteed birthright of freedom, opportunity, fairness, health, and well-being. We rely upon the institutions of government, society, and business to protect this birthright and behave justly.

We believe that our birthright has been violated, and we are inheriting a damaged future.

Enough is enough. We have been left worse off than prior generations for the first time in our nation's history.

We will not accept an unfair future of incomprehensible debt, punitive taxation, economic disparity, military conscription, chronic disease, and environmental disaster.

Many in the establishment are robbing our birthright, the American legacy, and the planet. These plunderers exploit the institutions of government, society, and business to create a global empire and a new nobility that controls all resources, manipulates the media and markets, exploits current events and disasters, and treats the world as their private property.

The plunderers have created a political and business machine based on short-term, selfish greed and thirst for absolute power. They are stealing our security, destroying our planet, and selling out the long-term interests of our generation and its descendants.

The United States was formed to protect the interests of all citizens, *including* its young people. Our Constitution mandates liberties, rights, duties, and protects the people from oppression.

Our Constitution also sustains our nation from one generation to the next, where defending the future and its legacy are as important as caring for the present.

We, the youth, have inherited an unfair and unsustainable state of affairs. Our future has not been defended. If the people of the United States do not acknowledge the problems that confront us and move to rectify them, we, the youth, may not have a future worth living.

We believe that the time has come for our government and the establishment to respect our birthright and begin to manage affairs based on long-term interests and the greater good. The nation's leaders must be held accountable for their actions and end the plundering of our future.

We believe that the American Dream is at risk.
We live in a world where:

Our Health Has Collapsed.

We are suffering an epidemic of chronic, preventable diseases of abuse and neglect. We are being poisoned by the food we are fed and the drugs we are prescribed. Media, education, and government all brainwash us into thinking poisons are good for us. As a consequence, we are on the path to be the sickest generation in history. As children, we have the diseased arteries of the elderly. One in three of us will develop diabetes, more than half of us will become obese, and half of us will get cancer. Our lifespan is expected to be less than that of our parents.

Our Educational System Is Unfair.

A quality education is now the private property of the rich. Too many of our public schools are ineffective and decrepit, especially in the inner cities and rural America. A decent education, one leading to equality of opportunity, is out of reach to most people. Our skills in reading, writing, mathematics, science, and engineering are far behind those of our peers in the nations with which we must compete. The education system is manipulated by special interests for their own purposes, rather than for the service to the youth.

Our Environment Is Being Destroyed.

The devastation is putting mankind at risk. Our natural resources are being pillaged, deserts are being created, and clean water is becoming a luxury. Raw materials are being consumed unsustainably. If this alarming exhaustion continues, our generation could have nothing left to live on. Global warming is changing

We believe that the time has come for our government and the establishment to respect our birthright and begin to manage affairs based on long-term interests and the greater good. The nation's leaders must be held accountable for their actions and end the plundering of our future.

> *"It was we, the people; not we, the white male citizens; nor yet we, the male citizens; but we, the whole people, who formed the Union."*
>
> SUSAN B. ANTHONY

the entire landscape of opportunity and risks, and little is being done to immediately fix what is known to be enduring damage. Some even deny its existence. Caring for the environment is considered a burdensome expense, rather than a necessity for our future.

Our Planet Is Toxic and Dirty.

Irresponsible agriculture, manufacturing, power generation, and extraction of fossil fuels and metals are poisoning our lives. Our food and water now poison us with a host of diseases. In cities all over the world the sun is obscured from view by a filthy screen of pollution. It's impossible for humankind to flourish in a habitat coated with toxic sludge and wrapped in putrid air.

Our Debt Is Incomprehensible, Immoral, and Unsupportable.

We are assuming an unbounded national debt and social welfare obligations, which increase dramatically day by day. We are told that that debt does not matter—by those who will be dead before payment is due. We are obliged under penalty of law to fund massive social programs that benefit the old, but which will sap our productivity and which are projected to be insolvent by the time we might benefit from them.

Our Livelihoods Are Imperiled.

We are inheriting an economy that imports too many of its needs, exports our jobs, and runs massive trade deficits, all in the name of short-term business profits. The gap between rich and poor is widening, poverty is spreading, real wages and purchasing power are decreasing for the middle class, gasoline is unaffordable, homes are being repossessed at record rates, and the prospect of earning a living wage with job security and healthcare is a relic of the past.

Our Lives Are Not Our Own.

We are being conscripted to fight the wars of the plunderers, serving their ambitions and settling their scores. Many leaders care more about the illusion of victory, despite the costs, than about living in peace. We are told by our leaders that the "war on terror" will last our entire lives, and perhaps that of our children. We are asked to breed children to fight this war which we did not start and which offers no prospect of peace or compromise.

Our Civil Rights Are Besieged.

We are being spied on by government and business, our right to read or write what we wish is being undermined, our freedom of inquiry is being legislated away, and the courts are becoming tools of special interests.

Our Public Servants Are, in Too Many Cases, Engaged in Scandal and Selling the Assets of the Government to the Highest Bidder or Closest Friend.

Corruption, graft, waste, fraud, and conspiracy have become so common that they are ignored by the media and swept under a rug. The contract of honor and fiduciary responsibility between the government and its people has been broken. The government cannot even perform its most basic function of security in times of disaster, with Hurricane Katrina as just one example.

Our Laws Are Made and Money is Spent to Pander to Large Special Interest Groups with Organized Lobbies and Voting Strength, like Baby Boomers and Seniors.

For the purpose of getting elected today, legislators ignore our long-term interests, granting earmarks, entitlements, and expanding our debt to buy votes.

Our Media Do Not Represent Our Interests or Give Us a Voice.

Media are regulated and manipulated by the government and the establishment. The large media conglomerates serve as instruments of power and special interests selling us consumer goods and propaganda. Because we cannot trust the mainstream media, we rely on the Internet. But now it too is being purchased and manipulated by the same conglomerates and special interests. Slowly and surely, the regulators and courts are limiting its freedoms of privacy, expression, and organization. Governments around the world are censoring the Internet and employing it as a tool of espionage and coercion.

Some of Our Elders Do Not Really Believe in the Future.

Many religious and political leaders in the United States and abroad wish to see an “end of times” that will fulfill scriptural prophecies. We wish to live and live well. We do not want to die, and we do not wish for the planet to perish.

Skeptics, and those who have vested interests in oil, gas, and coal, will argue that such a program is unrealistic and overly ambitious. A similar mentality doubted that we could put a man on the moon, decode the human genome, harness electricity, or establish American democracy. Humanity progresses when it is optimistic and dedicates itself to the challenge. Inventing the next generation of energy will take incredible dedication and a lot of money, but the results will yield returns that dwarf the sacrifice.

The United States has an intrinsic innovation advantage over the rest of the world, and we must not squander the opportunity to lead and own the most important inventions in energy. We believe that it is possible, given our rate of technology advancement, to achieve this in time to save our environment and avoid energy wars in the future.

Inventing the next source of energy is the single greatest thing that changes the world for the better. There is nothing more important to our society. It is the call and legacy of the Millennial generation. It will be the greatest achievement in the history of mankind.

Restore and Protect Our Environment and the Planet.

We must immediately reverse and repair environmental desecration. We are quickly entering an era where survival will be difficult for many humans. We must clean the toxicity from our living conditions, as it is causing unprecedented disease and suffering.

Eliminate Wars Caused by Scarcity, Resource Contention, Plunderers, Ethnic and Religious Intolerance, and Economic and Military Imperialism.

We support the need to protect and preserve our nation, our freedom, our allies, and our interests. We support our military and soldiers for their valor and patriotism, and we wish to create a world of peace.

Provide Quality Nutrition and Healthcare for All Youth.

Every child must have health insurance and proper nourishment, whatever his or her family's income, ethnicity, and class. We must eliminate preventable chronic diseases and end the poisoning that is leading to a generation of obesity and diabetes and other preventable miseries such as hunger and malnutrition.

Provide Equality of Education and Learning Resources for All People and Economic Classes.

This is our investment in our future livelihood and ability to compete in a global economy.

Balance the Fiscal Budget and Eliminate the 10-Plus-Trillion-Dollar National Debt.

Our liability is horrifying and is increasing at an unsustainable level. It is not fair to expect us to pay off the reckless spending and consumption of the plunderers. We must not be forced to live in a world where we are indebted to countries that are potential competitors or adversaries. Our economy could collapse if they call in their loans or stop buying our Treasury bills.

Restructure and Fully Fund Social Security, Medicare, and Other Social Insurance Commitments.

We believe, for the most part, benefit commitments must be fully funded, and we must not expect them to be paid for by later generations. Today, we have more than 50 trillion dollars of future Medicare commitments to our elders, up from 20 trillion dollars in the year 2000. It is criminal to pass unfunded liabilities of this size to one's children.

End Large Structural Trade Imbalances.

Current account deficits of nearly one trillion dollars per year are unsustainable, and now for the first time in history, the United States is a net debtor nation. Unabated, the trade and current account deficits will decimate American liquidity and damage our ability to invest in our infrastructure to maintain acceptable levels of economic growth.

Restore Our Industrial Base and Economic Security of the Middle Class.

More people are falling into poverty, and real wages for the middle classes have been declining for 30 years. Secure jobs with living wages and healthcare must not be rarities. Our shrinking middle class and growing lower class have virtually no savings and are deeply indebted. They cannot afford energy, and home ownership is becoming out of reach because of the mortgage crisis brought about by financial speculators.There are now two Americas, and our political stability and economic viability are at risk, because no democracy has ever survived without a vibrant middle class.

Implement a Strategy for National Economic Development.

We must ensure our industrial infrastructure is self-sufficient. Because we are highly dependent on a global economic supply chain, we are at the mercy of other nations for essential industrial components requisite for our defense and basic needs. As we have seen with oil, this is a dangerous predicament.

Protect Our Civil Rights and Restore Human Decency.

To sustain our democracy, we must protect our rights to privacy and freedoms of speech, inquiry, and petition. We must reverse the deterioration of a free press and unbiased media and ensure the survival of an unfettered Internet. We must stamp out governmental graft and pandering to special interests, and we must restore honor and transparency to business and politics.

We must vigorously pursue this agenda for the greater good and peacefully transform our government to once again reflect the values of our Founders. Together, we can cause our nation to be managed for the long term, preserving our planet, security, rights, well-being, health, and opportunity.

We believe that we can innovate ourselves out of the mess we are in and create the greatest society in history.

We must create a culture of plenitude rather than plundering, contention, and conflict.

We must create a future where our birthright is restored, and we create a legacy for our descendants.

This We Declaration is a call to action. It is the beginning of our heroic movement to restore our future, save our nation, and preserve our planet.

We call upon the sincere youth, the fair-minded, and the legacy bearers to join our movement.

We will succeed in our cause, because right always prevails over wrong.

–Eric H. Greenberg

"Let us never forget that government is ourselves and not an alien power over us. The ultimate rulers of our democracy are not a president and senators and congressmen and government officials, but the voters of this country."

FRANKLIN D. ROOSEVELT

ACKNOWLEDGMENTS

I owe thanks to so many people for inspiring, guiding, mentoring, helping, and sharing themselves with me in life and this endeavor. This book is a result of working diligently to make myself into a better human being. Through that hard work, I was rewarded with the insight that inspired the vision that is now in your hands. Work on the self is the hardest work of all, and that dedication earned me the gift of being in service to the world, which is now my life purpose.

Many people have helped me along the way. I first must thank the Angel in my life, my Grandpa Jack, who believed unwaveringly in me and enabled me to become educated and pursue my life dreams.

I thank my wife Carmel, whom I fell in love with the day we met and have shared my life with ever since.

Dr. Larry Brilliant opened my soul to spirituality and gave me a book to read, which, at first, I could not understand, but which held the key to living for a higher purpose. After a lot of hard work and dedication, I came to understand the wisdom it contained, and it has had a profound effect. There are turning points in life, and angels speak to us through people. Meeting Larry was one of those times. My wife had gotten me an Aum necklace, which I thought was a cool thing to wear. I showed it to a Hindu friend, Chirag Patel, who shared that he has worn one every day and it brought him nothing but good luck. At that point, I wore the necklace every day. I showed this to Larry at a dinner where we were seated next to each other, and our conversation about that good luck charm was the start of a great friendship, which resulted in synchronicities that enabled my life transformation.

Larry, a week later, introduced me to my dear friend, Dr. Dean Ornish, who was the catalyst in my losing 60 pounds and gaining back my health, and who inspired the vision and formation of my food and health business. Dean has touched me in so many ways, and I am blessed to have him in my life.

Bill Davidow gave me my break in Silicon Valley by backing Viant, and without this, I would not be in the position I am today. He is a second father to me and has given me the gift of his support at the most important times in my life. Life goes full circle, and now Bill is on the board of directors of my new company, Beautifull—www.beautifull.com—and was instrumental in getting the company financed.

My dear brother, Alberto Villoldo, gave me love and keys to his wisdom. I have been blessed to spend a lot of time in Peru, in the Amazon and Andes, and Alberto shared his 30 years of experience and relationships with me unconditionally to help me create a path of experience and learning mere words can never articulate. My experiences in Peru have been the most powerful and transformative of my lifetime.

I owe thanks to many in Peru and the United States who played a part in my spiritual path by working with me and sharing their time, friendship, and knowledge: Marcela, Martin, Panduro, Humberto, Bernardina, Francisco, Chino, Wilbert, Paul, Manuel, and Brian.

Alberto introduced me to Paul Ray, author of *The Cultural Creatives*. Paul worked diligently with me to craft the thesis of this book, and our early collaboration resulted in the We Declaration and the basis for the survey, focus groups, and research that underpin this book. Many thanks to Jason Pontin for editing the Declaration and helping us frame the book early on.

Pete Leyden and I engaged on the importance of the Millennials in early 2005, and it was insight gained from Pete that drove me to explore this cultural shift and phenomena more closely. Pete has collaborated on the book since the beginning and brought Ruy Teixeira into the project. Ruy focused on the massive job of sifting through all data and materials ever written on the generation and connecting the patterns that formed the thesis of what is behind the generational shift. Ruy then introduced me to Jim Gerstein and Karl Agne, who designed and conducted our breakthrough proprietary survey and the ancillary 12 focus groups where we tested and validated the thesis of the book and survey results.

My long-time friend Jerry Weissman introduced me to Karl Weber. Karl is an extraordinary human being and an incredible talent. He has been my deepest collaborator in the project and integrated reams of data and complex ideas into a simple and compelling narrative. I am deeply grateful that Karl took on this project and is now a part of my life.

Karl introduced me to Mike Shatzkin, and he immediately jumped into the project to assist with the publishing and launch efforts. His sense of urgency, knowledge, and pragmatism are invaluable. Mike has brought together a talented team consisting of Peta Moran, Brian O'Leary, and Rich Freese to take our work forward.

Maria Giudice of HOT Studio and her design team took on the project of helping us design and produce the book and website, and without her angelic spirit, this project would not have the beauty it does. Sandra Kelch of Designpool has done an outstanding job leading the day-to-day creative direction, design and production and assembled a talented team. Hannah Day led the team as layout manager, assisted by Jesse Rice, with incredible devotion to the design and production of the book. Others that assisted the team were Sharon Anderson, Vanita Torcato, Tim Carroll, Patrick Gruwell, Candice Jacobus, Joshua Short, Solange Phommachanh and Patricia Chytrowski. They have done incredible work in a very compressed period of time. Sue Collier of Lead Dog Communications did a fine job of copyediting the manuscript under extreme time pressure. Thank you to Julie Connery who assisted with proofreading. SourceN rapidly developed our website, and I thank Jim Weldon and Ajay Ramachandran for their dedication and sense of urgency. Further thanks to GSI hosting and Mark Fuqua.

I want to thank my public relations team at Rubenstein and Associates, starting with Steven Rubenstein, Bob Lawson, Trey Ditto, and Andrew Palladino. Thanks to Max Pulsinelli of Maximum Impact

PR for his assistance in our effort. Further thanks to J. C. Davis, Josh Shore, and Stephen Marshall for assisting with the effort to take the ideas behind the book and create a movement out of them.

I have been blessed with many friends and colleagues who have supported me during the course of my life. Paul Clemmons has been my best friend virtually my entire life. Manny Fernandez, the former CEO of Gartner Group, gave me the assignment at the company to build an online presence in 1994, which launched my Internet success. Lori Atherton has been my executive assistant for almost 10 years and during that time has been my right arm. Andy Arnold opened the doors at Scient and Beautifull and has been such an asset to me. Ken Jones has been there every time I have ever needed him, and we have shared many experiences that transcend words. Aron Dutta is another brother to me, and he is one of the most talented, loyal, and dedicated people I know. Kit Rodgers and Martin Esteverena have each been my right arm at many of the most important times in my career. Bob Howe was a father and brother to me in the creation of Scient, and without his partnership, my biggest business success would not have been possible. My early partnerships with Mohr Davidow Ventures, Kleiner Perkins Caufield and Byers, and Sequoia Capital were instrumental to me becoming established in Silicon Valley. There is a long list of friends and colleagues—too many to mention here—who have been with me at various stages of my career and life, many of whom have worked with me repeatedly. You all are always in my thoughts, and my gratitude is enormous.

Others have played important roles in helping me grow personally, physically, and spiritually. Caren Raisin was my nurse, working with Dean Ornish to restore my health, after which she became the first employee at Beautifull. Albert Salopek and John Segesta physically trained me and provided the support system to regain my health over a two-year period. Rogelio Nunez, referred by Girija Brilliant, was my yoga instructor and helped me transform my posture and regain Prana. Kristin Davis and Bryan Black made my food and reinforced the insight that others have the same need I did for prepared, fresh, and healthy food. Paula LeDuc has been a sister to me and opened up her many years of experience and goodwill to enable the start of my new business. She introduced me to Donna Insalaco, who has become a dear friend and the culinary genius for my food company. Bill Ericson has become a great friend, and he, along with Mohr Davidow Ventures, has been tremendous in supporting Beautifull and its mission.

I have developed a deep interest and commitment to working within our political system and supporting the public servants who fight every day to sustain our nation and make it a better place. I would like to thank Senator Harry Reid for his friendship and inspiration. He is a man who works tirelessly for the greater good, and, in my mind, Leader Reid is the ultimate role model for great public servants.

At a political retreat for Democratic senators, I met Ben Barnes, who told me of the plight of the Native Americans of the Great Plains and how their voting rights were being suppressed, in part to defeat Tom Daschle in the 2004 election cycle. I helped Ben raise funds to support a get-out-the-vote effort, and then, as a result of meeting the leadership of the Lower Brule Sioux Tribe, took on a labor of love to develop wind farms on Native American land. This project culminated in what is becoming the largest Native American alternative energy investment in U.S. history.

Ben enabled me to get to know Tom Daschle on a personal basis, and with great respect I thank my friend Tom for being the elder-statesman, enabling the deal to put the energy project in the hands of the largest wind developer in the world. The project would not have been successful without the hard work of my partner and dear friend Tracey LeBeau.

I thank all those people who fight the good fight every day on behalf of making the world a better place. Many of you toil anonymously but all toward the greater good. The reward is in the work, and contentment comes from recognizing that. I am most inspired by Mahatma Gandhi, who liberated a country without violence and taught human decency and compassion.

Finally, I would like to thank Nature. I live at the base of Mount Tamalpais in Marin, California, and I have spent countless hours hiking and running on the mountain and in the redwood trees and lakes that surround it. I have gained much strength and clarity from my time spent in the wilderness. I also thank Apu Pachatusan in Peru. The Quechua translation of the name is "he who sustains the world," and in Incan culture, this Apu is considered the axis of the world. One of my greatest life experiences was climbing to the 16,000-foot summit of the mountain. I felt as one with the Earth and the Spirit of greater good. The Indians who guided me up the mountain shared an incredible gift, and for that I am ever grateful.

— Eric H. Greenberg

THE GREENBERG MILLENNIALS STUDY

The Greenberg Millennials Study included several components. It began with an in-depth national survey of 2,000 individuals age 18 to 29, conducted from July 20 to August 1, 2007, which used a mix of methodologies to explore the unique beliefs and attitudes of the Millennial generation. By moving beyond standard questions of behavior and traditional political measures to a deeper understanding of the core values that animate their daily lives and vision for the future—both in their individual lives and for the nation as a whole—this survey provides critical insights into this potentially historic generation.

The study also included a series of 12 geographically and demographically diverse focus groups, conducted during the first week of December 2007. These focus groups were of mixed gender and included a mix of ages between 18 and 29. Each group focused on a particular demographic subset of the Millennial generation.

Our three focus groups conducted in New York City included one made up of white college graduates, one of white noncollege grads, and one of African Americans. We conducted two focus groups (one in Birmingham, Alabama, and one in Denver, Colorado) consisting of evangelical Christians, and two (in Denver and Los Angeles) containing Hispanics. Two groups were selected to include Millennials with children of their own.

Taken together, the 12 focus groups captured a unique cross-section of various slices of the Millennial pie, and provided some vivid personal stories and testimony to flesh out the more general observations made possible by the broader survey.

RESULTS OF THE SURVEY

2000 RESPONDENTS, JULY 20-AUGUST 1, 2007

Survey performed by
Gerstein Agne Strategic Communications
National Survey, 18-29-year-olds

What follows are the question-by-question results of our 2007 survey of 2,000 Millennials. They're numbered as they were in the original survey, and the totals shown in the right-hand column represent percentages. We think you'll find these data fascinating. Taken together, they create a more complete and detailed portrait of the attitudes, values, and beliefs of Generation We than has ever previously been available.

Q2

We often look at history in terms of generations—groups of people of similar age and experiences who often share specific attitudes and priorities regarding the world around them—such as the Baby Boomers or Generation X. As you look at your own generation of young adults under the age of 30, do you agree or disagree that your generation shares specific beliefs, attitudes, and experiences that set you apart from generations that have come before you?

Strongly agree	35	(Don't know/refused)	1
Somewhat agree	55		
Somewhat disagree	7	**Total agree**	**90**
Strongly disagree	2	**Total disagree**	**9**

Q3

How much do you feel your generation of Americans under the age of 30 has in common—in terms of attitudes, beliefs, and priorities—with young adults of your generation in other countries?

A great deal	12	(Don't know/refused)	1
A fair amount	56		
Just a little	28	**Great deal/fair amount**	**68**
Nothing at all	3	**Little/nothing**	**31**

Q4

Do you feel your generation of Americans under the age of 30 has more in common–in terms of attitudes, beliefs, and priorities–with Americans of older generations or with young adults of your generation in other countries?

Much more with older Americans	8
Somewhat more with older Americans	36
Somewhat more with young adults in other countries	42
Much more with young adults in other countries	11
(Don't know/refused)	2
Total older Americans	**44**
Total young adults in other countries	**54**

Q5

Please tell us how important each of the following has been in shaping the attitudes and beliefs of your generation of Americans under the age of 30, on a scale of 0-10, where 10 means it has been extremely important in shaping your generation's attitudes and beliefs, and 0 means it has not been at all important. You can choose any number between 0 and 10–the higher the number, the more important that factor has been in shaping the attitudes and beliefs of your generation.

	Mean	10	8-10	6-10	0-5	DK-Ref
5. The terrorist attacks of 9/11	7.9	36	67	83	17	-
6. Global climate change	6.5	18	41	65	35	0
7. The growing racial and ethnic diversity of the U.S.	7.1	21	51	74	26	0

Q5 Continued

	Mean	10	8-10	6-10	0-5	DK-Ref
8. The rise of the Internet, cell phones, text messaging, e-mail, and other advances in personal technology	8.3	46	73	85	15	-
9. America's dependence on foreign oil	7.2	22	52	75	24	0
10. America's dependence on fossil fuels like coal, natural gas, and oil	7.2	22	53	76	24	0
11. Declining quality and rising inequality in America's public education system	7.2	23	52	75	25	0
12. Rapid shift of U.S. economy from manufacturing to services, information and technology	7.0	18	48	73	27	0
13. The war in Iraq	7.7	31	63	81	19	0
14. Corporate scandals such as Enron	5.7	10	27	52	47	1
15. The partisan divide in U.S. politics	6.2	11	32	60	40	0
16. Lack of long-term job and retirement security	7.1	22	51	74	26	0
17. Increase in obesity and chronic disease	7.0	19	49	74	26	-
18. The rising cost of health care and growing number of uninsured	7.2	23	50	74	25	0

Q19

Next, please tell us whether your generation of Americans under the age of 30 is more likely or less likely than earlier generations of Americans to be characterized by each of the following.

	Much More Likely	Smwt More Likely	No Dif	Smwt Less Likely	Much Less Likely	DK-Ref	Total More Likely	Total Less Likely	More - Less
19. Embrace innovation and new ideas	44	34	15	5	2	0	78	7	71
20. Start a new business	27	37	22	10	4	0	64	14	50
21. Make environmental protection a top priority	27	40	20	9	4	0	67	13	54
22. Express patriotic pride	15	23	28	26	8	0	38	34	3
23. Support those in the armed forces	22	26	28	18	6	0	48	24	24
24. Trust government and political leaders	5	12	20	36	27	0	17	63	-46
25. Believe government has a positive role to play	8	17	27	33	16	0	24	49	-25
26. Support working with other countries to achieve shared goals	19	42	24	11	4	0	60	15	45
27. Engage in volunteer activities or community service	12	33	29	20	6	0	45	26	20
28. Try to directly influence and communicate with elected officials	12	32	26	22	8	0	45	29	15

Q19 Continued

	Much More Likely	Smwt More Likely	No Dif	Smwt Less Likely	Much Less Likely	DK-Ref	Total More Likely	Total Less Likely	More - Less
29. Engage in political activism	13	30	28	23	6	0	42	29	13
30. Join a church or other organized religious community	9	16	29	33	13	0	25	46	-21
31. Express personal spiritual beliefs outside of organized religion	24	31	22	16	6	0	56	22	33
32. Join an independent or issue-based political movement	16	33	27	18	6	1	49	23	25
33. Support an emerging third political party	18	38	25	12	6	0	56	18	38

Q34

Now I'm going to read you some pairs of statements. As I read each pair, please tell me whether the FIRST statement or the SECOND statement comes closer to your own views, even if neither is exactly right.

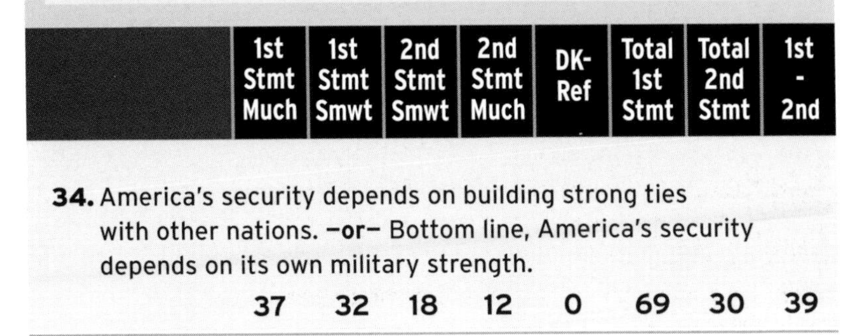

	1st Stmt Much	1st Stmt Smwt	2nd Stmt Smwt	2nd Stmt Much	DK-Ref	Total 1st Stmt	Total 2nd Stmt	1st - 2nd
34. America's security depends on building strong ties with other nations. **–or–** Bottom line, America's security depends on its own military strength.	37	32	18	12	0	69	30	39

	1st Stmt Much	1st Stmt Smwt	2nd Stmt Smwt	2nd Stmt Much	DK-Ref	Total 1st Stmt	Total 2nd Stmt	1st - 2nd
35. Addressing the big issues facing my generation starts with individuals willing to take a stand and take action. **–or–** Individuals can't make a real difference in addressing the big issues facing my generation.	47	33	15	5	0	80	20	60
36. The two-party political system in our country is working because it offers voters a clear choice between two different visions for our country's future. **–or–** Democrats and Republicans alike are failing our country, putting partisanship ahead of our country's needs and offering voters no real solutions to our country's problems.	12	18	31	39	0	29	70	-41
37. Businesses and corporate leaders have a responsibiilty to try to make the world a better place, not just make money. **–or–** Businesses and corporate leaders' responsibility to their shareholders is to make money, not to worry about making the world a better place.	44	30	17	9	0	74	26	48
38. Government has a responsibility to pursue policies that benefit all of society and balance the rights of the individual with the needs of the entire society. **–or–** The primary responsibility of government is to protect the rights of the individual.	27	35	23	14	0	63	37	25
39. The needs and goals of my generation are fundamentally at odds with those of older generations, and accomplishing our goals will require removing those currently in power and replacing them with ourselves. **–or–** The needs and goals of my generation are similar to those of older generations, and our best course is to work together to advance common interests.	19	30	34	16	1	49	50	-1

Q34 Continued

	1st Stmt Much	1st Stmt Smwt	2nd Stmt Smwt	2nd Stmt Much	DK-Ref	Total 1st Stmt	Total 2nd Stmt	1st - 2nd
40. Government needs to do more to address the major challenges facing our country. - OR - Government is already too involved in areas that are better left to individuals or the free market.	34	29	22	15	0	63	37	26
41. I believe that spending money with companies that reflect my values and priorities is an effective way to express my values and to promote change through my daily life. **–or–** My consumer choices are based on economics, not values, and I don't see my purchasing decisions as an effective way of expressing my values or promoting change.	23	31	29	16	0	55	45	10
42. We must make major investments now to innovate the next generation of non-fossil fuel based energy solutions. **–or–** We should continue on our current path, gradually shifting the mix of sources used to meet our energy needs.	46	29	17	8	0	74	26	49

Q43

Now we're going to review some statements. As you read each statement, please tell us whether you agree or disagree with the statement.

	Strng Agree	Smwt Agree	Smwt Dis-agree	Strong Dis-agree	DK-Ref	Total Agree	Total Dis agree	Agree - Dis
43. In our country, each generation has a responsibility to wisely use the country's resources and power so that they can provide the next generation a secure, sustainable country that is stronger than the one they inherited.	53	38	8	1	0	91	9	82
44. Our current political and corporate leaders are abusing their power for selfish gains, wasting our nation's resources for their own short-term gain and threatening our long-term security.	45	37	15	3	0	82	18	64
45. Young Americans must take action now to reverse the rapid decline of our country. If we wait until we are older, it will be too late.	48	41	9	1	0	89	11	78
46. Life in the future in America will be much worse unless my generation of Americans takes the lead in pushing for change.	42	43	13	2	0	85	15	70
47. I am willing to personally make significant sacrifices in my own life to address the major environmental, economic, and security challenges facing our country.	27	51	18	4	0	78	22	56
48. My generation of Americans has better opportunities to make a difference and produce structural change than previous generations.	31	48	17	3	0	79	20	59

Q43 Continued

	Strng Agree	Smwt Agree	Smwt Dis-agree	Strong Dis-agree	DK-Ref	Total Agree	Total Dis-agree	Agree - Dis
49. Throughout our history, America's success has been built on innovation and entrepreneurship. As we confront the many challenges facing us today, it is that same spirit of innovation and entrepreneurship that is needed to maintain America's strength in the 21st century.	38	49	11	2	0	87	13	75
50. When something is run by the government, it is necessarily inefficient and wasteful.	14	40	36	9	0	54	45	9
51. There should be a third political party in our country that fits between the Democrats and Republicans and offers a viable alternative to the two major parties.	35	41	18	6	1	76	24	52

Q52

Do you believe that, 20 years from now, your generation will live in a country that is better off or worse off than the one we live in today?

Much better off 9	Much worse off. 18
Little better off 25	(Don't know/refused) . . . 1
About the same. 20	**Total better off. 34**
Little worse off 28	**Total worse off. 46**

Q53

Now we're going to review some more statements about some of the issues facing our country. Once again, as you read each statement, please tell us whether you agree or disagree with the statement. (IF AGREE) Does this situation represent a crisis that our country must address immediately, a major problem that must be addressed soon, or a minor problem that should be addressed eventually?

	Agree Crisis	Agree Major Prob	Agree Minor Prob	Disagree	DK-Ref	Total Agree
53. Our nation's continuing dependence on oil has weakened our economy and stifled innovation, left us dependent on foreign countries—some of whom sponsor terrorism against us—and dragged us into unnecessary wars.	37	42	15	6	1	93
54. With costs rising out of control and the quality of health coverage declining, the health care system in our country is broken, and we need to make fundamental changes.	38	42	16	4	-	96
55. The growing burden placed on our country by our massive national debt is hurting our economy, stifling job growth and investment and making it harder for American businesses and entrepreneurs to be competitive in the global marketplace.	22	43	27	8	0	92
56. The health of our country is collapsing under an epidemic of chronic, preventable diseases as we slowly poison our own bodies through environmental pollution, overmedication, and unhealthy diets.	28	43	22	7	0	93

Q53 Continued

	Agree Crisis	Agree Major Prob	Agree Minor Prob	Dis-agree	DK-Ref	Total Agree
57. We have an unequal education system in our country, where students in affluent areas enjoy better resources and learning environments while those in rural areas and inner cities too often receive an inferior education.	31	40	21	8	0	92
58. Man-made causes are destroying our environment and the Earth's delicate ecosystem. As a result, we could see massive, irreversible damage to the Earth's landscape during our lifetimes.	35	39	18	9	0	91
59. Our country must take extreme measures now, before it is too late, to protect the environment and begin to reverse the damage we have done.	33	41	20	6	-	94
60. The federal debt is exploding, with no end in sight, shifting a tremendous burden onto future generations to pay for the failed leadership of the current generation and weakening America's economic growth for decades to come.	30	44	21	5	0	94
61. The changing nature of America's economy, where we import most of our goods and export millions of jobs to developing countries, is threatening America's middle class.	26	43	24	7	0	92
62. Long-term jobs that provide comprehensive health benefits and retirement security are becoming athing of the past, and individuals in our generation will have to provide for their own health care and retirement security.	32	42	18	7	0	93

Q53 Continued

	Agree Crisis	Agree Major Prob	Agree Minor Prob	Dis-agree	DK-Ref	Total Agree
63. Americans' basic civil rights are being undermined more every day. Government and business have compromised our privacy, the corporate media tells us what they want us to hear rather than the facts, and justice is for sale to anyone who can afford the right lawyers.	31	38	24	7	0	92
64. From the failed response to Hurricane Katrina to persistent fraud, corruption, and abuse, our government has failed to meet its most basic responsibilities and violated the very taxpayers who fund it.	30	41	20	9	0	90
65. Government is dominated by special interests and lobbyists, who give millions of dollars in campaign contributions to politicians, who in turn give even more back to those special interests, while the rest of us are left holding the bag.	31	42	21	5	0	95
66. Hurricane Katrina revealed the extent to which our country is divided into two Americas, one of which lacks many basic needs and is largely ignored by our government. The growing gap between the wealthy and the rest of us must be addressed, because no democracy can survive without a large, vibrant middle class.	30	40	20	9	0	90
67. Our reliance on fossil fuels is a by-product of the interests of those currently in power. We need to invest in and innovate new energy sources in order to protect our quality of life and prosperity.	33	43	19	4	0	96

Q68/69

Thinking about the many challenges facing our country, do you feel the best way to address these challenges is...through individual action and entrepreneurship, through a collective social movement, through the media and popular culture, through government action, or through international cooperation? And what do you feel is the second best way to address these challenges?

	Comb	1st	2nd
A collective social movement	60	38	22
Government action	40	16	24
Individual action and entrepreneurship	35	16	19
Media and popular culture	33	16	17
International cooperation	30	12	18
(Don't know/refused)	1	1	1

Q70

Now let's look at some potential solutions for some of the major challenges facing our country today. For each, please tell us how effective you feel each of the following would be in addressing that issue, on a scale of 0-10, where 10 means it would be extremely effetive in addressing that challenge and 0 means it would not be at all effective. You can choose any number between 0 and 10—the higher the number, the more effective you feel the solution would be in addressing that issue.

	Mean	10	8-10	6-10	0-5	DK-Ref
70. Launch a concerted national effort, similar to the Apollo Program that put a man on the moon, with the goal of moving America beyond fossil fuels and inventing the next generation of energy, based on new technologies such as hydrogen or fusion. This aggressive plan would require a huge national investment but would produce millions of new jobs, could dramatically reduce environmental damage, and free us from our dependence on fossil fuels and foreign oil.	7.0	21	49	71	29	0
71. Commit ourselves to a comprehensive effort to not only reduce the pollution we are putting into the environment but reverse the damage we have done. That damage is not only polluting the earth, it is causing unprecedented disease and suffering in communities throughout our country and across the globe.	6.9	20	46	69	30	0
72. Provide quality health care and nutrition for all children in our country, regardless of their financial condition. Poor nutrition is creating an epidemic of preventable chronic diseases, including diabetes and obesity, that will cost our country billions of dollars and ruin the lives of millions of children.	7.3	29	53	75	25	-

Q70 Continued

	Mean	10	8-10	6-10	0-5	DK-Ref
73. Provide equal funding for public education and learning resources for all children and all communities, regardless of economic class. This is a critical investment in the human potential of our country and its ability to compete in a global economy.	7.2	27	53	73	27	0
74. Balance the federal budget, but also eliminate the 8 trillion dollars of national debt that have been built up over decades of irresponsible spending. This debt makes it impossible for our country to keep pace and leaves us indebted to other countries who are potential competitors.	6.8	16	43	69	31	0
75. Fully fund Social Security, Medicare, and other social insurance commitments being passed on to future generations, which have doubled to over 40 trillion dollars just since 2000 and are increasing by several trillion every year. These commitments must be met by current generations because it would be morally wrong to pass on unfunded liabilities of this size to our own children.	6.7	17	43	66	33	0
76. End trade imbalances that see us importing nearly 1 trillion dollars per year more than we export to other countries by restoring our industrial base. Restoring our industrial base and eliminating our trade deficit will provide secure jobs with good wages and benefits and rebuild our shrinking middle class.	6.6	16	39	66	33	0

Q70 Continued

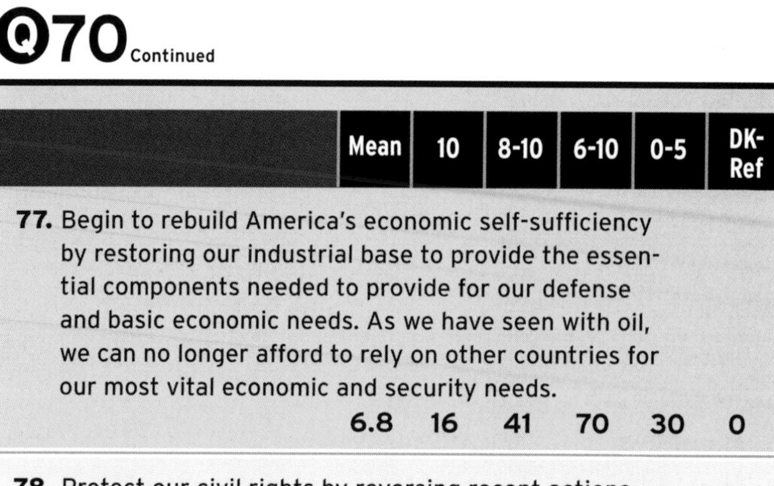

	Mean	10	8-10	6-10	0-5	DK-Ref
77. Begin to rebuild America's economic self-sufficiency by restoring our industrial base to provide the essential components needed to provide for our defense and basic economic needs. As we have seen with oil, we can no longer afford to rely on other countries for our most vital economic and security needs.	6.8	16	41	70	30	0
78. Protect our civil rights by reversing recent actions to restrict our right to privacy and to limit access to government information, ensuring survival of a free and unrestricted Internet, and restoring an objective, unbiased media. Protecting our civil rights also requires eliminating the influence of special interests over our government and creating more transparency in government and business.	6.6	17	40	65	35	0

Q79

Finally, a few questions for statistical purposes. First, what is your gender?

Male . . . . .51 Female 49

Q80

What is the last year of schooling that you have completed?

1-11th grade 5
Noncollege post H.S. . . . 2
College graduate 23
Post-graduate school. . . 6
High school grad 22
Some college 42
(Don't know/refused) . . .0

Q81

In what year were you born? (age)

18. 7
19. 8
20 9
21. 9
22 8
23 9
24 9
25 9
26 9
27 8
28 8
29 8

Q82

Are you married, single, separated, divorced, or widowed?

Married 30
Separated 1
Widowed 0
Single 68
Divorced 1
(Don't know/refused) . . .0

Q83

Do you have any children?

Yes	30	(Don't know/refused)	.0
No	70		

Q84

Regardless of any religious affiliation or beliefs, do you consider yourself to be a spiritual person?

Yes	.73	(Don't know/refused)	.0
No	26		

Q85

Do you consider yourself to be a member of a specific religious community? (IF YES) Which of the following best describes your religion?

Roman Catholic	.15	Charismatic	.1
Baptist	11	Buddhist	.1
Non-denominational Christian	.10	Christian Scientist	.1
Lutheran	3	Hindu	.1
Methodist	3	Islam	.1
Presbyterian	2	Seventh Day Adventist	.0
Congregational/ United Church of Christ	2	Eastern Orthodox	.0
Pentecostal	2	Anglican/Episcopal	.0
Mormon	2	Unitarian Universalist	.0

Q85 Continued

Jewish 2	(Other) 8
Evangelical 1	No religious affiliation. . 33
	(Don't know/refused) . . .0

[731 Respondents]

Q86

(IF LUTHERAN, PRESBYTERIAN, CONGREGATIONAL, EVANGELICAL, CHARISMATIC, BAPTIST, METHODIST, SEVENTH DAY, PENTECOSTAL, OR NON-DENOMINATIONAL) Do you consider yourself to be a born-again Christian?

Yes 58	(Don't know/refused) . . .0
No 42	

Q87

Have you done any volunteer work in the last 12 months? (IF YES) How often do you participate in volunteer work?

Volunteer on a weekly basis 9
Volunteer once or twice a month 13
Volunteer several times a year 19
Volunteer once or twice a year 20
No volunteer work in last 12 months 40
(Don't know/refused) 1

Q88

How effective do you think community volunteerism is as a means of solving the major challenges facing our country?

Very effective. 26
Somewhat effective . . 47
A little effective. 23
Not at all effective 4
(Don't know/refused) . . .0
Very/somewhat 73
Little/not. 27

Q89

How effective do you think political activism is as a means of solving the major challenges facing our country?

Very effective. 18
Somewhat effective . . .51
A little effective. 25
Not at all effective 6
(Don't know/refused) . . . 1
Very/somewhat 69
Little/not. 31

Q90

Are you registered to vote?

Yes 75
No 24
(Don't know/refused) . . .0

Q91

I know it's a long way off, but what are the chances of your voting in the election for President next year?

Almost certain to vote . 63
Probably will vote. 16
50-50 11
Will not vote 9
(Don't know/refused) . . . 1

Q92

Generally speaking, do you think of yourself as a Democrat, a Republican, or what?

Strong Democrat 16
Weak Democrat. 20
Independent-lean Democrat 11
Independent. 22
Independent-lean Republican 6
Weak Republican. 14
Strong Republican 10
(Don't know/refused) . . . 1

Q95

How often do you talk about politics with your friends and co-workers?

Frequently. 19
Sometimes 45
Hardly ever 26
Never 10
(Don't know/refused) . . . -
Frequently/sometimes 64
Hardly ever/never . . . 36

Q97

In terms of your job status, are you...

Employed full-time . . . 46
Employed part-time . . . 14
Unemployed, looking for work. 7
Student 23
Homemaker. 9
(Don't know/refused) . . . 0

Q98

Are you a member of a labor union? (IF NO) Is any member of your household a union member?

Yes, I'm a union member 6
Household member belongs to union 10
No union members in household 83
(Don't know/refused) 1

Q99

Which of the following three statements is most accurate for you and your household?

Everyone in the household has health insurance coverage 63
Some people in the household have health coverage, and some currently do not have coverage 28
Nobody in the household currently has health coverage . . 9
(Don't know/refused) 0

Q100

What racial or ethnic group best describes you?

White. 65
African-American or Black 13
Hispanic or Latino 15
Native American 1
Asian or Pacific Islander .4
(Other) 2
(Don't know/refused) . . .0

Q101

Last year, that is in 2006, what was your total household income from all sources, before taxes?

Less than $10,000 9
$10,000 to $19,999. . . . 11
$20,000 to $29,999 . . .15
$30,000 to $49,999 . . 23
$50,000 to $74,999 . . .19
$75,000 to $99,999. . . 10
$100,000 to $249,999 . .8
$250,000 or more. 2
(Don't know/refused) . . .3

SOURCE NOTES

For a detailed listing of polls, surveys, and research studies regarding the Millennial generation, see the Bibliography. Other sources used in this book appear below.

[1] "Educational Attainment in the United States: 2005." U.S. Census Bureau. Online at http://www.census.gov/population/www/socdemo/education/cps2005.html.

[2] In this chapter, we cite a number of surveys by date, sponsoring organization, and title (if appropriate). As we went to press, information on all the surveys we mention is available online. Further details can be found in the Bibliography to this book. The organizations whose surveys we cite are as follows:

Center for Information and Research on Civic Learning and Engagement (CIRCLE). Surveys, available at http://www.civicyouth.org.

Democracy Corps. Surveys available at http://www.democracycorps.com.

Greenberg, Quinlan, Rosner Research. Surveys available at http://www.gqrr.com.

Guttmacher Institute, "U.S. Teenage Pregnancy Statistics National and State Trends and Trends by Race and Ethnicity." Updated September 2006. Online at http://www.guttmacher.org/pubs/2006/09/12/USTPstats.pdf.

Harvard Institute of Politics. Surveys available at http://www.iop.harvard.edu.

National Institute on Drug Abuse. Survey designed and conducted by the University of Michigan, "32nd Annual Monitoring the Future Survey." Available at http://monitoringthefuture.org/data/06data.html#2006data-drugs.

New York Times/CBS News/MTV Poll, "17 to 29 Year Olds." June 15–23, 2007. Online at http://graphics8.nytimes.com/packages/pdf/politics/20070627_POLL.pdf.

Pew Research Center. Surveys available at http://people-press.org/reports.

University of Michigan, American National Election Study, 2004. Available at http://sda.berkeley.edu/cgi-bin/hsda?harcsda+nes2004p.

[3] U.S. Census Bureau, International Data Base, Table 94. Online at http://www.census.gov/cgi-bin/ipc/idbagg.

[4] *Millennials Rising: The Next Great Generation*, by Neil Howe and William Strauss. New York: Vintage Books, 2000, pages 298–299.

[5] "The 50 Year Strategy: A New Progressive Era (No, Really!)" by Simon Rosenberg and Peter Leyden. *Mother Jones*, November/December, 2007.

[6] See, for example, the National Election Studies in the 1950s and 1970s, which found that "Party identification was the most stable attitude measured...indeed almost perfectly stable." *Oxford Handbook of Political Psychology*. Oxford:

Oxford University Press, page 79. Also see *The American Voter*, by A. Campbell, et. al. Survey Research Center, The University of Michigan, 1964.

[1] The Physical Science Basis of Climate Change—Summary for Policymakers, Intergovernmental Panel on Climate Change, Working Group 1. Online at http://ipcc-wg1.ucar.edu/wg1.wg1-report.html. Cited in *Freedom from Oil: How the Next President Can End the United States' Oil Addiction*, by David Sandalow. New York: McGraw-Hill, 2008, page 29.

[2] Details on coal here and in the following paragraph from "Dirty Coal Power," The Sierra Club. Online at http://www.sierraclub.org/cleanair/factsheets/power.asp.

[3] "Coal Facts 2007." World Coal Institute. Online at http://www.worldcoal.org/pages/content/index.asp?PageID=188.

[4] "Water for People, Water for Life: The United Nations World Water Development Report." UNESCO, March 2003. Online at http://www.unesco.org/water/wwap.

[5] "Half the world facing water shortages by 2025," by Francoise Kadri. ABC News, March 11, 2003. Online at http://www.abc.net.au/science/news/stories/s803659.htm.

[6] "Water shortages and drought are the next scourge, warns U.S. group," by David Gow. *The Guardian*, May 29, 2008. Online at http://www.guardian.co.uk/business/2008/may/29/generalelectric.greenbusiness.

[7] "Message from the Director-General," in *The World Health Report 2007—A Safer Future: Global Public Health Security in the 21st Century.* The World Health Organization. Online at http://www.who.int/whr/2007/en/.

[8] "The Growing Crisis of Chronic Disease in the United States." Partnership to Fight Chronic Disease. Online at www.fightchronicdisease.org/pdfs/ChronicDiseaseFactSheet.pdf

[9] "Hint of Hope As Child Obesity Rate Hits Plateau," by Tara Parker-Pope. *New York Times*, May 28, 2008. Online at http://www.nytimes.com/2008/05/28/health/research/28obesity.html.

[10] *Money-Driven Medicine: The Real Reason Health Care Costs So Much*, by Maggie Mahar. New York: Collins, 2006, page xiv.

[11] Statistics from "Facts on the Cost of Health Care," website of the National Coalition on Health Care. Online at http://www.nchc.org/facts/cost.shtml.

[12] "The First National Report Card on Quality of Health Care in America: Research Highlights." RAND Health. Online at http://rand.org/pubs/research_briefs/RB9053-2/index1.html.

[13] "Why Not the Best? Results from a National Scorecard on U.S. Health System Performance." The Commonwealth Fund Commission on a High Performance Health System. 20 September, 2006. Online at http://www.

commonwealthfund.org/publications/publications_show.htm?doc_id=401577.

[14] *Money-Driven Medicine*, page 159.

[15] *Condition of America's Public School Facilities: 1999*. National Center for Education Statistics, Statistical Analysis Report, June 2000. Online at http://nces.ed.gov/pubs2000/2000032.pdf.

[16] "U.S. Teens Trail Peers Around World in Math-Science Test," by Maria Glod. *Washington Post*, December 5, 2007, page A7. Online at http://www.washingtonpost.com/wp-dyn/content/article/2007/12/04/AR2007120400730.html.

[17] "New Research Finds Students' Weak Cognitive Skills Adversely Affect U.S. Economic Growth Rate," by Eric. A. Hanushek, Stanford University. Business Wire. Online at http://www.reuters.com/article/pressRelease/idUS138590+03-Mar-2008+BW20080303.

[18] "U.S. Debt: $30,000 per American." *USA Today*, December 3, 2007.

[19] *Financial Audit, IRS's Fiscal Years 2006 and 2005 Financial Statements*, U.S. Government Accountability Office Report to the secretary of the Treasury, page 152. Online at www.gao.gov/cgi-bin/getrpt?GAO-07-136

[20] "America 101," by Bill Moyers. Speech delivered October 27, 2006, to the Council of Great City Schools in San Diego, California.

[21] *Data in Supercapitalism: The Transformation of Business, Democracy, and Everyday Life*, by Robert B. Reich. New York: Alfred A. Knopf, 2007, page 103.

[22] Ibid., page 106.

[23] "The World Distribution of Household Wealth," by James B. Davies, et. al. UNU-WIDER (World Institute for Development Economics Research), Discussion Paper No. 2008/03, February 2008, page 4.

[24] "How the Democrats Can Keep the Youth Vote," by Paul Rogat Loeb. Online at http://www.paulloeb.org/articles/financialaidandyouthvote.html.

[25] "Youth Quake," by Michelle Conlin. *BusinessWeek*, January 21, 2008, p. 34.

[26] *The End of America: Letter of Warning to a Young Patriot*, by Naomi Wolf. White River Junction, VT: Chelsea Green Publishing, 2007.

[27] "Outsourcing Torture: The Secret History of America's 'Extraordinary Rendition' Program," by Jane Mayer. *The New Yorker*, February 14, 2005.

[28] "Day 1: America's prison for terrorists often held the wrong men," by Tom Lasseter. McClatchy Newspapers, June 15, 2008. Online at http://www.mcclatchydc.com/259/story/38773.html.

[29] *The End of America*, pages 97–100.

[30] "Message Machine: Behind TV Analysts, Pentagon's Hidden Hand," by David Barstow. *New York Times*, 20 April 2008.

[31] "Media Backtalk," by Howard Kurtz. *Washington Post*, April 28, 2008. Online at http://www.washingtonpost.com/wp-dyn/content/discussion/2008/04/25/DI2008042502539.html.

[32] "Saudi says he nixed Fox News 'Muslim riots' banner," by Art Moore. *WorldNetDaily*, December 9, 2005. Online at http://www.worldnetdaily.com/news/article.asp?ARTICLE_ID=47771.

[33] *Alwaleed: Businessman, Billionaire, Prince*, by Riz Khan. New York: Harper Collins, 2005.

[34] "Water Wars of the Near Future," by Marq de Villiers. *ITT Industries Guidebook to Global Water Issues.* Online at http://www.itt.com/waterbook/Wars.asp.

[35] Data on military spending from "World Military Spending" by Anup Shah. From GlobalIssues.org. Online at http://www.globalissues.org/Geopolitics/ArmsTrade/Spending.asp.

[36] "A Parable For Our Times," by Bill Moyers, December 22, 2006, TomPaine.com. Online at http://www.tompaine.com/articles/2006/12/22/a_parable_for_our_times.php.

[37] The Nobel Lecture, Al Gore, December 10, 2007. Online at http://nobelprize.org/nobel_prizes/peace/laureates/2007/gore-lecture_en.html.

CHAPTER 5

[1] "The Fourth Turning, Part II—Rise of the Anti-Boomers: Millennial Generation 1, Imus 0," by M. A. Nystrom. Bullnotbull website at http://www.bullnotbull.com/archice/fourth-turning-2.html.

[2] *Millennial Makeover: MySpace, YouTube & the Future of American Politics*, by Morley Winograd and Michael D. Hais. New Brunswick, NJ: Rutgers U.P., 2008, page 148.

[3] *Youth to Power: How Today's Young Voters Are Building Tomorrow's Progressive Majority*, by Michael Connery. Brooklyn: Ig Publishing, 2008, page 174.

[4] *Millennial Makeover*, pages 134–135.

[5] "The 50 Year Strategy: A New Progressive Era (No, Really!)" by Simon Rosenberg and Peter Leyden. *Mother Jones*, November/December, 2007.

[6] Harvard University Institute of Politics, "The 12th Biannual Youth Survey on Politics and Public Service March 8–26 2007." Cited in *Youth to Power*, page 166.

[7] "Progressive Re-Generation," by Ben Adler. *The American Prospect*, 25 February 2008. Online at http://www.prospect. org/cs/articles?article=progressive_re_generation.

[8] Ibid.

[9] "Youth Voters Make History as Turnout Shatters Records in 2008 U.S. Presidential Primaries." Fox Business, June 6, 2008. Online at http://www.foxbusiness.com/story/youth-voters-make-history-turnout-shatters-records--presidential-primaries/#.

[10] *Youth to Power*, pages 95–96.

[11] *Youth to Power*, pages 97–99.

[12] *Youth to Power*, pages 99–100.

[13] "February 15, 2003 anti-war protest." Wikipedia. Online at http://en.wikipedia.org/wiki/February_15,_2003_anti-war_protest.

[14] "The Invisible Children Movement." Invisible Children website. Online at http://www.invisiblechildren.com/theMovement/.

[15] "The Home Maker," by Angus Loten. Inc.com. Online at http://www.inc.com/30under30/2007/the-home-maker.html.

[16] "MIT Vehicle Design Summit 2.0—Executive Summary." Online at http://vehicledesignsummit.org/website/content/view/25/107/. "The People We Have Been Waiting For," by Thomas L. Friedman. *New York Times*, December 2, 2007.

[17] "About Mobilize.org." Mobilize.org website. Online at http://www.mobilize.org/index.php?tray=topic_inline&tid=top358&cid=20.

[18] Free the Children website. Online at http://www.freethechildren.com/index.php.

[19] "2 Young Hedge-Fund Veterans Stir Up the World of Philanthropy," by Stephanie Strom. *New York Times*, December 20, 2007. Online at http://www.nytimes.com/2007/12/20/us/20charity.html?_r=1&scp=1&sq=karnofsky&st=cse&oref=slogin.

[20] "About Facebook" by Ari Melber. TPMCafe, December 26, 2007. Online at http://www.tpmcafe.com/blog/tableforone/2007/dec/26/about_facebook. Also, "Inside the Backlash Against Facebook," by Tracy Samatha Schmidt. *Time*, September 6, 2006. Online at http://www.time.com/time.printout/0,8816,1532225.00.html.

[21] "The Age of Ambition," by Nicholas D. Kristof. *New York Times*, January 27, 2008, page A18.

6 CHAPTER

[1] New York: Harmony, 2000.

[2] "The New Political Compass," Version 7.5.5, by Paul H. Ray. Integral Partnerships LLC, 2003, pages 17–18.

[3] Prison Statistics: Summary Findings. Bureau of Justice, U.S. Department of Justice, June 30, 2007. Online at http://ojp.usdoj.gov/bjs/prisons.htm.

[4] *Millennials Rising*, by Neil Howe and William Strauss. New York: Vintage Books, 2000, page 8.

CHAPTER 7

[1] "Exxon Shatters Profit Records," by David Ellis. CNNMoney.com, February 1, 2008. Online at http://money.cnn.com/2008/02/01/news/companies/exxon_earnings/.

[2] *Freedom from Oil: How the Next President Can End the United States' Oil Addiction*, by David Sandalow. New York: McGraw-Hill, 2008, page 42.

[3] "A New Manhattan Project for Clean Energy Independence," by Lamar Alexander. May 9, 2008. Online at http://www.lamaralexander.com/index.cfm?Fuseaction=PressReleases.View&PressRelease_id=566d4645-41fb-403b-904f-30bfbd240bc9.

[4] "Introduction to the Grand Challenges for Engineering." National Academy of Engineering of the National Academies. February 16, 2008. Online at http://www.engineeringchallenges.org/cms/8996/9221.aspx.

[5] "A Global 'Manhattan Project' for the Energy Crisis," by David J. Eaglesham. MRS Bulletin, Volume 30, December 2005, page 923.

[6] "In Defense of the Campus Rebels," by I.F. Stone. May 19, 1969. In *The Best of I.F. Stone*, edited by Karl Weber. New York: Public Affairs, 2006, page 47.

[7] The Nobel Lecture, Muhammad Yunus, December 10, 2006. Online at http://nobelprize.org/nobel_prizes/peace/laureates/2006/yunus-lecture-en.html.

[8] "On The Need of Our Time: The Need is for a Planetary Wisdom Civilization," draft v.5.1, by Paul H. Ray, 2003, 2005, page 5.

CHAPTER 8

[1] "1848: When America Came of Age," by Kurt Andersen. *Time*, March 8, 2007. Online at http://www.time.com/time/magazine/article/0,9171,1597503,00.html. Cited in *Millennial Makeover: MySpace, YouTube & the Future of American Politics*, by Morley Winograd and Michael D. Hais. New Brunswick, NJ: Rutgers U.P., 2008.

[2] "Discovering What Democracy Means," by Bill Moyers. Speech delivered to the Woodrow Wilson National Fellowship Foundation, February 7, 2007.

[3] "Progressive Voter Registration," by Kay Steiger. *TAPPED*, December 12, 2007. Online at http://www.prospect.org/cs/blogs/tapped_archive?month=12&year=2007&base_name=progressive_voter_registration#103144.

[4] "High Court Upholds Indiana's Voter ID Law," by Bill Mears, CNN. April 28, 2008. Online at http://www.cnn.com/2008/POLITICS/04/28/scotus.voter.id/.

[5] "Think Globally, Protect the Vote Locally," by Paul Rogat Loeb. Online at www.thenation.com.

BIBLIOGRAPHY

The following Bibliography lists many research studies, reports, and surveys that offer further insights into the Millennial generation. The first section lists materials available free online; the second section lists materials for which a fee is charged.

AVAILABLE FREE ONLINE

- Associated Press/Ipsos Poll. **"The Decline of American Civilization, Or at Least Its Manners,"** October 14, 2005. Topline and detailed tables available online to subscribers at http://www.ipsos-na.com/news/pressrelease.cfm?id=2827.

  Provides a comparison between the behavior of the Millennial generation and older generations from the perspective of adults.

- Baylor Institute for Studies of Religion, **"American Piety in the 21st Century: New Insights to the Depth and Complexity of Religion in the U.S."** Interviews conducted 2005; report released September 2006. Available at http://www.baylor.edu/content/services/document.php/33304.pdf

  The most in-depth survey on religion in America to date. It breaks down the issue of religion to its many variables, discerning who people pray to so regularly, which god they believe in, and what kind of god they believe in, for example. It covers religious beliefs, practices and consumerism—including both standard and nonstandard religions.

- Bridge Ratings & Research, **"Internet Behaviors."** Study conducted between January 2, 2007, and April 27, 2007. Available online at http://www.bridgeratings.com/press_05.02.07.Internet%20Consumer%20FactFile.htm.

  This survey looks generally at how everyone used technology from music and video downloads to getting news. It does devote some time to the 18- to 34-year-old age group, which it describes as "addicted to Web." The 18- to 34-year-old age group had a significantly higher percentage of users for all of the activities the study looked at: general comfort with technology; shared videos and music; listening to radio stations; and getting their news. It found that this age group relied on the Web regardless of where they are, even accessing it from friends' houses, etc.

- Bridgeland, John M., et al. **"The Silent Epidemic: Perspectives of High School Dropouts."** Report by Civic Enterprises for the Bill and Melinda Gates Foundation. March 2006. Available online at http://www.gatesfoundation.org/nr/downloads/ed/TheSilentEpidemic3-06FINAL.pdf.

  Provides statistics on dropout rates and looks at the primary reasons why students dropout of high school. It found that the reasons can vary drastically, from not being adequately challenged academically to being academically overwhelmed; low expectations on the part of teachers and adults were cited as one reason for students to dropout. Personal reasons also influenced dropout rates, with students reporting that they had become parents, or needed the income of working, or had to care for one of their parents.

- Carey, Kevin. **"One Step from the Finish Line: Higher College Graduation Rates are Within Our Reach,"** A report by the Education Trust. January 2005. Available online at http://www2.edtrust.org/NR/rdonlyres/5ED8CD8A-E910-4E51-AEDB-6526FFED9F05/0/one_step_from.pdf

  Although more students are starting college following high school than in the past, the number of students completing college remains rather low. This is particularly true for minority and low-income students, some of whom are the first generations to attend college in their families. This report also looks at the high rate of transfers between colleges. It disputes assertions that student mobility has increased over the past decade but accedes that the transfer rate is higher than it was in the 1970s.

- Caruso, J. B., & Kvavik, R. B. (2004). **ECAR study of students and information technology, 2004: Convenience, connection, and control (Key Findings).** Retrieved September 10, 2007, from http://www.educause.edu/ir/library/pdf/ERS0405/ekf0405.pdf

  A 2004 survey of technology use among college students, including how frequently they use it and for what purposes.

- Caruso, J.B. & Gail Salaway (September 2007). **The ECAR study of students and information technology, 2007.** Boulder, CO: EDUCAUSE Center for Applied Research. Retrieved September 15, 2007, from http://www.educause.edu/ir/library/pdf/ERS0706/ekf0706.pdf.

  Follow up to the 2006 survey of college students' use of technology.

- Salaway, Gail, et al. (2006). **The ECAR study of students and information technology, 2006.** Boulder, CO: EDUCAUSE Center for Applied Research. Retrieved September 15, 2007, from http://www.educause.edu/ir/library/pdf/ERS0607/ERS0607w.pdf.

  Follow up to the 2004 survey of college students' use of technology. This report is the most detailed, including a copy of the survey administered.

- Centers for Disease Control and Prevention, **"Youth Risk Behavior Surveillance—United States, 2005,"** Morbidity and Mortality Weekly Report, Vol. 55: No. SS-5. June 9, 2006. Report available online at http://www.cdc.gov/mmwr/PDF/SS/SS5505.pdf.

  This survey questioned and the subsequent report outlined youth participation in risky behavior, which included a broad swath of activities from eating habits, to bicycle helmet wearing, to illicit drug and alcohol use. The report includes a section that compares trends in risky behavior from 1991–2005. Many of the variables compared had increased from 1991 to 2003, but then did not change significantly from 2003–2005. Healthy eating habits declined and the rate of overweight students increased in the 1991–2005 timeframe. Other risky behaviors such as alcohol and most drug use did not change significantly.

- Center for Information and Research on Civic Learning and Engagement (CIRCLE), **"Young Voter Mobilization Tactics: A compilation of the most recent research on traditional and innovative voter turnout techniques."** Available at http://www.civicyouth.org/PopUps/Young_Voters_Guide.pdf

  Compilation of research on voter turnout, focused on the youth vote. The surveys compiled describe which tactics are most successful at increasing the likelihood of young people turning out to vote; as well as which tactics are the least effective and are essentially a waste of a campaign's time and money.

  — **"Young Voters in the 2006 Elections."** Available at http://www.civicyouth.org/PopUps/FactSheets/FS-Midterm06.pdf Information derived from data in the National Election Pool's Election Day Exit Poll.

  Fact sheet that presents information on the youth vote: their political preferences, issues that concern them, and turnout estimates. Most of the data in the fact sheet comes from the National Election Pool's Election Day Exit Poll.

—**2006 CIRCLE Civic and Political Health of the Nation survey**, available at http://www.civicyouth.org/PopUps/2006_CPHS_Report_update.pdf

This survey sought to look at how young Americans are participating in politics and communities. In addition to participation, it examined attitudes toward government and current issues. It looked at the level of civic engagement on the part of young Americans, the level of their political knowledge and partisanship, as well as their views on elections and politics. The survey included young people age 15 to 25 and adults age 26 and higher.

—**"Youth Demographics,"** November 2006. Available at http://www.civicyouth.org/PopUps/youthdemo_2006.pdf

Fact sheet on the demographics of young people with information drawn from the March Annual Demographic Supplement of the Current Population Survey from 1968 to 2006. It breaks them down by racial and ethnic diversity, marital status, military service records, etc., and then compares them with their counterparts of 30 years ago. It finds that they are more racially diverse, less likely to be married or have a military service record, and more likely to live in the West and be unemployed. Although the number of young people is growing, its share of the American population is declining.

—**"Electoral Engagement Among Non-College Attending Youth,"** July 2005. Available at http://www.civicyouth.org/PopUps/FactSheets/FS_04_noncollege_vote.pdf

Fact sheet on the electoral engagement of American youth who are not in college. Those young Americans who do not attend college make up about 48 percent of the young adult population. They are more likely to be male and minority than their college attending counterparts; they are also less likely to vote or be otherwise involved in the political process. Among other findings, those who are not attending college are less likely to consider voting a responsibility and more likely to consider themselves incapable of making a difference in their communities.

—**"Volunteering Among High School Students,"** Karlo Barrios Marcelo, July 2007. Available online at http://www.civicyouth.org/PopUps/FactSheets/FS07_High_School_Volunteering.pdf

This report compiles data from the Current Population Survey and Monitoring the Future survey looking at volunteer activities of 16- to 18-year-olds. It includes a comparison of volunteer activities of this age group dating back to 1976, illustrating a steady increase in the percentage of high school students volunteering. The report also breaks down the data by region and type of volunteer activity.

—**"College Experience and Volunteering,"** Karlo Barrios Marcelo, July 2007. Available online at http://www.civicyouth.org/PopUps/FactSheets/FS07_College_Volunteering.pdf.

With data compiled largely from the Current Population Survey, this fact sheet explores the correlation between volunteering and college experience. It provides statistics and graphs on the recent history of volunteering for those with college experience. From 2002–2006, the volunteer rate of youth with college experience (19–25 year olds) rose and then fell back to where it started, peaking in 2004. In addition to volunteer rates, it also looks at where youth volunteer and in what capacity.

—**"Volunteering Among Non-College Youth,"** Karlo Barrios Marcelo, July 2007. Available online at http://www.civicyouth.org/PopUps/FactSheets/FS07_Noncollege_Volunteering.pdf.

Using data from the Current Population Survey, this fact sheet looks at the volunteer

rate of youth (19–25 year olds) who do not have college experience. From 2002–2005, the volunteer rate was steady but in 2006 the rate dropped. In addition to volunteer rates, it also looks at where youth volunteer and in what capacity.

- CIGNA, **"Workplace Report III,"** October 2003. Available online at http://www.prnewswire.com/cigna/newsfiles/02132004.

Millennials are less likely to participate in or value their employers' 401(k) plans than the Boomers generation. This survey looks at what is competing for the younger generation's money, their outlook on retirement, and their primary financial concerns. Some of the contrasts between the generations' participation in 401(k) plans can be attributed to the age difference, but the participation gap is too wide for it to be entirely attributed to that. Most Millennials (67%) say that their employer's 401(k) plan has little to no effect on their decision to stay with their current employer or accept another job. Boomers are more likely to consider their 401(k)s when changing jobs, with only 54 percent saying that it does not effect their decision.

- CNN, **"America Votes 2006."** Available at http://www.cnn.com/ELECTION/2006/pages/results/states/US/H/00/epolls.0.html

General topline election data on whether subgroups voted Republican or Democrat. The data are disaggregated by gender, ethnicity, age, religious beliefs, union membership, etc.

- College Parents of America, **"Survey of Current College Parent Experiences."** Released March 30, 2006. Available online at http://www.collegeparents.org/files/Current-Parent-Survey-Summary.pdf.

The parents of college (Millennial) students were surveyed concerning how frequently the communicated with their students (very often: 74.1% communicated two to three times/week); how they communicated with their students (overwhelmingly by cell phone); and what they were most worried about (academics and finances topped the list). When questioned, the large majority admitted to being "more involved or much more involved" than their parents were in their college experience. In terms of how colleges are addressing increased parental involvement, parents gave mixed reviews on how satisfied they were with the colleges' communications with them.

- Collins, S.R., et al. **"Rite of Passage? Why Young Adults Become Uninsured and How New Policies Can Help,"** The Commonwealth Fund. Updated May 24, 2006. Available online at http://www.commonwealthfund.org/usr_doc/Collins_riteofpassage2006_649_ib.pdf?section=4039.

The report looks at why so many Millennials are uninsured, focusing primarily on those between the ages of 19 and 29. It provides data on the growing number of uninsured young adults since 2000, the demographics of uninsured young adults, as well as data on the numerous cases that arise from being uninsured such as the number of young adults unable to pay their medical bills. Many of the data are compiled from the Commonwealth Fund Biennial Health Insurance Survey, 2005—see below.

— **"Gaps in Health Insurance: An All-American Problem, Findings from the Commonwealth Fund Biennial Health Insurance Survey."** April 2006. Available online at http://www.commonwealthfund.org/usr_doc/Collins_gapshltins_920.pdf?section=4039.

A general survey of whether or not Americans' had health insurance. If they did not, it looked at how long and how frequently they had been uninsured. The survey also asked respondents about problems with medical bills and accrued medical debt; difficulty in accessing needed healthcare; managing chronic conditions; utilization of routine preventive care, like mammograms and colonoscopies; and coordination and efficiency of care.

The survey took all of this information in the context of employment, income, and other demographics.

- Cone, Inc. **"2006 Cone Millennial Cause Study,"** October 24, 2006. Unable to access full study. Press release with statistics and contact information available online at http://www.coneinc.com/Pages/pr_45.html. Report of study available online at http://www.solsustainability.org/documents/2006%20Cone%20Millennial%20Cause%20Study.pdf.

  Millennials are conscientious of the social responsibility accepted by companies, both for when they're choosing which products to purchase as well as when choosing where to work. According to the study, Millennials reward companies that are associated with good causes and are socially and environmentally responsible. When choosing an employee, Millennials want a company that "cares about how it impacts and contributes to society." More than half (56%) said that they would "refuse to work for an irresponsible corporation." The study also found that although large numbers of Millennials "give back"—through activities such as recycling, educating others on social and environmental issues, volunteering, and donating money—a much smaller number of Millennials actually believe that their actions will make a difference on a particular issue.

- Cooperative Institutional Research Program, Higher Education Research Institute. **"CIRP Freshman Survey,"** December 2006. Available at http://www.gseis.ucla.edu/heri/PDFs/06CIRPFS_Norms_Narrative.pdf (summary)

  The CIRP Freshman Survey is administered to incoming college freshman and covers many things: demographics; expectations of college; high school experiences; degree goals and career plans; college finances; attitudes, values, life goals; and reasons for attending college. The Freshman Survey has been administered for over 40 years and can be used to track generational shifts in attitudes and practices.

- Corporation for National and Community Service, **"Volunteering in America: 2007 City Trends and Rankings."** July 2007. Available online at http://www.nationalservice.gov/pdf/VIA_CITIES/VIA_cities_fullreport.pdf.

  This report tracks the rates and demographics of volunteers around the country, as well as what kinds of volunteer work they're doing. In 2006, 23.4 percent of 16- to 24-year-olds around the country spent an average of 39 hours volunteering.

- Democracy Corps (survey conducted by Greenberg, Quinlan, Rosner), **"The Democrats' Moment to Engage,"** June 2005. Available at http://www.democracycorps.com/reports/surveys/Democracy_Corps_June_2005_Survey.pdf

  A survey of registered voters who voted in the 2004 presidential election that examines what voters thought of current politics in the United States at the time of the survey. It asked questions about both the Republican Party, in general, as well as about specific figures within the party. Respondents were questioned on their opinions general policy issues, such as immigration and the Iraq war. The conclusion drawn from the survey was that the Republican Party's position with Americans is drastically weakened and that Democrats have the opportunity to step into positions of power.

  —**"Solving the Paradox of 2004,"** November 2004. Available at http://www.democracycorps.com/reports/surveys/Post_Election_Survey_November_2-3_2004.pdf (survey); http://www.democracycorps.com/reports/analyses/solving_the_paradox.pdf (analysis).

  This survey sought to understand how Bush was reelected to office in 2004, with a majority of the popular vote, despite weak numbers pre-election and a general sentiment of dissatisfaction with what he had done in office. Among other things, the survey posed questions that pressed voters on what they considered the differences between Bush and Kerry, which may have influenced their votes. Voters were questioned on the impact positive and negative media had on their votes: what the most important issues were facing the country; their approval for Bush; their feelings on the two political parties, generally; the top reasons why they did or did not vote for the candidates, etc.

—Democracy Corps/GQR, **"Republicans Collapse Among Young Americans."** July 27, 2007. Survey conducted May 29–June 29, 2007. Analysis available online at http://www.democracycorps.com/reports/analyses/Democracy_Corps_July_27_2007_Youth_Memo.pdf. Survey available online at http://www.democracycorps.com/reports/surveys/Democracy_Corps_May_29-June_29_2007_Youth_Survey.pdf.

GQR looks at the current position of the Republican Party among young Americans in this survey. It finds that young Americans no longer identify with Republicans, particularly in terms of social issues, leaning strongly left instead. In terms of the 2008 election, this gives Democrats an advantage. However, GQR pointed out that the most important issue young people are considering when thinking about the election is their economic situation, which Democrats need to be sure to address in order to secure their vote.

- Experience, Inc. **"2006 Online Advertising: Habits,"** January 30, 2006. Press Release available online at http://www.experience.com/corp/press_release?id=press_release_1138662942335&tab=cn1&channel_id=about_us&page_id=media_coverage_news.

  A survey of 18- to 34-year-olds concerning their spending habits online. It questions the amount of time that they spend online researching products, how frequently they purchase products online, and which methods of advertisements are the most effective.

- Fabrizio, McLaughlin & Associates, **"The Elephant Looks in the Mirror Ten Years Later: A Critical Look at Today's Grand Old Party."** June 2007. Available online at http://www.youngvoterstrategies.org/index.php?tg=fileman&idx=get&inl=1&id=1&gr=Y&path=Research&file=%29.pdf.

  This National GOP Study found that young Republicans are more and less conservative than their older counterparts. On many of the questions, responses were fairly similar, but not all. In terms of issues, young Republicans seem more conservative on some issues (34% of young Republicans agreed that abortion should be illegal under any circumstances, whereas 28% agreed with that overall) and less on others (only 29% of young Republicans think that the government is too involved in education compared to 43% overall; and 39% of young Republicans actually think that the government should be more involved in education). Young Republicans were also found to be more supportive of private investment for retirement than their older counterparts.

- Farkas, Steve, and Jean Johnson, et al. **"A Lot Easier Said than Done: Parents Talk about Raising Children in Today's America,"** Public Agenda, 2002. Available for purchase online at http://www.publicagenda.org/specials/parents/parents.htm.

  Survey of American parents that captures their concerns with parenting and their parenting styles, which provides insight to how the Millennial generations is being raised.

- Furstenberg, Frank F., Jr., et al. **"Growing Up is Harder to Do,"** Contexts: Understanding People in Their Social Worlds, vol. 3, no. 3. Summer 2004: University of California Press. Available at http://www.contextsmagazine.org/content_sample_v3-3.php.

Furstenberg and his colleagues look at the changing perception of "growing up" in the United States. They compare previous generations with more recent generations, finding significant differences. Whereas previous generations generally defined "adulthood" as marriage and children and was achieved by most in their late teens or early twenties, current generations have a much looser definition of "adulthood," and rarely reach it before their mid-twenties. This prolonged transition to adulthood has been labeled "early adulthood," and is largely attributed to growing demands on families, schools, and governments. Young Americans have to put in more time at school and on the job to achieve the same goal of supporting a family their predecessors sought.

- GFK Technology. **"Backpacks, Lunch Boxes and Cells? ...Nearly half of US Teens and Tweens Have Cell phones According to Gfk NOP mKids Study."** GFKamerica.com. March 9, 2005. Press release available online at http://www.gfkamerica.com/news/mkidspressrelease.htm

  Marketing survey that tracked the number of teens and tweens who own cell phones and looked at the extent of brand recognition and loyalty teens and tweens have within the industry. The survey found that teens and tweens are generally loyal to their phone carriers and that service upgrades are more common than changing carriers.

- Greenberg, Quinlan, Rosner Research. **"Coming of Age in America, Part I,"** April 2005. Available at http://www.gqrr.com/articles/814/712_ym1survey.pdf (survey); http://www.gqrr.com/articles/814/2617_COA10605.pdf (report).

  GQR conducted this survey in an effort to understand young Americans as they mature into adults. To do this, the survey questioned them on their view of politics, social issues, and values. It also looked at how they perceived themselves and how often and in what manner they incorporated various technologies into their lives. The survey concluded that many young Americans are in the dilemma of a strong clash between their individualistic personal goals and their values and world-view. As they mature, they are being forced to confront that conflict and "negotiate their principles."

—**"Coming of Age in America, Part II,"** Youth Monitor: Frequency Questionnaire, August 10–17, 2005. Available at http://www.gqrr.com/articles/814/3408_COA2081705fq.pdf (survey); http://www.gqrr.com/articles/1010/2618_COA20905.pdf (report).

A continuation in its effort to understand the current generation of young Americans entering adulthood, GQR used this survey to explore Generation Y's family life. The survey questioned how the subjects were raised and by whom, closeness to their parents, and the potential impact of this family life on their politics, world-view, and their perceptions of family and marriage.

—**"Coming of Age in America, Part III—Eschatism in Generation Y,"** Youth Monitor: Frequency Questionnaire, December 8–13, 2005. Available at http://www.gqrr.com/articles/1699/3405_COA4050206fq.pdf (survey); http://www.gqrr.com/articles/1659/2619_COA30106.pdf (report).

Further explores Generation Y, this time focusing on "their attitudes toward the future, their level of uncertainty in a world of uncertainty: how safe do they feel today amidst a new round of disasters, do they trust our government to protect us, and do they hold an apocalyptic vision to account for the spate of recent disasters?"

—**"Coming of Age in America, Part IV—The MySpace Generation,"** Youth Monitor: Frequency Questionnaire, April 25–May 1, 2006. Available at http://www.gqrr.com/articles/1699/3405_COA4050206fq.pdf (survey); http://www.gqrr.com/articles/1699/2620_COA40506.pdf (report).

Fourth in the Generation Y series, this survey explores "the role of the Internet in the lives of Gen Yers; how it influences the way they connect with the world around them; what they perceive to be the benefits and risks of the online world; and what, if anything, they are doing to protect themselves from the potential dangers it can present."

- Guttmacher Institute, **"U.S. Teenage Pregnancy Statistics National and State Trends and Trends by Race and Ethnicity."** Updated September 2006. Available at http://www.guttmacher.org/pubs/2006/09/12/USTPstats.pdf

  Outlines the statistics and trends of teenage pregnancy in the United States, looking back as far as 1986. The data are disaggregated by ethnicity and state.

  —Abma, JC, et al., Teenagers in the United States: sexual activity, contraceptive use, and childbearing, 2002, Vital and Health Statistics, 2004, Series 23, No. 24. Available at http://www.cdc.gov/nchs/data/series/sr_23/sr23_024.pdf

  Cited by the Guttmacher Institute in its "Facts on American Teens' Sexual and Reproductive Health." This report presents data on the sexual activity of males and females between the ages of 15 and 19 in the United States. The data comes from the 2002 National Survey of Family Growth as well as the 1988 and 1995 NSFGs and the 1988 and 1995 National Survey of Adolescent Males.

- Harris Interactive, **"360 Youth College Explorer Study,"** Fall 2003. News release on report available online at http://www.harrisinteractive.com/news/allnewsbydate.asp?NewsID=835 Access to the survey itself is unavailable.

  Although a little dated, the study details the financials habits of college students (18–24 years old): both earning and spending their money. "Overall, the data point to college students as savvy, capable and influential consumers, balancing the rising cost of tuition with a hardy work ethic, spending a fair portion of their considerable discretionary income on high-end technology, and holding considerable sway over the purchasing decisions of their peers."

  — **"Generation 2001: A Survey of The First College Graduating Class of the New Millennium."** February 1998. Fieldwork: November 11, 1997–January 12, 1998. Available online at http://www.nmfn.com/tn/learnctr--studiesreports--first_study.

  In addition to looking at the social and political concerns, goals and aspirations, beliefs and values, etc., this survey also looks at the Millennial generation's take on finances—the importance not simply of financial security, but the means of financial security (having life insurance and retirement accounts and the kind of retirement accounts). It also looks at the "typical week" of a member of the Millennial generation and their perception how they look, what they spend their time doing, and what they would like to spend their time doing.

  — **"Generation 2001: A Second Study of The First College Graduating Class of the New Millennium,"** Final Report April 17, 2001.Field Dates: February 7–March 3, 2001. Available online at http://www.nmfn.com/tn/learnctr--studiesreports--second_study.

  In their final year of college, students were wired into the Internet with most saying it was their primary source of news, means of correspondence, and center of their job search. Over half planned on beginning work immediately following graduation and had already begun their job search. Most also said they expected to have to sacrifice family time to get ahead in their careers and had modest expectations for their starting salaries. They continued to express concern on other issues, such as the direction of the county, race relations, the environment, and healthcare.

— **"The Third Study: No Longer Students, the Millennium Generation Finds the World and Unfriendly Place."** Fall 2001. Email study conducted October 11–October 22, 2001. Summarized findings available online at http://www.nmfn.com/tn/learnctr--studiesreports--third_study.

Interesting change in this survey, which was taken shortly after September 11, is that the willingness of respondents to fight for their country declined. Men also earned less money than they expected and a high salary became more important—almost doubling among respondents. Entrepreneurship remained strong.

— **"The Fourth Study: Adjusting to Life in Hard Times."** 2002. Email study conducted July 17–July 26, 2002. Summarized findings available online at http://www.nmfn.com/tn/learnctr--studiesreports--fourth_study.

The same group of Millennials that was interviewed in the previous three studies was contacted again, this time about one year after they had graduated from college. This study assessed the general level of optimism felt by the participants—their perception of 9/11's impact on the economy and their own job security, as well as revisited goals and job priorities that participants held.

— **"Millennium Generation Studies: The Fifth Study, The Class of 2004 and the Class of 2001—Three Years Later"** Revised Report June 13, 2004. Field Dates: March 23–April 4, 2004. Available online at http://www.nmfn.com/tn/learnctr--studiesreports--fifth_study (full report).

The fifth in a series of studies following the Millennial class of 2001 and introducing the class of 2004. It described the Millennials as a "We" generation instead of the "Me" generation that preceded it. The study captures the general sentiments of participants' on the economy, government and society: pessimistic. It also looks at how they see the world: perceived advantages (more opportunities for minorities and women) and disadvantages (forced to grow up too quickly) unique to their generation. Finally, the study looks at what Millennials are looking for in life: careers that allow them to help others but with the freedom to spend time with family. Many are interested in pursuing entrepreneurial endeavors at some point in their lives; some have already started their own businesses.

- Harrison Group (for Deloitte), **"2007 State of the Media Democracy."** Survey was conducted online from February 23 to March 3, 2007. Survey not available online. Article with extensive citations of Millennials' habits available online at http://www.tvweek.com/news/2007/05/Millennials_defying_the_old_mo.php (Dominiak, Mark. "'Millennials' Defying the Old Models," TelevisionWeek. May 7, 2007.)

  Designed to look at how generations use modes of communication, the survey focused largely on new technologies but also touched on older means such as television and word-of-mouth. Among other findings, the survey found that Millennials desire control over the media that they use—particularly online. Of the time spent online, the majority of it is spent on user-generation content versus company-generated. Millennials also expressed more eagerness for advancements in technology than other generations.

- Harvard Institute of Politics, October 2006. **"The 11th Biannual Youth Survey on Politics and Public Service."** http://www.iop.harvard.edu/pdfs/survey/fall_2006_topline.pdf.

  The IOP has been conducting regular polling of America's college students for six years, highlighting key trends and issues related to politics and public service. Although there are some questions on respondents' participation in community service, this particular survey focuses strongly on the respondent's political views: how they would rate the

Bush Administration, their take on the Iraq war, how 9/11 has influenced politics, their general view of politics as positive or negative, etc.

—April 10, 2006 Survey. Available at http://www.iop.harvard.edu/pdfs/survey/spring_poll_2006_topline.pdf

As one of its regular surveys of college students to track trends, this survey questioned participants on their political affiliations, their opinions on the direction the country is taking, the administration in office and key policy issues. One of the policy issues examined was the participants' willingness to sacrifice certain degrees of civil liberties in order to be more secure. The survey also looked at participants' own religiosity and their view of its real and ideal influence on policy issues and politics.

- Howe, Neil and William Strauss. **Millennials Rising: The Next Great Generation.** New York: Vintage Books, 2000.

- IHRSA, **"Trend Report,"** Vol. 11: No. 4. October 2004. Report available online at http://download.ihrsa.org/trendreport/10_2004trend.pdf. Cited study (Yankelovich, Inc. 2003) unavailable online without subscription.

  This report compiles data on the health habits of Millennials, Generation Xers, and Boomers. It looks at what forms of exercise they participate in, which health habits they follow, as well as how interested and concerned they are about their health.

- Johnson, Jean and Ann Duffett, with Amber Ott. **"Life After High School: Young People Talk about Their Hopes and Prospects,"** Public Agenda. 2005. Executive summary available online at http://www.publicagenda.org/research/pdfs/life_after_high_school_execsum.pdf. Full-report available for purchase online at http://www.publicagenda.org/research/research_reports_details.cfm?list=31.

  This survey asks young people between the ages of 18 and 25 about their lives. It follows both those who are pursuing college degrees as well as those who have chosen not to attend college. It looks at what factors were involved in their choices to attend or not attend college, as well as their views of the future and, in the case of those who chose not to pursue a higher degree, their perceptions of where they currently are: how they see their jobs, reflections on high school, etc.

- Josephson Institute, **"2006 Report Card on the Ethics of American Youth: Part One-Integrity."** October 2006. Available online at http://www.josephsoninstitute.org/reportcard/ (summary of data); http://www.josephsoninstitute.org/pdf/2006reportcard/reportcard-all.pdf (complete data tables).

  According to this survey of middle and high school students by the Josephson Institute, youth place a high importance on having integrity. This includes having integrity in the workplace, though many are cynical of how realistic it is to succeed and have integrity at work. Despite the high value they place on integrity and the fairly high score they award themselves on integrity (74% say they are better at "doing what is right" than people they know), the vast majority have lied and/or cheated in the past year (82% admitted to having lied to parents about "something significant" in the past year and 60% admitted to cheating on an exam at school in the past year).

  — **"What Are Your Children Learning? The Impact of High School Sports on the Values and Ethics of High School Athletes,"** Released February 2007. Available online at http://www.josephsoninstitute.org/pdf/sports_survey_report_022107.pdf.

  Survey of high school athletes on how participating in athletics impacts their values. This survey found that most high school athletes admire and respect their coaches, valuing the lessons taught by them. On the positive side, it found that slightly fewer athletes steal than their nonathletic counterparts. On the other side, however, athletes are more likely to cheat in school than their nonathletic peers and many of their coaches' lessons seem to be ethically questionable in terms of what is acceptable "sportsmanlike behavior." Certain sports had higher rates of cheating than others, with baseball, basketball, and football being the worst for males; and basketball and softball having the highest rate of cheating for females. Gender differences were visible with female athletes across the board considerably more likely to express a deeper conviction for ethical behavior than their male counterparts.

- The Henry J. Kaiser Family Foundation, **"Parents, Children & Media,"** June 2007. Available online at http://www.kff.org/entmedia/upload/7638.pdf.

  Survey of parents concerning their view of the role that media plays in their children's lives. It explores how much control parents feel that they have; how appropriate they consider the content; what role they think the government should have in controlling media content; etc.

- Kamenetz, Anya. **Generation Debt: Why Now is a Terrible Time to be Young.** New York: Riverhead Books, 2005.

- Lake Research Partners, **"Lifetime Women's Pulse Poll,"** conducted by Lake Research Partners (Celinda Lake) and the WomanTrend division of The Polling Company, Inc (Kellyanne Conway), March 4-8, 2007. Press release available online at http://www.prnewswire.com/cgi-bin/stories.pl?ACCT=ind_focus.story&STORY=/www/story/03-22-2007/0004551691&EDATE=THU+Mar+22+2007,+03:48+PM.

  Interviewing 500 18- to 29-year-old women and 200 18- to 29-year-old men, pollsters found that women in Generation Y have few aspirations in politics—preferring to pursue corporate advancement over political—but that they largely support female candidates. The perception of these women is that the best way for them to influence politics is by voting, and volunteering and/or donating money to campaigns. Women in Generation Y are less drawn to ideology and more drawn to leadership on issues that concern them.

  — **"Generation Why?"** conducted by Lake Research Partners and WomanTrend. February 27–March 1, 2006. Executive summary available online at http://www.pollingcompany.com/cms/files/Executive%20Summary%20Layout%20FINAL.pdf.

  For this study, interviews were conducted with women from three generations (Boomers, X, and Y) and compiled to create a comparison of their responses. Issues it looked at were ideal ages for marriage and children; the role of technology in their lives; shopping habits; and discrimination among others. The sharpest contrast between generations was in terms of technology use in their lives, which was much higher for the youngest generation. Generation Y was also the most in favor of settling down sooner rather than later with marriage and children. The generations were very similar in terms of perceived sacrifices for getting ahead in a career; retirement dreams and realities; and the continued presence of discrimination.

- Lancaster, Lynne C. and David Stillman. **When Generations Collide: Who They Are. Why They Clash. How to Solve the Generational Puzzle at Work.** HarperCollins: New York, 2002.

  This book addresses the differences between the current generations that are coexisting in society and, in particular, at work. After outlining those differences, it examines the ways in which they clash and looks at what businesses need to consider when recruiting, hiring, and retaining Millennial employees. In this context, it looks at the employment habits and expectations of Millennials.

Life Course Associates, **"High School Class of 2000 Survey,"** April–May 1999. Available online at http://www.lifecourse.com/news/ms_hssurvey.html.

This survey was given only at Fairfax County, Virginia, public high schools to rising seniors. It questioned them on their perceptions of previous generations as well as their own. Among similar topics, it asked what expectations they thought their parents had for them; what events had had the greatest impact on them (top two at the time were the Columbine massacre and the war in Kosovo); how optimistic they were about the United State's future; and how civically engaged they thought their generation would be compared to their older brothers' and sisters' generation.

— **"Teachers' Survey,"** April-May 1999. Available online at http://www.lifecourse.com/news/ms_teachersurvey.html.

According to teachers in the Fairfax County, Virginia, public schools (elementary, middle, and high) who have been teaching for at least the past 10 years, student performance has gone up over the years. Other changes include that teachers are increasingly "teaching to the test," with 95 percent of elementary and middle school teachers saying they are teaching "more" to the test than in the past. When questioned, teachers indicated that more emphasis in being placed on team work, good behavior, and citizenship. And although problems with racial taunting have declined, gender taunting has actually increased.

Magid Associates, **"The Politics of the Millennial Generation,"** March 2006. Available at http://www.newpolitics.net/files/MillennialGenerationPolitics.pdf (report).

This survey compared three generations: the Millennials, Gen Xers, and Baby Boomers. Within the Millennials, they did a further break out between subgenerations: Teen Millennials, Transitional Millennials, and Cusp Millennials. Since each generation was born into such distinctive social situations and raised in distinct manners, the survey explores how that has impacted their politics: political identification, opinions on social issues, terrorism, etc.

MTV/CBS News Poll: Environment. Telephone Interviews between May 30 and June 9, 2006. Available online at http://www.mtv.com/thinkmtv/about/pdfs/mtv_environment_poll.pdf.

Survey of 13- to 24-year-olds on their perception of the environment. It found that the majority of young people are concerned about global warming, with the majority (56%) believing that it is happening right now; only 3 percent don't believe it will ever happen. Concern for global warming increases with age: 18- to 24-year-olds express higher levels of concern than 13- to 17-year-olds. More than 80 percent say that action on global warming needs to be taken "right away" and most believe that they can do something to help. Although considered important by young people, the environment is not always at the top of young people's minds. When given five choices, "environment" was chosen as the "most important" concern for their generation; but when given the freedom to just name the most important concern, "drugs" was first and "environment" didn't even make it into the top five.

MTV/Think, **"Just Cause: Today's Activism,"** April 27, 2006. Available online at http://www.mtv.com/thinkmtv/research/pdf/Just.Cause.FNL.APX.pdf.

Survey sought to understand what "being involved" means to young people (12–24 years old) in today's society. It looked at what prevented young people from participating and what has prompted those involved to become involved. There was a strong level of interest in volunteering among young people but that interest did not translate directly into involvement, with a much large percentage of people expressing interest and a considerably smaller percent actually following through. Lack of time, hanging out with friends, and "just not for me" was a few of the top reasons for not becoming involved.

- MTV/Associated Press, **"Young People and Happiness,"** August 20, 2007. Interviews conducted April 16–23, 2007. Available online at http://www.mtv.com/thinkmtv/about/pdfs/APMTV_happinesspoll.pdf (full survey); http://www.mtv.com/thinkmtv/research/ (press release).

  How happy are young people (13–24 year olds)? What makes them happy? What are they doing to ensure their future happiness? This survey sought to answer those questions, looking at all aspects of young Americans' lives from sex to money to religious faith. It found that young Americans are generally happy and optimistic about their futures. They value time spent with friends and family over most other activities; and religion and spirituality play an important role in many young people's lives (44%). With technology so intricately woven into their lives, unsurprisingly nearly two-thirds said that having different types of technology in their lives makes them happier. In terms of finance, the survey found that few young people attributed having money to happiness; but many cited the lack of money as a source of unhappiness. White young Americans are the happiest (72%), trailed by Blacks (56%), and Hispanics (51%).

- National Center for Education Statistics, **"Chapter 3: Postsecondary Education,"** Digest of Education Statistics: 2005. Available online at http://nces.ed.gov/programs/digest/d05/ch_3.asp

  This is the National Center for Education Statistics' most current Digest of Education Statistics. The Digest's "primary purpose is to provide a compilation of statistical information covering the broad field of American education from prekindergarten through graduate school." Chapter 3, which solely addresses postsecondary education, has education statistics that include the number of colleges, teachers, enrollments and graduates; as well as education attainment, finances, federal funds for education, and so on. "Supplemental information on population trends, attitudes on education, education characteristics of the labor force, government finances, and economic trends provides background for evaluating education data."

- **"National Election Pool Poll # 2006-NATELEC: National Election Day Exit Poll."**

- National Institute on Drug Abuse, survey designed and conducted by the University of Michigan, **"32nd Annual Monitoring the Future Survey."** Available at http://monitoringthefuture.org/data/06data.html#2006data-drugs

  Survey compares the number of adolescents who used illicit drugs or drank alcohol in 2006 with those in previous years. It found that there is a general trend down in illicit drug use since the 1990s but in recent years that trend seems to have slowed. For some age groups the downward trend seemed to have stopped altogether from 2005 to 2006.

- New American Media. **"California Dreamers: A public opinion portrait of the most diverse generation the nation has know,"** April 25, 2007. Executive summary available online at http://media.newamericamedia.org/images/polls/youth/california_dreamers_executive_summary.pdf.

  This survey of young Californians between the ages of 16 and 22 years old found that they were generally optimistic, held a strong belief in the "American Dream" that if they work hard enough they can achieve all of their goals, and were committed to making society more inclusive and tolerant. When questioned on how they identified themselves, respondents were as likely to say their music and fashion preferences as their race or religion. But they didn't view the world entirely through rose-colored glasses as they did harbor concerns about family stability, citing the breakdown of the family as the biggest challenge facing their generation.

New York Times/CBS News/MTV Poll, **"17 to 29 Year Olds."** June 15–23, 2007. Available online at http://graphics8.nytimes.com/packages/pdf/politics/20070627_POLL.pdf.

This survey of 17- to 29-year-olds focuses largely on the politics of the 2008 election and how the age group was responding to the individual candidates and which issues they considered most important. It found that more than half of the respondents would probably vote for a Democratic candidate if they were voting immediately; the economy and Iraq were the most pressing issues they were considering when choosing their candidates; and they did not think the candidates were are making the issues they considered important enough of a priority.

Noel-Levitz, **"National Freshman Attitudes Survey."** 2007. Available online at https://www.noellevitz.com/NR/rdonlyres/3934DA20-2C31-4336-962B-A1D1E7731D8B/0/07FRESHMANATTITUDES_report.pdf.

This survey and report look at the attitude that college freshmen have at the beginning of their experience: how open they are to assistance in academics and career direction; how determined they are to complete their degree; whether or not they expect to work while earning their degree; etc.

—**"Embracing Diversity: Looking at Freshman Attitudes by Race/Ethnicity."** 2007. Available online at https://www.noellevitz.com/NR/rdonlyres/0F09D72F-7A65-48D6-A21A-6045DA330CBF/0/Freshmanattitudesdiversityreport2007.pdf.

This survey and report is also a look at the attitude that college freshmen have at the beginning of their experience: how open they are to assistance in academics and career direction; how determined they are to complete their degree; whether or not they expect to work while earning their degree; etc. It breaks all of the information down and compares it in terms of racial demographics.

NORC at the University of Chicago, **"General Social Survey 1972–2006: Gender Issues."** Available at http://sda.berkeley.edu/archive.htm

"The questionnaire contains a standard core of demographic and attitudinal variables, plus certain topics of special interest selected for rotation (called "topical modules"). Items that appeared on national surveys between 1973 and 1975 are replicated. The exact wording of these questions is retained to facilitate time trend studies as well as replications of earlier findings.... Items include national spending priorities, drinking behavior, marijuana use, crime and punishment, race relations, quality of life, confidence in institutions, and membership in voluntary associations."

Patterson, Thomas E. **"Young People and News,"** Joan Shorenstein Center on the Press, Politics and Public Policy. July 2007. Available online at http://www.ksg.harvard.edu/presspol/carnegie_knight/young_news_web.pdf.

A survey of people, disaggregated by age groups, found that young people are significantly less likely to routinely consume the news in any form than people older than them. The news they do consume is primarily via television, not the Internet. This limited consumption of news reflects a shift in young people from a couple decades ago when the gap between news consumption of the various age groups was considerably narrower.

- Pew Hispanic Center, **"The Changing Racial and Ethnic Composition of U.S. Public Schools,"** August 30, 2007. Available online at http://pewhispanic.org/files/reports/79.pdf (report); http://pewhispanic.org/files/reports/79.1.pdf (appendix).

  The Millennial generation is more diverse than its predecessors, but in terms of education, many remain racially isolated in their schools. Because of demographic shifts, white students are less likely to be in nearly all-white schools than 12 years ago; minority students (Hispanics and Blacks) are slightly more likely to be in nearly all-Hispanic or nearly all-black schools.

  —Tables referenced in the Pew Hispanic Survey are available at the Institute of Education Sciences: Department of Education, **"Public Elementary/ Secondary School Universe Survey Data,"** Common Core of Data. Available online at http://nces.ed.gov/ccd/pubschuniv.asp.

- Pew Research Center, **"Report: A Portrait of Generation Next,"** released January 2007. Gen Next Survey interviews were conducted September 6–October 2, 2006. Available at http://people-press.org/reports/pdf/300.pdf (report); http://people-press.org/reports/questionnaires/300.pdf (questionnaire).

  Survey of 18- to 25-year-olds aka "Generation Next" that looks at their voting trends, attitudes on social issues, religion, finances, networking, family, perceptions of the future, etc.

  —**"2005 Typology Survey: Beyond Red vs. Blue,"** embargoed for release May 10, 2005. Interviews conducted December 1-16, 2004 and re-interviews conducted March 17–27, 2005. Available at http://people-press.org/reports/pdf/242.pdf (report); http://people-press.org/reports/print.php3?PageID=951 (questionnaire, part one); http://people-press.org/reports/print.php3?PageID=952 (questionnaire, part two).

  The 2005 Typology Survey sorted voters into homogenous groups that were based on values, political beliefs, and party affiliation. Despite beliefs that the country is divided into two strong political parties, the surveys found that each party is divided internally over issues such as immigration, environmental protection, and the role of government. Since the last Typology Survey, foreign policy and national security have become more central issues for voters—both Democrats and Republicans. Although the left remains strong, more voters in the middle are leaning further right than they did in previous surveys.

  —**"Once again, the Future Ain't What It Used to Be,"** embargoed for release May 2, 2006. Interviews conducted February 8–March 7, 2006. Available at http://pewresearch.org/assets/social/pdf/BetterOff.pdf.

  Measures the optimism of adults for their children's futures. The survey found that Whites and Blacks are generally more pessimistic about the future than they have been in the past, with most believing that their children will not be better off than they are; Hispanics were the most optimistic that their children would be better off than they are, but they are also the least satisfied with the quality of their lives. It also found that young adults are more optimistic than older adults about the future.

  —**"Public Says American Work Life is Worsening, But Most Workers Remain Satisfied with Their Jobs,"** Labor Day 2006. Interviews conducted June 20–July 16, 2006. Available at http://pewresearch.org/assets/social/pdf/Jobs.pdf

Explores how Americans perceive the job market, how they think it has changed, job security, and their satisfaction with their jobs.

—**"Trends in Political Values and Core Attitudes: 1987-2007: Political Landscape more Favorable to Democrats,"** Released March 22, 2007. Available at http://people-press.org/reports/pdf/312.pdf (report); http://people-press.org/reports/questionnaires/312.pdf (questionnaire).

Broad survey of how the public's political values and core attitudes have shifted over the past 20 years. The survey touches on political affiliation, levels of social liberalism/conservatism, religiosity, etc. It found that there is increased public support for social safety nets and concern over income inequality, and less support for "assertive national security policies."

—**"Iraq Views Improve, Small Bounce for Bush,"** June 14–19, 2006. Available at http://people-press.org/reports/questionnaires/278.pdf (questionnaire).

Survey of public sentiments on Bush, including approval and disapproval of how Bush is handling Iraq.

—**"Election 2006 Online,"** January 17, 2007. Lee Rainie, Director. Available online at http://www.pewinternet.org/pdfs/PIP_Politics_2006.pdf.

Overview of how widely used the Internet was for acquiring information about the candidates and issues leading up to the 2006 elections. Amid this information are some data broken out by age groups, including 18- to 29-year-olds. These look at how frequently these subgroups use the Internet for political information; the percentage of the subgroups that belong to the group of "campaign Internet users"; etc.

—**"Luxury or Necessity?"** December 14, 2006. Available online at http://pewresearch.org/assets/social/pdf/Luxury.pdf.

This survey questions respondents on the necessity of 14 items, including such things as microwaves, air conditioning, cell phones, and cable television. It found that many items that were not considered necessary in 1996 have come to be considered increasingly vital to everyday life for Americans. Young Americans, 18 to 20 years old, consider technological items, such as high-speed Internet and home computers, as necessities while older Americans place more importance on items such as air conditioning and washers and dryers.

—**"A Barometer of Modern Morals: Sex, Drugs and the 1040,"** March 28, 2006. Available online at http://pewresearch.org/assets/social/pdf/Morality.pdf.

Based on respondents' evaluations of 10 behaviors, Pew sought to gauge Americans' perceptions of morality. In terms of age differences, it found that older Americans are more likely than young Americans to consider homosexuality morally wrong. But it also found that there was no significant difference between old and young Americans on the question of the morality of abortion. Unfortunately, age groups are not split out very far, clumping 18- to 49-year-olds together.

—**"Eating More; Enjoying Less,"** April 19, 2006. Available online at http://pewresearch.org/assets/social/pdf/Eating.pdf.

This survey looks at the eating habits of Americans, garnering such information as how often they eat out, how often they consume fast food, how much they enjoy eating, and how much they enjoy cooking. It found that young adults (18–29) eat out the most frequently of all adults ages 18 to 65-plus and that they are the most likely to eat at a fast food restaurant at least once weekly.

—"'Information Age' Bills Keep Piling Up: What Americans Pay For—And How," February 7, 2007. Available online at http://pewresearch.org/assets/social/pdf/Expenses.pdf.

Pew looks at what bills Americans are paying and how they pay for them. Young adults (18–29) have most of the same bills as other age groups, with a larger percentage paying school tuition and repaying student loans, and a slightly higher rate of people paying child support or alimony and having an in-store payment plan. Young adults are also most likely to pay with cash for everyday expenses and least likely, by far, to pay with check (only 5%).

—**"We Try Hard. We Fall Short. Americans Assess Their Saving Habits,"** January 24, 2007. Available online at http://pewresearch.org/assets/social/pdf/Saving.pdf.

Americans say they are instinctive savers, but most don't think they're saving enough. Young adults follow the trends of older adults in many categories. Forty-two percent of 18- to 29-year-olds say they spend more than they can afford, which is even with 30- to 49-year-olds but higher than older age groups. Thirty-five percent said they have felt as though their financial situation was "out of control." In terms of splurging, 18- to 29-year-olds splurge most on eating/dining out and shopping/personal items; a much smaller percentage of young adults splurge on entertainment/recreation than any of the other age groups.

—**"Americans Social Trust: Who, Where and Why?"** February 22, 2007. Available online at http://pewresearch.org/assets/social/pdf/SocialTrust.pdf.

This short Pew survey of Americans sought to create a picture of which demographic groups, one of which was age, have the highest social trust. It found that young adults (18–29) have the lowest social trust index of all the age groups, with 49 percent of young adults registering low on the social trust index and only 23 percent registering high.

—**"Generations Online,"** December 2005. Available online at http://www.pewinternet.org/pdfs/PIP_Generations_Memo.pdf.

This memo compares how the different generations utilize the Internet. It found that users between the ages of 12 and 28 are more likely to use the Internet for chatting via IM, creating blogs, and gaming; whereas users over the age of 28, but younger than 70, use the Internet for travel reservations and online banking. Younger users also outnumber older users.

—**"Teen Content Creators and Consumers,"** November 2, 2005. Available online at http://www.pewinternet.org/pdfs/PIP_Teens_Content_Creation.pdf.

American teenagers (12–17 years old) are active Internet users—not only using but also creating content on the web. This survey found that more than half of online teens have created web content. The survey distinguishes between bloggers and nonbloggers, with bloggers being more active online, comparing the extent of the online activity. The survey also questions teenagers on their use of music downloads and their opinions on its regulation; their use of peer-to-peer services; as well as what other activities they use the Internet for (news, political info, college info, entertainment, health info, etc.).

—**"Protecting Teens Online,"** March 17, 2005. Available online at http://www.pewinternet.org/pdfs/PIP_Filters_Report.pdf.

Eighty-seven percent of teenagers (12–17) use the Internet. Of those, 87 percent have access to the Internet at home. Some of those 13 percent who do not use the Internet stopped using it because of bad experiences they had on it. According to this Pew study, most parents say they are checking up on their teens' online activities and most teens say that they don't think their parents are monitoring their online activities. Both teens and parents expressed the belief that teens do things they shouldn't online: 79 percent of teens said they share personal information online more freely than they should; and 64 percent say they do things online they wouldn't want their parents to know about. In addition to providing statistics on Internet usage and perceptions, the study looks at how parents are coping with the freedom the Internet offers their teens and how they're limiting that freedom.

—**"Cyberbullying and Online Teens,"** June 27, 2007. Available online at http://www.pewinternet.org/pdfs/PIP%20Cyberbullying%20Memo.pdf.

One-third of teens say they have experienced bullying online, with teenage girls more likely to have experienced it than their male counterparts. Bullying online is most commonly in the form of "making private information public." This is done by maliciously forwarding emails, photographs, and IM messages. It is commonly used as a means of generating and spreading rumors more rapidly. In addition to spreading rumors and publicizing private information, teenagers also report receiving threatening emails, text messages and IMs.

—**"Teens and Technology: Youth are leading the transition to a fully wired and mobile nation,"** July 27, 2005. Available online at http://www.pewinternet.org/pdfs/PIP_Teens_Tech_July2005web.pdf.

Teens are more wired than adults, reporting high uses of the Internet, instant messaging, and cell phones. Pew found that teenagers prefer instant messaging to emails, though most still use email more than IM. Teenagers use the Internet for everything from gaming, to finding information on colleges and health, to reading the news. Along with the ubiquitous use of technology has come cyberbullying, which is looked at more closely in the Pew study on the subject. Despite the prevalence of technology in their lives, teenagers say "face time" still beats screen time in terms of relationships.

—**"Social Networking Sites and Teens: An Overview,"** January 3, 2007. Available online at http://www.pewinternet.org/pdfs/PIP_SNS_Data_Memo_Jan_2007.pdf.

More than half of all American teenagers use online social networking sites—of those, the majority is female. For the most part, teens use the sites to "manage" their friendships with people they see regularly, though to a lesser degree, some teens do use the sites to stay in touch with friends who live further away. And males are both more likely than females to say they use the sites to make new friends as well as to flirt.

—**"Most Parents Encourage their Kids to Follow the News: Growing Up with the News,"** May 23, 2007. News Interest Index with Project for Excellence in Journalism. Available online at http://people-press.org/reports/pdf/330.pdf (report); http://people-press.org/reports/questionnaires/330.pdf (topline questionnaire).

Parents of school-age children generally encourage their kids to follow the news, although that figure depends on the parents' own news following habits. The more parents follow the news, the more likely they are to encourage their children to do so. It also depends on the age of the children, with considerably more parents encouraging their 12- to 17-year-olds to follow the news than their younger children. More than half of the parents surveyed shielded their children under 12 years old from the news. Pew found no significant difference between the practices of Republicans and Democrats; it did find that independents were slightly less likely to encourage their kids to follow the news.

—**"Mixed Views on Immigration Bill: Democratic Leaders Facing Growing Disapproval, Criticism on Iraq,"** June 7, 2007. Available online at http://people-press.org/reports/display.php3?ReportID=335 (report); http://people-press.org/reports/questionnaires/335.pdf (topline questionnaire).

Young Americans (18–29 years old) are in the age group most inclined to favor providing immigrants with a way to obtain citizenship. They also look more kindly on amnesty than any of the other age groups, although they view it less favorably than the path to citizenship. In terms of Iraq, young Americans are the least like to believe that withdrawing troops would hurt the morale of troops.

- Public Agenda. **"Life After High School: Young People Talk about Their Hopes and Prospects,"** 2005. Survey conducted between August 14 and September 4, 2004. Available online at http://www.publicagenda.org/research/pdfs/life_after_high_school.pdf.

Most young adults (18–25 years old), regardless of race, consider education beyond high school to be important in getting ahead in life. Despite this, many never make it. And many of those who do go to college drop out before successfully earning a degree. This survey looks at how young people make their decisions to continue with their education following high school or begin working. Money is a large barrier for young people when considering college, but many also said they "just didn't like school." Respondents all said they felt unprepared entering four-year colleges, admitting that they should have worked harder while in high school but also arguing that their teachers and schools didn't prepare them properly. The study concludes that society has successfully instilled the importance of attending college in the minds of American youth but questions whether it has provided the means for all youth to successfully attain or even pursue that goal.

- 2004 Reboot Study, **"OMG! How Generation Y is Redefining Faith in the iPod Era."** Available at http://www.rebooters.net/poll/rebootpoll.pdf (report); http://www.rebooters.net/poll/rebootfq.pdf (questionnaire), August 7–November 18, 2004.

"The result of this partnership is a unique survey examining issues of identity, community, and meaning, from Catholic, Protestant, Jewish and Muslim youth, ages 18–25, across racial and ethnic lines. The findings, although remarkable in and of themselves, also represent a snapshot of tomorrow, a glimpse of what may happen when Generation Y matures to the peak of its member's participatory experiences."

- Resource Interactive. Research unavailable online. Company's website is http://www.resourceinteractive.com/aboutus/Default.aspx. Data cited in article on DMNews: Abramovich, Giselle. **"Millennials work as teams, not individuals: Mooney at Shop.org,"** DMNews, October 12, 2006. Available online at http://www.dmnews.com/cms/dm-news/research-studies/38545.html.

Conducted a study that looked at how Millennials spend their money. It addressed issues like Millennials' reluctance to pay shipping and how companies can get around that (one example was Levi Strauss, which came up with a plan that let shoppers email advertisements to friends in exchange for free shipping); asked Millennials how best to target them with marketing (use new communication tools available; "keep it real"; ask young people their opinions on items; etc.).

- Snyder, Howard N. and Melissa Sickmund. **"Juvenile Offenders and Victims: 2006 National Report,"** National Center for Juvenile Justice, March 2006. Available at http://ojjdp.ncjrs.org/ojstatbb/nr2006/downloads/NR2006.pdf.

This report "offers a clear view of juvenile crime and the justice system's response at the beginning of the 21st century." It looks at the trends in juvenile crime, including changes in the racial and gender makeup of perpetrators of juvenile crime, as well as its prevalence.

- Twenge, Jean. **Generation Me: Why Today's Young Americans are More Confident, Assertive, Entitled—and More Miserable Than Ever Before.** Free Press: New York, 2006.

  Includes research based on the Marlowe-Crowne Social Desirability Scale about babies of the 1970s, 1980s, and 1990s. Twenge "says her findings suggest the young don't care as much about making a good impression or displaying courtesy as their parents and grandparents did when they were growing up."

- University of Michigan, **American National Election Study, 2004.** Available at http://sda.berkeley.edu/cgi-bin/hsda?harcsda+nes2004p; can be downloaded directly and analyzed, if you have SPSS, SAS, or STATA at http://www.electionstudies.org/studypages/download/datacenter_all.htm.

  The ANES has been around since 1948. It focuses on voter perceptions of the major political parties, the candidates, national and international issues, and of the importance of the election. The survey also explores voters' expectations about the outcome of the election, the degree of voter interest in politics, political affiliation and voting history, as well as participation in the electoral process. Interviews for the ANES are conducted before and after presidential elections and after national congressional elections. In post-election interviews, respondents are also asked about actual voting behavior and voter reflections about the election outcome.

- U.S. Census Bureau, **"Voting and Registration in the Election of November 2004,"** Issued March 2006. Available at http://www.census.gov/prod/2006pubs/p20-556.pdf.

  "This report examines the levels of voting and registration in the November 2004 presidential election, the characteristics of citizens who reported that they were registered for or voted in the election, and the reasons why registered voters did not vote."

  —U.S. Census Bureau Population Projects 2000 to 2050, available at http://www.census.gov/ipc/www/usinterimproj/usproj2000-2050.xls

  —**"Income, Poverty, and Health Insurance Coverage in the United States: 2005."** Issued August 2006. Available at http://www.census.gov/prod/2006pubs/p60-231.pdf.

  "This report presents data on income, poverty, and health insurance coverage in the United States based on information collected in the 2006 and earlier Annual Social and Economic Supplements (ASEC) to the Current Population Survey (CPS) conducted by the U.S. Census Bureau." Data is disaggregated by variables such as age, race, ethnicity, nativity, and region.

- USA Today/National Endowment for Financial Education, **"Young Adults' Finances Poll."** Interviews conducted October 26-November 14, 2006. Available online at http://www.nefe.org/Portals/0/NEFE_Files/USATodaySurvey.pdf.

  This survey questioned respondents, 22 to 29 years old, on their financial lives. It asked about things such as the recent financial regrets they've had; whether or not they have and follow a budget; what areas of life they would be willing to cut back their spending on; their largest financial concerns; and how their current financial situation compares with where they thought they would be financially at this point in their lives.

- Young Voter Strategies, **"Young Voter Battleground Poll I,"** May 16, 2006. Available at http://www.youngvoterstrategies.org/index.php?tg=articles&idx=

More&article=117&topics=37 (press release); http://www.youngvoterstrategies.org/index.php?tg=fileman&idx=get&inl=1&id=1&gr=Y&path=YVS+Polling&file=Battleground+Poll+April+2006+BANNERS.pdf (crosstabs).

Conducted in the months leading up to the 2006 elections, this survey questioned young voters on what they would be considering when they went to the polls, the best way for candidates to frame the issues being considered to reach them, how many were actually planning on going to the polls, etc.

—**"Background on the Millennial Generation."** February 2007. Available at http://www.youngvoterstrategies.org/index.php?tg=fileman&idx=get&inl=1&id=1&gr=Y&path=Factsheets&file=Background+on+the+Millennial+Generation.pdf.

A snapshot fact sheet looking at the Millennial generation as a political body: voting potential, party affiliation, influencing factors, and demographics.

—**"Young Voter Battleground Poll III,"** November 2–7, 2006. Polls conducted by Lake Research Partners. Available at http://www.youngvoterstrategies.org/index.php?tg=fileman&idx=get&inl=1&id=1&gr=Y&path=YVS+Polling&file=Nov+Poll+Banners+2006.pdf (crosstabs); http://www.youngvoterstrategies.org/index.php?tg=fileman&idx=get&inl=1&id=1&gr=Y&path=YVS+Polling&file=11+8+06+Toplines.pdf (toplines); http://www.youngvoterstrategies.org/index.php?tg=fileman&idx=get&inl=1&id=1&gr=Y&path=YVS+Polling&file=Democratic+Analysis+Post+Election+Young+Voter+Poll+2006.pdf (Democratic analysis); http://www.youngvoterstrategies.org/index.php?tg=fileman&idx=get&inl=1&id=1&gr=Y&path=YVS+Polling&file=Republican+Analysis+Post+Election+Young+Voter+Poll+2006.pdf (Republican analysis); http://www.youngvoterstrategies.com/index.php?tg=articles&idx=More&topics=37&article=282 (press release).

Another snapshot of the Millennial generation's politics and political engagement. Conducted during the midterm elections, it tracked participation and voting preferences. It found that most Millennials continue to be largely supportive of Democrats and disapproving of Bush's agenda. Among those still in school, education and its cost were the primary concern. Of those out of school, the economy was the greatest concern.

REPORTS FOR A PRICE:

> **"The Millennials: American Born 1977–1994, 3rd Edition."** New Strategist Publications, Inc. Market Research.com. June 1, 2006. Available for purchase ($69.95) online at http://www.marketresearch.com/product/display.asp?productid=1297225&g=1.

This is a comprehensive report that looks at the Millennial generation in terms of everything from education to health to family relationships and so forth. The website also has links to other related reports, also available for purchase.

> Deloitte, **"2007 State of the Media Democracy,"** April 16, 2007. Online survey conducted between February 23 and March 6, 2007 by the Harrison Group. Available online at http://www.deloitte.com/dtt/press_release/0,1014,cid%253D153732,00.html (press release); http://www.marketingcharts.com/television/Millennials-like-traditional-not-just-new-media-1117/ (additional summary of data by MC Marketing); http://www.tvweek.com/news/2007/05/Millennials_defying_the_old_mo.php (another summary of the data).

This survey found that although Millennials have an affinity for new technology, they still frequently use traditional media as well. Seventy-one percent, for example, like to read magazines to find information on fashion trends in clothes, cars, and music. Although Millennials are increasingly utilizing new forms of technology to communicate, their favorite pastime remains hanging out with one another—decidedly "low tech," as pointed out by researchers. Surveyors found that word of mouth was the most common reason Millennials visited a website; and when Millennials like something, such as a television show, they broadcast that information to friends and acquaintances at a higher rate than other age groups.

- The Gallup Organization, **"Minority Rights and Relations,"** June 6–25, 2005. Access available to members online at http://www.galluppoll.com/content/?ci=19033.

  Looks at the level of acceptance people have for interracial dating, broken down by race, age, and gender.

- Harris Interactive, **"Youth Pulse 2006."** Available for purchase ($6,000!) online at http://www.harrisinteractive.com/services/youthpulse.asp.

  Broad information on people between the ages of 8 and 21 years old. Survey is directed toward marketers.

- Integrated Media Measurement, Inc. **"Television Viewing."** Available online at http://www.immi.com/marketTests.html (scroll to the link at the bottom).

  This survey indicates that children do not actually watch as much television as their parents do.

- Javelin Strategy & Research, **"Generation Y Banking Behaviors and Attitudes: Expanding the Banking Relationship on Their Terms."** August 2007. Available for purchase online at http://www.javelinstrategy.com/. Preview available online at http://www.javelinstrategy.com/uploads/717.F_GenYBankingBehaviorsandAttitudes_Brochure.pdf.

  Essentially marketing advice for banks that want to target Millennial consumers. Research focused on what services Millennials wanted provided; what their banking habits and attitudes are; etc.

INDEX

F

G

H

I

J

K

L

ERIC H. GREENBERG

PHOTO: ELIOT HOLTZMAN

Eric H. Greenberg is President and Chief Executive Officer of Beautifull (www.beautifull.com), a prepared, fresh-food company focused on providing tasty, healthy, and real food for retail and home delivery.

Eric has founded and established many businesses in his entrepreneurial career, including wind farms in partnership with Native American tribes in the Great Plains; Acumen Sciences and the Acumen Journal of Life Sciences; Scient, a consulting firm focused on eBusiness and emerging technology; and Viant, an Internet systems integrator.

Mr. Greenberg received a Bachelor of Business Administration degree in finance from the University of Texas at Austin. Mr. Greenberg serves on the board of directors of the Shoah Foundation, received Shoah's Ambassador to Humanity Award for 2001, was on the fundraising campaign committee at UCSF for their new Mission Bay Campus where the human genetics lab is named after him, has endowed genetic research treatments at Columbia/Cornell for breast cancer and pediatric cardiology, is a recipient of the Einstein Technology Innovation Award from the State of Israel and the Jerusalem Fund, and was named by *Worth* magazine as one of the 10 Most Generous Americans Under 45.

KARL WEBER

Karl Weber is a writer, editor, and book developer with over twenty-five years' experience in the book publishing industry. He is an expert in general-interest non-fiction publishing, specializing in topics in business, politics, and current affairs.

Weber's recent projects include the *New York Times* bestseller *Creating a World Without Poverty*, co-authored with Muhammad Yunus, winner of the 2006 Nobel Peace Prize (2008); *The Triple Bottom Line*, a guide to sustainable business co-authored with Andrew W. Savitz (2006); and *The Best of I.F. Stone*, a collection of pieces by the famed independent journalist which Weber edited (2006). Weber served as project editor on the number one *New York Times* bestseller *What Happened: Inside the Bush White House and Washington's Culture of Deception* by Scott McClellan (June, 2008).

Weber has advised and assisted authors in a wide range of non-fiction areas, including, for example, former president Jimmy Carter, author of several *New York Times* bestsellers, including *An Hour Before Daylight* (2000), which Weber edited; business guru Adrian Slywotzky, a director at the consulting firm of Oliver Wyman, and author of *The Upside* (2007), *How To Grow When Markets Don't* (2003), and *How Digital Is Your Business?* (2000), all of which Weber co-authored; and executive Jonathan M. Tisch, who wrote *Chocolates on the Pillow Aren't Enough* (2007), and *The Power of We: Succeeding Through Partnerships* (2004) in collaboration with Weber.

"Never doubt that a small group of thoughtful, committed citizens can change the world; indeed, it's the only thing that ever has."

MARGARET MEAD